PROPHETS
SEERS & VISIONARIES

PROPHETS
SEERS & VISIONARIES

MELANIE KING

Quercus

Contents

Moses

Cassandra

Jeane Dixon

INTRODUCTION

The word 'prophet' comes from the Greek *pro* ('before') and *phétés* ('speaker'). A prophet is therefore someone who speaks of events before they happen, while the word 'seer' was originally a Middle English term describing, literally, someone who sees: a 'see-er' of the future, often by means of visions.

Belief in the power to see the future and predict coming events, especially wars and other catastrophes, is an ancient and widespread cultural phenomenon. Prophecy is found everywhere, from the Ancient Greeks and Hebrews (the latter of whom had more than 50 prophets) to Muslims, medieval Christians, Native Americans, and the Xhosa people of South Africa. Some of those claiming contact with God or the power to foretell the future gained tremendous political and spiritual power, founding major religions, from Christianity to Scientology. Other prophets have been imprisoned, murdered by mobs, burned at the stake, or confined in mental asylums. Still others have led their followers to mass suicide.

PROMISES AND WARNINGS

No matter how diverse the cultures, prophets and prophecies are often remarkably similar. For thousands of years, many of the same themes have run through prophetic utterances. The end of the world is a common refrain, from the fire-and-brimstone predictions of Old Testament prophets, through the apocalyptic pronouncements of the Arthurian wizard Merlin, to modern doom-mongers such as Hal Lindsey and Elizabeth Clare Prophet. Another recurrent theme, more optimistic in nature, has been the promise of return to a homeland: Old Testament prophets such as Moses relayed messages from God promising that the Israelites would one day return to the land of Israel, thus giving hope to an exiled people. In 1880s Nevada, Wovoka, a Paiute medicine man, foretold the creation of a new world – a land free from white men – for the Plains Indians of North America. Fifty years later, Wallace Fard Muhammad, founder of the Nation of Islam, also prophesied a world free of white domination.

Other prophetic messages have predicted that dreadful calamities would occur unless morals were improved. Jonah was told to go to Nineveh and warn its inhabitants of the Lord's intention to destroy the city because of their wickedness; Elijah warned that a drought would follow if the Israelites continued to worship Baal; and Girolamo Savonarola preached that if the Florentines did not mend their wicked ways God's wrath would befall them.

A MULTIPLICITY OF METHODS

Just as prophecies cover a variety of universal themes, so too are they delivered by remarkably similar methods. Many prophets claim the ability to talk directly to God or the gods. Among these were several Old Testament prophets, including Moses and Jonah, along with the Sibyls of Ancient Greece. Others received God's messages via angels (Muhammad, Mani, Joseph Smith Jr. and William Wadé Harris), from saints (Joan of Arc and Guy Ballard), or through the medium of the Virgin Mary, as in the case of Hildegard of Bingen, the three Portuguese children from Fátima, and the six Croatian children from Medjugorje in the former Yugoslavia.

Knowledge of the future can also be gained through the observation of natural phenomena. To make their predictions, Ancient Roman seers practised an art known as auspices, examining the entrails of animals, the flight patterns of birds, and the occurrences of thunder and lightning. Both Merlin and the Brahan Seer, a Scottish Highlander, trusted to the elements and local habitat for their portents of the future. Nostradamus and Jeanne Dixon, on the other hand, looked to the stars, using astrology for their predictions. Sometimes messages were received through objects such as the blue stone used by the Brahan Seer.

A TROUBLESOME GIFT

The lot of a prophet is by no means always a happy one. As Jesus said: 'A prophet is not without honour, but in his own country' (Mark 6:4). Speaking the truth to power, or making unpopular pronouncements, often resulted in mockery, tribulations or violent death. Cassandra, though gifted with the powers of prophecy, was beset by the curse that caused no one to believe her words. The Trojan seer Laocoön was strangled by sea serpents, while Jonah was swallowed by a 'great fish'. Joan of Arc was burned alive, Savonarola hanged, and the Brahan Seer thrown into a vat of boiling oil.

Where do prophetic visions come from? Perhaps inevitably in our increasingly sceptical age, some scientists have tried to argue that prophetic visions are, so to speak, all in the mind. Matthew Alper, author of *The 'God' Part of the Brain: A Scientific Interpretation of Human Spirituality and God* (2001), claims that we are innately 'hard-wired' to perceive a spiritual reality. God, he claims, does not necessarily exist, but is a product of our evolutionary process, an inherited instinct which triggers parts of the brain as a survival mechanism. Prayer in particular sets it off. On the other hand, Dean Hammer, from the US National Cancer Institute, thinks that God is actually in our genes. After studying nine genes promoting brain chemicals, he identified a 'God gene', VMAT2 (vesticular monamine transporter). Volunteers who claimed to have had a religious or spiritual experience were found, when tested, to have a nucleic acid cytosine (c) that appeared in a particular position on the gene.

Other neurologists, such as Jeffrey Saver and John Tabin from the UCLA-Reed Neurologic Research Centre, argue that there is a distinctive personality type prone to religious experience. This tendency is often related to temporal-lobe epilepsy, which can affect the limbic system located in the middle part of the brain associated with emotions and memories. Temporal-lobe epilepsy often begins with partial seizures involving the hearing of voices and an awareness of smells, tastes, forgotten memories and unusually intense feelings. Vilayanur Ramachandran, director of the Centre for Brain and Cognition at University of California, San Diego, claims that temporal-lope epilepsy can trigger a religious or spiritual experience. Ramachandran uncovered a 'God circuit' in the brain which showed that the stronger the belief in God or religion, the more enhanced this part of the brain's electrical circuitry. On the other hand, Michael C. Jackson argues in his PhD thesis 'A Study of the Relationship Between Psychotic and Spiritual Experience' (Oxford University, 1991) that spiritual experiences form a central component in the normally adaptive process of problem-solving. Which might explain, he claims, why intimations of a divine presence are relatively common in the general population.

Whatever the scientists and academics believe, humankind clearly needs its prophets. Throughout the ages, prophets and seers have mirrored our anxieties and given a voice to many of our deepest fears. The Brahan Seer, for example, expressed concerns about social change in 17th-century Scotland, while Savonarola lambasted the 'decadent' culture of Florence during the Italian Renaissance. During the 1980s, at the height of the Cold War, prophets such as Hal Lindsey and Elizabeth Clare Prophet foretold nuclear Armageddon. Whether the predictions of prophets, seers and visionaries actually come true, all have left us with a legacy of religious traditions, cultural beliefs and examples of astonishing artwork. A world not populated by such creatures would surely be a far less interesting place to live.

The reader should note that the subjects treated in this book, while organized along broadly chronological lines, have been arranged according to the date (actual or speculative) of their most famous and resonant prophecy.

Melanie King 2008

abraham

c.2000 BC

Father of Great Nations

So central a prophet is Abraham in Judaism, Christianity and Islam that they are known as the 'Abrahamic religions'. Jews regard him as the first patriarch of their people and the man through whom the Promised Land was given to them, while St Paul calls both the Christians and the Jews 'the seed of Abraham' (2 Corinthians 11:22). In the Qur'an, where he is known as Ibrahim and mentioned in more than 70 verses, he is described as the 'father' of all believers (22:78), with Islam called the 'Religion of Ibrahim' (2:30). Through the annual *hajj* pilgrimage, which symbolically re-enacts events from his life, he has brought together Muslims from all over the world for more than 14 centuries.

According to both the Bible and the Torah, Abraham, originally known as Abram, was a sheep farmer born in Ur, in Mesopotamia (modern-day Iraq). He seems to have led a largely uneventful life when suddenly, aged 75, he received instructions from God: 'Go forth out of thy country, and from thy kindred, and out of thy father's house, and come in the land that I will show you, and I will make of thee a great nation.' Trusting in God's promise, the old man and his equally elderly wife, who were childless, duly abandoned their home and set forth for this new land. It was there, in a region that includes modern-day Israel, the West Bank and Gaza, parts of Lebanon and Syria, that God appeared once more to Abram, saying: 'To your descendants, I will give this land.'

SUMMONED BY THE LORD

Abram's arrival there was only the start of further peregrinations and adventures. A famine in this promised land forced him to move on to the more fertile region of Egypt. His wife Sar'ai, despite her advancing years, was frequently admired for her beauty, and Abram, worried he would be killed for being her husband, instructed her to say that she was his sister. It wasn't long before news of her beauty reached the pharaoh and, as Abram's sister, she was urged to join the royal household. In return, Abram was given sheep, oxen, asses, servants and camels. The Lord, however, was displeased with this arrangement and sent plagues to the pharaoh's household. When the pharaoh discovered the cause of these calamities, he was furious with Abram for deceiving him over his relationship with Sar'ai, sending both of them on their way with a scolding.

FATHER OF NATIONS

From Egypt, Abram journeyed with Sar'ai and Lot, his nephew, to Negeb, the hilly desert region of southern Israel, now named Ne-gev. From there, they continued on to Bethel, thought to be 10 miles (16 km) north of Jerusalem, on the west bank of the River Jordan. Both Abram and Lot had grown rich in cattle, silver and gold, but once they were settled near Bethel their herdsmen clashed, and it became clear that the area was too small for the two of them and

Rembrandt's Abraham's Sacrifice *(1634) shows an angel
stopping the prophet from killing Isaac.*

their entourages. Not wishing to fall out with his kinsman, Abram asked Lot to move on and settle elsewhere. They parted amicably, Abram remaining in Canaan and Lot travelling to pastures new in Jordan, where he was captured by warring tribes. Hearing of Lot's misfortune, Abram immediately set out to rescue his nephew with a force of 318 men.

The raiding party was successful and, returning home laden with their booty and retrieved possessions, Abram was greeted by the kings of Sodom and Salem. King Mechiz'edek, ruler of Salem, was enormously impressed with Abram's heroism and blessed him. In return, Abram gave the kings tithes and kept nothing of the booty for himself, having sworn to the Lord that he would take nothing apart from his retrieved belongings. God was also pleased with Abram, telling him in a vision: 'Fear not, Abram, I am your shield; your reward shall be very great.' But Abram was unconvinced, as he was a man of advancing years and still remained childless. God instructed him to sacrifice animals and make a covenant with Him, promising once again that his descendants would receive land and great possessions: 'To thy seed I will give this land, from the river of Egypt even to the great River Euphrates.'

Convinced that the Lord had prevented her from having children, Sa'rai offered their Egyptian servant, Hagar, to Abram in order to fulfil the Lord's promise. Hagar quickly became pregnant, whereupon Sar'ai, consumed with jealousy, inflicted much cruelty on the servant girl, who was so terrified of her mistress's wrath that, heavy with child, she fled into the desert. As Hagar wept by a stream, an angel appeared to her and ordered her to return, telling her: 'I will so greatly multiply your descendants that they cannot be numbered for multitude.' And so Hagar returned to Abram's household; shortly afterwards, in the 86th year of Abram's life, Ish'mael was born.

Ish'mael was not destined to remain Abram's only child. Thirteen years later, the Lord renamed Abram, calling him Abraham, meaning 'Father of the Multitude'. He told Abraham that his wife should be given the name Sarah and that she would soon bear him a son to be called Isaac ('Laughter'). Abraham greeted the news that his 90-year-old wife would give birth to a son with incredulity. God also instructed him that all males should in future be circumcised at eight days old, as a sign of covenant between God and his followers. Dutifully, Abraham set about organizing the circumcision of all the males in his settlement, including both himself and his 13-year-old son Ish'mael.

> ' SHALL A CHILD BE BORN TO A MAN WHO IS A HUNDRED YEARS OLD? SHALL SARAH, WHO IS NINETY YEARS OLD, BEAR A CHILD? '

ABRAHAM, ISH'MAEL AND ISAAC

Eventually, as God promised, Sarah did give birth to Isaac, even though she was over 90 and her husband 100. Yet tensions remained. Despite her joy in finally having her own child, Sarah still harboured feelings of jealously towards Hagar's son, Ish'mael. Regarding him as a threat to Isaac's position as heir to the household, she asked her husband to banish the boy. Abraham consulted God, who told him to do as his wife requested, saying, in a repetition of his promise to Hagar: 'I will make a nation of the son of the slave woman also, because he is your offspring.' Ish'mael was duly banished, growing up in the wilderness, becoming an archer and marrying an Egyptian woman. Ish'mael, or Ismail, is vitally important in Islam, since in the Qur'an he is the sacrificial son. He and Hagar (Hajarah) are taken by Ibrahim to a dry hill called al-Marwa near present-day Mecca. After nursing Ish'mael until their water and food were exhausted, Hajarah, in search of help and deceived by mirages, walked back and forth in the scorching heat between al-Marwa and a neighbouring hill, as-Safa. Following her seventh trip back from as-Safa, water miraculously began flowing from what is now celebrated by Muslims as the Well of Zamzam. Today, in commemoration of Hajarah, Muslim pilgrims performing the *hajj* pass seven times between as-Safa and al-Marwa; they also drink water drawn from the Well of Zamzam.

The Bible, the Qur'an and the Torah all describe how God decided to test Abraham's devotion one more time, ordering him to take his son Isaac (or Ish'mael in the Qur'an) to the land of Mori'ah, which some scholars believe to be Mount Gerizim in the West Bank. Once there, Abraham was instructed by God to sacrifice his beloved son. On completion of a sacrificial altar, Abraham bound Isaac with rope and was preparing to slit his throat when an angel intervened and spared the young man. The spirit of sacrifice shown by Ibrahim and Ish'mael, as recounted in the Qur'an, is commemorated in the three-day Islamic festival Eid al-Adha, the 'Festival of the Sacrifice'. The Qur'an also describes how Ibrahim and Ish'mael were later commanded by Allah to rebuild the Kabah, the 13-metre (43-ft) high granite shrine that Islamic tradition maintains was originally built by Adam as a reflection of a heavenly structure called the 'Primordial House'. The holiest site in Mecca, the Kabah is the focus of the *hajj*, with pilgrims walking anticlockwise around it seven times in a ritual known as the *tawaf*.

PATRIARCH OF THREE FAITHS

According to the Bible, Sarah died in Hebron at the age of 127 years and was buried in the nearby cave of Machpelah that had been purchased by Abraham from a Hittite named Ephron. Abraham lived for several more decades, marrying a woman named Ketu'rah, who bore him six children. After his death at the age of 177, he was buried beside Sarah at Machpelah, where he was joined later by Isaac and his wife Rebekah, their son Jacob and his wife Leah. In the sixth century AD a Christian church was built over the cave; in the following century it was converted into a mosque. Machpelah, now situated in Palestine, remains a place of worship for Jews, Christians and Muslims alike.

As the Lord promised, Abraham did become the 'father of nations': he was an ancestor of both Christ (through Isaac) and Muhammad (through Ish'mael), and the religion of the Israelites and their special relationship to Jehovah has its origins in the promise given to Abraham that he and his descendants would inherit Canaan.

moses

c.1400 BC

Lawgiver and Prophet

Moses is known in Hebrew as Moshe Rabbenu ('Moses our teacher') and to the Muslims as Musa. He is credited with authoring the first five books of the Bible – Genesis, Exodus, Leviticus, Numbers and Deuteronomy – in addition to receiving the Ten Commandments. God gave Moses remarkable powers to help free his people from slavery, and he foretold the exile, scattering and persecution of the Hebrews, with the eventual restoration of the Promised Land – Israel. He is an important prophet in Christianity, Judaism, Islam and the Bahá'í faith (see pages 93–96).

Moses was born to Amram and Jochebed, of the house of Levi, at a time when Jews were living as slaves in Egypt. Feeling threatened by the growing numbers of the Israelites, the pharaoh (thought by many scholars to be Rameses II; r. 1279–1213 BC) ordered that all male babies born to the Hebrews should be drowned. To save her infant son, Moses' mother placed him in a basket made of reeds and set him adrift on the River Nile. Hearing the

*Moses shows his people the way across the wilderness,
as depicted in a 19th-century engraving.*

infant's cries, the pharaoh's daughter, who was bathing nearby, rescued him and then brought him up in the palace as her own child, schooling him in the wisdom of the Egyptians and naming him Moses ('one saved from the water'). Despite living a life of luxury, Moses never lost touch with his origins, as his mother, without revealing her identity to the pharaoh's daughter, assumed the role of his nursemaid.

Moses was not destined to remain at the pharaoh's court. When, as an adult, he witnessed the beating of a Hebrew slave he was so incensed that he slew the perpetrator and buried his body in the sand. To avoid the pharaoh's wrath, he fled into exile in Midian – a region that today covers parts of Saudi Arabia, southern Jordan, southern Israel and the Sinai.

MOSES' MISSION

For some 40 years, Moses led what seems to have been a quiet life in Midian. After marrying Zipporah, daughter of Jethro, a priest, he produced two sons, Gershon and Eliezer. He worked for many years as a shepherd until one day, while tending his flock, he heard the voice of God calling from a burning bush. God told Moses that he had heard the cries of the Israelites and wanted the shepherd to ask the pharaoh to release them so that they could be delivered to Canaan, the 'land of milk and honey'. Moses, by then an unassuming man of 80, was deeply concerned that he was not equal to the task. Yet God reassured him by telling him to place his staff on the ground, whereupon it miraculously turned into a serpent; and when, on God's instruction, Moses reached to pick up the serpent, it once again became a staff.

Moses duly embarked on the long journey from Midian back into Egypt, accompanied by his brother Aaron. They sought an audience with the pharaoh, asking for the release of the Hebrews. The pharaoh's refusal provoked God into unleashing a succession of plagues – a river of blood, frogs, gnats, flies, the death of livestock, boils, hail, locusts, darkness, and finally the slaughter of the first-born. In between each calamity, Moses and Aaron tried to persuade the pharaoh to change his mind. The final, terrible plague convinced him to accede to God's demands. However, almost immediately he went back on his word, sending an army of 600 charioteers after the fleeing slaves. But Moses was given powers to save his people. Using his magical staff, he was able to part the Red Sea, thus enabling his people to escape the Egyptian soldiers. One further swipe of the staff caused the parted waters to roll back, engulfing and drowning the pursuers.

> ## Moses at Mount Sinai
>
> During Moses' first 40 days of solitary communication with the Lord, the Israelites waiting at the foot of the mountain became restless and disillusioned. They approached Aaron, one of Moses' deputies, asking him to make gods for them to worship. Melting down earrings provided by the people, Aaron created a golden calf as an idol. When Moses came down from Sinai and saw what they had done, he threw down the stone tablets on which the Lord had engraved the Ten Commandments, smashing them. It subsequently took all his persuasive powers to stop God from destroying his 'stiff-necked people'. Moses demolished the golden calf, and Aaron was told that, as punishment, he and his descendants would never enter the Promised Land. Moses then called those 'on the Lord's side' to join him, while the remaining 3000 idolators were slaughtered.
>
> When Moses descended from his second 40-day audience with God he was carrying a second set of Ten Commandments. His face, emblazoned in a brilliant light, inspired awe and fear. 'You cannot see my face, for no man shall see Me and live,' God had told Moses, but his protégé was permitted the great honour of gazing on God's back. This vision caused Moses' face temporarily to shine so brightly that he covered it with a veil in order not to frighten his people.

IN THE WILDERNESS

At first the Israelites were in awe of Moses, but when food and water became scarce in the desert they were quick to blame their leader. With the aid of his staff once again, Moses satisfied them by causing manna (small white flakes of grain resembling coriander seed and tasting of 'flour and honey') to fall from the sky, together with quails and water. The staff was further deployed when Amalekite raiders attacked the Israelites as they rested in the Sinai desert: Moses stood on a nearby hill with his hand raised, holding aloft the staff of God. If it remained upright and elevated, God told Moses, the Amalekites would be defeated. When he tired, his brother Aaron, together with Hur from the tribe of Judaea, propped up his arms until the aggressors were finally defeated.

It was too perilous for Moses to lead his people directly into Canaan, which was inhabited by belligerent tribes. Instead, after three months wandering in the desert, the Israelites finally reached Mount Sinai, and it was here God made a covenant with Moses. The Lord gave him 613 commandments, known as the Torah, which represented an entire way of living, covering law, family, personal hygiene and diet. The commandments included a ban on eating anything without fins found in the rivers or seas, the requirement to offer a young bull as a sin-offering following a transgression against the Lord, and the necessity of bathing after sexual intercourse. The most famous are the Ten Commandments, which, among other things, forbid worshipping other gods, making graven images, taking the Lord's name in vain, and committing homicide, adultery and theft.

REACHING THE PROMISED LAND

By the time he made his covenant with the Lord, Moses was the leader of more than 600,000 people. God instructed him to erect a Tabernacle, a portable place of worship which would hold His manifest presence as it went everywhere with the Israelites. During the day it would be shrouded by a cloud; when the cloud lifted, the Israelites were to follow it until it stopped moving and thereby indicated the spot to make camp. On reaching the borders of Canaan, Moses sent 12 spies into the land to report on the viability of entering. Ten returned, saying they should not enter, as warring tribes awaited them; not even God, they said, would be able to protect them. Caleb and Joshua, two other spies who disagreed, were nearly stoned to death for voicing their contrary opinion. God was furious at this example of his people's lack of faith and, as a punishment, condemned them to 40 years of wandering in the desert, until all those over the age of 20 had perished. Caleb and Joshua alone were exempt. Even Moses was barred from entering the Promised Land, as he had trespassed against God in the episode known as the Water of Contradiction. This transgression involved an occasion when the Israelites had complained about the lack of water: God had told Moses to speak to a rock and water would flow, but Moses instead tapped the rock with his magical staff – an act of disobedience against a direct command from the Lord.

> ' WHO AM I THAT I SHOULD GO TO PHARAOH, AND BRING THE SONS OF ISRAEL OUT OF EGYPT? '

Moses died at the age of 120 and was buried at an unknown location in the valley of Moab. Like Abraham, he spent many of his earlier years in obscurity, herding sheep. But his vocation as a liberator and lawgiver was an eventful one. He led over 600,000 men (not counting women and children) from slavery in Egypt and for 40 years wandered with them in the wilderness, in search of God's Promised Land. Encountering many hardships, enemy tribes and discontentment among his own people, Moses – with God's backing – ordered the slaughter of all those who stood in his way. Before he died in exile, he made a series of prophecies regarding the 12 Tribes of Israel, including the one that 'thy enemies shall deny thee, and thou shalt tread upon their necks' (Deuteronomy 33:29). He also passed on a further message to his people: 'The Lord your God will raise up for you a prophet like me.' The Christians believe this Messiah was Jesus Christ; some Muslims see parallels with Muhammad, while the Jews still await the arrival of Moses' twin.

laocoön

c.1200 BC

Seer of Ancient Greece

In Greek mythology, Laocoön, a Trojan prince and seer, was the man who uttered the famous phrase 'Beware of Greeks bearing gifts'. During the Trojan War, he warned the inhabitants of Troy not to allow the wooden horse – filled with heavily-armed Greek warriors – inside the walls of their city. When his advice was ignored, Laocoön threw his spear against the horse. His action angered the gods, who sent sea serpents to strangle the seer and his sons.

*l*aocoön's grim fate in the coils of these reptiles is graphically described in the *Aeneid*, the epic poem by the first-century BC Roman writer Virgil. It is also the subject of one of the world's most famous sculptures, now in the Vatican Museums in Rome. The story of Laocoön exemplifies the difficult path that prophets tread when they dare to speak an unpopular truth.

PARIS'S FATEFUL CHOICE

The story of the Trojan War appears throughout Greek literature, notably in Homer's *Iliad* and *Odyssey*, in other epic poems and tragedies, and in poetical works by the Roman poets Virgil and Ovid. According to these sources, the Trojan War, which lasted ten years, began when the mischievous goddess of strife, Eris, threw a golden apple inscribed with the words 'for the fairest' before the goddesses Athena, Hera and Aphrodite, causing them to argue bitterly among themselves as to which one of them deserved the prize. Unable to agree, they asked the god Zeus to decide. Not wishing to get involved in the squabble, Zeus passed on the task to Paris, son of King Priam of Troy. Each of the goddesses

An ancient Greek statue (c.50 BC) of Laocoön and his sons in their death throes.

then attempted to bribe Paris to look favourably on her. Hera offered him power and riches with dominion over the whole of Asia; Athena promised to make him a hero with amazing skills on the battlefield; and Aphrodite tempted him with marriage to Helen of Sparta, the most beautiful woman in the world after herself. Needless to say, Paris chose Aphrodite.

At this time, Paris was married to Oenone, a mountain nymph, and was living on Mount Ida, where he worked as a shepherd. Despite being warned by his brother and sister, Helenus and Cassandra, that his journey to Sparta would cause the destruction of Troy, he abandoned his wife and sailed to Greece to claim his prize. Helen, likewise, was already married. She had enjoyed the attentions of many powerful Greek suitors: so many, in fact, that her father Tyndareus, king of Sparta, was afraid that any choice his daughter made would be bound to offend the rejected suitors. Odysseus, king of Ithaca, came up with a solution to the problem, suggesting that each suitor should swear an oath to defend the interests of Helen's new husband. Helen chose Menelaus, son of Atreus, as her husband; following the marriage, he became king of Sparta when his father-in-law, Tyndareus, abdicated in his favour.

Unaware of Paris's intentions, Menelaus welcomed the young Trojan prince as his guest. By the time Menelaus had unexpectedly to leave the island on the tenth day of Paris's visit in order to attend his father's funeral in Crete, Helen (with a little divine help from Aphrodite) had already fallen in love with the visitor. The lovers seized the opportunity to flee to Troy, taking with them many of Sparta's treasures. The war against Troy, waged in what is now Turkey, was a direct consequence of Paris's action, since the armies of the Achaeans (the Mycenaean Greeks) joined with the cuckolded Menelaus to help him retrieve his wife from Troy.

A TREACHEROUS GIFT

The Trojan War dragged on for ten years, by which time the Achaeans, who had been unable to capture the impregnable city of Troy, were becoming weary. Versions hold that the idea of the wooden horse came from Helenus, Paris's brother, who had either been captured or deserted, while others claim it was Odysseus's plot. In any event, the architect Epeius was hired with orders to construct an enormous wooden horse that would secretly house armed warriors. The horse was to be left outside the city of Troy in the guise of an offering to the goddess Athena. Despite its sinister purpose, it was to be a magnificent work of art, featuring a mane of purple and gold fringe, amethyst eyes, hooves of bronze, and a bridle of ivory and bronze. To make it look as though they really had retreated, the Achaeans burnt their tents before sailing to a nearby island. Sinon, a member of the Achaean force, was appointed to stay behind, pretending to be a deserter, and confirming to the Trojans that the enemy had genuinely departed. All that remained of their presence was the magnificent wooden horse that, once safely ensconced within the city's walls, would set in motion the final defeat of Troy. Sinon, the Achaean spy, told the Trojans that if they left the horse outside the walls 'the spear of the Achaeans shall capture Troy', but if Athena received it as a holy offering at her shrine, then the Achaeans would flee.

This is the point at which Laocoön takes the stage. Nothing is known about his childhood or youth (he should not be confused with the figure of the same name who was one of the Argonauts who accompanied the mythical hero Jason in

Fact or Fiction?

The ancient Greeks regarded the Trojan War as an historical event which had taken place in the 12th or 13th centuries BC. This claim was generally dismissed as fanciful until, in 1870, the German archaeologist Heinrich Schliemann (1822–90) excavated a site in the vicinity of the Dardanelles (in modern-day Turkey), where it was believed the war had been waged. It is now thought that this was indeed the site of the city of Troy, although no evidence suggests that the episode of the Trojan horse, still less the gruesome death of Laocoön, ever took place.

his quest for the Golden Fleece). Virgil informs us that he was elected a priest of Poseidon, god of the sea, and was married with at least two children. Whether through divine guidance or his own reason, he was not deceived by the ruse. 'O my unhappy friends, you must be mad indeed,' he told the Trojans, pointing out that the offering was clearly a strategy devised to conquer Troy. He accused Sinon of being a fraud and, to emphasize his point, thrust his spear into the horse's side so that, in Virgil's words: 'the echoing spaces of the cavernous womb growled and rang.' Many Trojans began to believe Laocoön's warnings about not accepting the wooden horse. However, his sudden death in horrific circumstances changed their minds.

CAUGHT IN THE DEADLY COILS

Soon after he made his warnings, Laocoön, in his capacity as priest of Poseidon, set out to sacrifice a huge bull. As he did so, two enormous snakes with bloodshot eyes and blood-red crests slithered from the sea towards him and his two sons, Antiphantes and Thymbraeus. The serpents hissed and spat, arching their gigantic bodies as they approached their prey. Seizing Laocoön's sons, they promptly devoured them. Laocoön grabbed his sword in an attempt to defend himself, but the serpents, according to Virgil: 'seized and bound him in their huge scaly coils, twice around his middle, twice around his throat, their heads and necks towering over him.' Struggling in vain to free himself, he was covered in black venom and his piercing screams, 'like a bull's bellow when an axe has struck awry', filled the sky.

There are several different theories as to why Laocoön died in such a horrific manner. One version states that Apollo had sent the snakes, angered by the fact that the priest had married and produced children. Another suggests that Laocoön had sex with his wife under Apollo's statue, an act that enraged the god. A further version claims that Athena, thinking the Trojans were about to pay heed to Laocoön, shook the earth under his feet as a warning; when he persisted, she blinded him and sent the serpents to devour his sons. In this latter version, Laocoön himself escaped. Whatever the reason for his fate, the Trojans believed that Laocoön had been punished for damaging the 'sacred woodwork' with his spear, and that his death proved his warning was mistaken. 'All were loud in their desire for the horse to be towed to its rightful place,' reports Virgil. The huge wooden horse was dragged up the hill and through the gates of Troy.

> ' IS IT THUS YOU KNOW ODYSSEUS? TROJANS, TRUST NOT THE HORSE. WHATEVER IT BE, I FEAR THE GREEKS, AND WHEN BRINGING GIFTS. '

A BLOODY CONCLUSION

After spending the day celebrating and placing garlands around the statues of their gods, the Trojans, for the first time in ten years, slept peacefully in their beds, all except for the seeress Cassandra (see pages 18–20), who had also warned her countrymen against bringing the horse into the city. Later that night, the warriors, released from the horse by Sinon, killed the guards and opened the gates of Troy. Sinon then signalled to the Achaeans, who were waiting offshore in their ships, whereupon they poured through the city gates, slaughtering everyone in their path.

Paris was killed by deadly arrows shot by the Greek hero Philoctetes, weapons once owned by Hercules. Helen was married off to Deiphobus, Paris's brother, but he too was slain when the Achaeans sacked Troy. Helen was finally reunited with Menelaus who, having set out to kill her for her defection, was once again overwhelmed by her beauty and ended by welcoming her home. They returned to Sparta, where they lived out their remaining days.

Cassandra

c.1200 BC

Prophetess of Doom

According to Greek mythology, the seeress Cassandra ('she who ensnares men') was the beautiful daughter of King Priam of Troy and his wife Hecuba. Blessed with the power of prophecy by the god Apollo, she joined Laocoön in warning that an armed force was hidden inside the wooden horse left outside the gates of Troy by the Achaeans. Yet no one in Troy heeded this warning, or indeed any of her other prophecies, for Apollo, in revenge for spurning his amorous advances, had also laid upon her the curse of never being believed.

There is also another, less popular, Greek legend describing how Cassandra and her twin brother Helenus both acquired the gift of prophecy after being left overnight as infants in the temple of Thymbraean Apollo. When their parents arrived the next morning, they found the children entwined with the god's sacred serpents, which were licking their ears and mouths. This enabled the children henceforth to divine the future.

CAUSE OF STRIFE

Apollo's curse meant Cassandra lived her life knowing that terrible events would come to pass and that she would be powerless to prevent them. In some versions of her story, this knowledge drove her mad. Literature frequently portrays her shouting her desperate prophecies while running about with her hair undone and streaming behind her. In the Greek playwright Euripides' tragedy *Andromache*, when her younger brother Paris is born, she screams: 'Kill him! Kill the destroyer of Priam's city! Kill that child!' This underscores her mother Hecuba's own dream before Paris's birth that she would produce a firebrand who would burn down Troy; even so, Cassandra's warning is still ignored. However, when Hecuba's dream is interpreted by Cassandra's half-brother Aesacus, Priam becomes so concerned that he gives his baby son to his servant Agelaus, with instructions to leave him to die on Mount Ida. Paris survives after he is suckled by a bear; a few days later, Agelaus, discovering that the child is still alive, rescues him and brings him up as his own on his farm on the mountainside.

Some time later, King Priam sent his servants to Mount Ida to fetch a bull to be given as a prize in the funeral games. As the beast chosen was Paris's favourite bull, he decided to enter the games himself. In securing victory, he so angered one of his fellow contestants, the young Trojan Deiphobus, that he drew his sword on Paris. Frightened for his life, Paris took refuge at the altar of Zeus. It was there that Cassandra, recognizing her brother, informed her father of his reappearance. Priam, delighted, welcomed his son back as the long-lost prince.

Yet before the games Paris had been called upon to play a central role in a fateful contest. Seeking to sow discord among her fellow deities, Eris, the goddess of strife, had embroiled Hera, Athena and Aphrodite in a dispute about who was the most beautiful. The prize was a golden apple. Reluctant to make judgement himself, the supreme god Zeus chose the young shepherd boy to adjudicate. Each goddess tried to bribe Paris, but Aphrodite won by promising him the love of Helen of Sparta, the most beautiful woman in the world and the wife of King

Cassandra prophesies the fall of Troy, as seen on this fresco from the ruined Roman city of Pompeii.

Menelaus. Paris duly chose Aphrodite, abandoned his wife – the mountain nymph Oenone – and set sail to claim Helen as his bride. In Ovid's poem *Heroides*, it is at this point that Cassandra prophesies to her brother: 'You will bring conflagration back with you. How great the flames are that you are seeking over these waters, you do not know.' When Paris returns with Helen, Cassandra tears her hair and flings her golden veil to the ground. Her prediction is indeed fulfilled; Paris's action triggers the decade-long Trojan War as Helen's husband, Menelaus, calls in favours and the Achaean armies unite to help the king of Sparta retrieve his errant wife.

THE FALL OF TROY

When the wooden horse was left in the deserted camp of the Achaeans, Cassandra made one of her most famous – and tragically disregarded – prophecies. She warned the Trojans that there was an army hidden within the horse's belly and that the Achaeans had merely feigned retreat. In Tryphiodorus's epic poem *The Capture of Troy* she rages in vain against the Trojans who insist on dragging the 'unfriendly horse' into the city and thereby bringing down upon themselves what she calls 'the sleep that knows no waking'. Only the Trojan priest Laocoön supports her claim, and he too is disbelieved (see pages 15–17). When he dies in horrific circumstances – enormous sea serpents squeezing him and his sons to death – the Trojans misinterpret the episode as a sign that his prediction was wrong. Rejoicing at the apparent Achaean retreat, they haul the wooden horse to the shrine of Athena, the very goddess who is misleading them.

Accounts vary wildly on the number of warriors hidden inside the horse, from 23 to the unfeasibly large figure of 3000. However, there were most likely to have been just a dozen, including Menelaus. Once released from the horse by an Achaean spy, they killed the guards and opened the city's gates so their compatriots, who were waiting in ships nearby, could storm in. Troy was then ruthlessly destroyed, as Virgil recounts in the *Aeneid*: 'No tongue could describe the carnage of that night and its orgy of death; no tears could match such agonies.' Most of the buildings were set on fire, and anyone found alive was slaughtered, in their homes, in the temples or on the streets. 'All was a torment of suffering and fear,' Virgil writes, 'with death in a thousand forms.'

> ' HAVE I MISSED THE MARK, OR, LIKE TRUE ARCHER, DO I STRIKE MY QUARRY? OR AM I PROPHET OF LIES, A BABBLER FROM DOOR TO DOOR? '

In an attempt to escape the slaughter, King Priam fled to the temple of Zeus, but was murdered there by Neoptolemus. Cassandra ran for safety to the temple of Athena, where she clung to the statue of the goddess; however, the warrior Ajax followed her, dragged her away by the hair, and then raped her. Coroebus, son of the deceased king of the Bebrycians, who had travelled to Troy in the hope of marrying Cassandra, arrived on the scene in time to witness her capture by Ajax; he leapt to her defence but died in his attempt to save her. He was the second of her suitors to have met with a sudden death, the first being Othryoneus, who had been promised her hand by her father, but who was killed in battle by Idoneneus, king of Crete. As Cassandra was violated, the goddess Athena, appalled at what she had set in train, is said to have averted her eyes.

Following the fall of Troy, the Achaeans divided up the spoils of war, giving Cassandra to Agamemnon as his concubine. Ajax's brutal rape of Cassandra had greatly angered the Achaean leaders, but they were unable to agree on a punishment and so no reprisal was taken. The gods too were displeased, especially Athena, who, in Euripides' play *The Trojan Women*, tells Poseidon, god of the sea: 'I will impose on them a return that is no return.' And so, as Ajax sailed home, the furious Athena hurled a thunderbolt at his ship, causing the vessel to break up and Ajax himself to be tossed into the sea, where he clung desperately to a rock. Poseidon then took it upon himself to split the rock in half with his trident, and Ajax fell back into the sea and was drowned.

THE POWERLESS PROPHET

Agamemnon returned to Mycenae with his prize, Cassandra. During his absence, his wife Clytemnestra, who had never forgiven Agamemnon for sacrificing their daughter, Iphigenia, at the beginning of the Trojan War, had been having an affair with Aegisthus. On the arrival of Agamemnon and Cassandra, Clytemnestra persuaded her husband to walk into the palace across crimson carpets that she had laid specially in his honour. Cassandra warned him against this action, but the curse of Apollo was too strong and Clytemnestra too persuasive. 'Now, my beloved, step down from your chariot,' Clytemnestra coos in Aeschylus's play *Agamemnon*, 'and let not your foot, my lord, sacker of Troy, touch the earth.' Ignoring Cassandra's warning, Agamemnon steps from the carriage and strides across the carpet to his death: Clytemnestra murders the returning warrior with three strokes of a knife as he relaxes in his bath.

Cassandra knew that she too would be murdered if she entered the palace: 'for me waits destruction by the two-edged sword,' she says in *Agamemnon*. Resigned to her fate, however, she proceeds and is killed by Clytemnestra's lover, Aegisthus. Another version of the story claims that she bore twins by Agamemnon, Teledamus and Pelops, and that they too were murdered by Clytemnestra's paramour.

The point of prophecy is usually to effect a change, to convince people to mend their ways or modify their actions. But the accursed Cassandra was tragically unable to avert anything, including her own death. She therefore stands as a witness to the terrible events that she had so successfully forecast. It is for this reason that she is often referred to as a prophet of doom, and today she has given her name to anyone whose valid predictions are ignored or disbelieved.

elijah

c.900 BC

Old Testament Prophet

According to the author of Ecclesiastes, Elijah was 'as a fire, and his word burnt like a torch'. He was truly one of the most formidable of the Old Testament prophets. Known in the Hebrew Bible as Eliyahu, meaning 'My God is called Yahu', he is mentioned in the Bible, Talmud and Qur'an. Castigating the Israelites for their worship of the Canaanite weather god Baal, their introduction of foreign priests and their general corruption, he foretold a great drought in Israel, which duly came to pass. He raised a child from the dead and defeated the priests of Baal in a remarkable mountain-top duel.

Such great favour did Elijah enjoy with the Lord that a fiery chariot ultimately carried the prophet off to heaven in a whirlwind so he would never have to taste the bitterness of death. According to the Hebrew prophet Malachi, there Elijah will remain until his eventual return before 'the great and terrible day of the Lord' – that is, the coming of the Messiah on the Day of Judgement.

Little is known of the origins of Elijah other than that he was a 'Tishbite', a possible reference to a place called Tishbe in Gilead. A true ascetic, he wore animal skins and lived in caves and under waterfalls. He arrived on the scene at a time when the Israelites had been tempted away from the commandments of Moses (see pages 11–14). This apostasy had been set in motion by previous kings of Israel. One king in particular, Omri, had built altars for sacrificial offerings, appointed priests from outside the family of Levites and allowed temples to be dedicated to Baal. To secure peace with the Sidonians, Omri also arranged for his son Ahab to marry the Sidonian princess Jezebel, a priestess of Baal. With her arrival came more priests of Baal and of another pagan god, Asherah, while the prophets of the Lord were hunted down and killed.

Elijah reviving the widow's son, as depicted by the French engraver Gustave Doré (1832–83).

FAMINE STALKS THE LAND

'Depart from here and turn eastward,' the Lord commanded Elijah after the prophet had informed the new king, Ahab, that God was determined to avenge the apostasy of Israel by inflicting drought on the land. God instructed Elijah to hide himself by a brook, Cherith, east of Jordan, where he would have water to drink, and where the ravens would feed him twice daily with bread and flesh. When the brook ran dry, God commanded Elijah to go to Zarephath, in Sidonia, where a starving widow was about to make her last meal before she and her son lay down to die. Elijah assured the woman that the Lord would not allow her flour and oil to run out if she shared her last meal with him. Amazed to find that this promise came true, the widow was, however, devastated a short time later when her son died. Full of remorse,

Elijah fell to his knees and prayed to the Lord to restore the boy to life. The Lord was so moved by the plea that 'the soul of the child returned to him, and he revived' (I Kings 17:21).

In the third year of the famine, God instructed Elijah to show himself to King Ahab 'that I may give rain upon the face of the earth' (I Kings 18:1). On his way he met Obadiah, a member of Ahab's household who had been responsible for saving 100 prophets from Jezebel's massacre by hiding them in caves. Explaining his mission, Elijah asked Obadiah to find Ahab and inform him of his return. Obadiah was afraid that he would be killed as the messenger of ill tidings, but Elijah was persuasive. When Elijah eventually met with Ahab, the king shouted angrily: 'Is it you, you troubler of Israel?' To which Elijah replied: 'I have not troubled Israel but you have, and your father's house, because you have forsaken the commandments of the Lord and followed the Baals.' He admonished the king and the people of Israel for 'limping' between two different opinions – God and Baal. He then proposed a test to prove which God was the most powerful between himself and the prophets of Baal.

TESTS OF FAITH

Elijah suggested to Ahab that he should send for the prophets of Baal to meet him at Mount Carmel. He proposed that Baal's prophets should select a bull for sacrifice, cut it up, lay it on wood and offer it to their god. He would do the same. Each would then call upon their god, and the one that answered with fire would be the true deity. Accepting the challenge, the prophets of Baal danced and wailed throughout day, even slashing their own bodies so their own blood flowed as they beseeched their god – but to no avail. 'Cry with a louder voice,' Elijah taunted them, suggesting that their god was perhaps on a journey or else asleep. Then, using 12 stones that represented the 12 Tribes of Israel, Elijah constructed his own altar. Laying on it a dismembered bull, he dug a trench surrounding it which he filled with 12 barrels of water. As he began praying, 'the fire of the Lord fell', consuming the offering and licking up even the water in the trench. The assembled crowd fell to the ground in awe. Elijah ordered the slaying of the 450 prophets of Baal, at which point the rains fell, ending the drought and famine.

Ahab's wife Jezebel, furious that her priests had been slaughtered, threatened to kill Elijah. Fearing for his life, the prophet fled to Beersheba. Believing himself the only one still following the word of the Lord, a depressed Elijah wandered alone in the desert. Before falling asleep under a juniper tree, he asked God to take his soul. However, an angel woke him and offered him food and a vessel of water. After eating, Elijah fell asleep again; the angel returned a second time with further sustenance and informed him that a long journey awaited him. Fortified, Elijah walked for 40 days and nights to reach his destination, Horeb, 'Mount of God'. God, seeing that Elijah was still despondent, asked him the cause. 'I, even I only, am left,' the prophet lamented, 'and they seek my life, to take it away.' God was unimpressed, and, after sending a terrible wind, earthquake and fire to show

ELIJAH
Life and Times

*c.*872 BC Jezebel, a priestess of Baal, marries Ahab, son of Omri, the king of Israel; Elijah prophesies a period of drought and departs into the wilderness

*c.*869 BC Elijah flees following his massacre of the prophets of Baal; Jezebel retaliates by murdering the prophets of Jehovah

*c.*860 BC Naboth of Jezreel is stoned to death on Jezebel's orders after he refuses to sell Ahab his vineyard

*c.*843 BC Elijah departs to heaven and is succeeded by his disciple Elisha; Elisha anoints Jehu as king of Israel and incites him to kill the royal household; Jezebel is brutally murdered and eaten by dogs, fulfilling Elijah's prophecy

Elijah his power, ordered the prophet to go to Damascus and anoint Hazael as king of Syria, Jehu as king of Israel and Elisha as his own protégé. When Elijah found Elisha ploughing in a field, he threw his mantle over him, making him his trusted disciple. Elisha accepted the task, first sacrificing his 12 oxen and sharing them with his people.

VENGEANCE FOR TYRANNY

With Elisha now at his side, Elijah continued his mission. Once again, God sent him to confront Ahab. Ahab desired the vineyard of Naboth of Jezreel, but was refused because Naboth had no wish to part with the legacy of his fathers. Ahab reluctantly accepted this rebuff, but Jezebel was not so easily appeased. Forging Ahab's signature, she invited Naboth to a celebration at which he was falsely accused of cursing God and the king. As a consequence he was stoned to death – and Ahab was able to claim the vineyard for himself. On God's instructions, Elijah presented Ahab with a dire prophecy: 'In the place where dogs licked up the blood of Naboth shall dogs lick your own blood.' He also informed him that dogs would eat Jezebel, and that their descendants would be eaten either by dogs or birds.

These prophecies eventually fulfilled themselves. Jezebel got her come-uppance when she was thrown headlong from the window of her palace by her eunuchs, trampled by horses and then eaten by dogs so that nothing remained but her skull, hands and feet. Ahab was killed by an arrow while in battle against the Syrians, his pooled blood licked by dogs from his chariot.

Elijah was a great champion of people's rights and an enforcer of God's laws. What made him unique, however, is that he did not die, like other prophets. Prior to his departure, Elijah roamed the land with Elisha, and on approaching the River Jordan was able, like Moses, to part the waters – in this case by striking the water with his mantle. Safe on the far side of the river, the two men walked side by side, until a chariot, drawn by horses and engulfed in fire, descended from the heavens, separating the two men. Elijah leapt into it and ascended to heaven in a whirlwind, leaving Elisha in a state of ecstatic awe. Elisha took up Elijah's mantle from where it had fallen and returned to the riverbank, where he, too, was able to part the waters. The spirit of Elijah, as predicted by God, lived on in Elisha, who was to continue to spread the word of God.

'IT IS ENOUGH; O LORD, TAKE AWAY MY LIFE, FOR I AM NO BETTER THAN MY FATHERS.'

jonah
c.700 BC
The Reluctant Prophet

The Bible states that even great prophets such as Elijah were men 'passable like unto us' (James 5:17) – that is, men with the same faults and weaknesses as everyone else. The Hebrew prophet Jonah is perhaps the best example of a flawed, ordinary man who receives the gift of prophecy. He had the distinction of being the first Hebrew prophet despatched to preach to a heathen nation, an unwelcome task that earned him the nickname the 'reluctant prophet'.

Jonah's story reveals the price of disobeying the Lord as well as the potential perils of speaking unpopular words to an unsympathetic audience. The best-known episode in the Old Testament Book of Jonah – the three days and three nights the prophet spent in the belly of a great fish – has been interpreted as foreshadowing Christ's death and resurrection (which took place over the same period).

Jonah came from Gath-hepher, a village near Nazareth in Galilee. He lived during the reign of King Jeroboam II of Israel (r. *c.*786 – *c.*746 BC. Little is known about Jonah's early life, although he is recorded in II Kings 14:25 as having foretold the military successes of Jeroboam in restoring Israel's ancient borders against the encroachments of the Assyrians. His life story really begins on the day that the Lord commanded him to go to the capital of Assyria: 'Arise and go to Nineveh, the great city, and preach in it: For the wickedness thereof is come up before me' (Jonah 1:2). Assyria occupied northern and central Mesopotamia, between the Tigris and Euphrates. Nineveh, with a population of 120,000, was situated on the site of Mosul, in modern-day Iraq. Jonah dreaded the assignment, surmising that his prophecy about Nineveh's imminent destruction would not go down well (and also, perhaps, suspecting that the Lord would not actually fulfil this fire-and-brimstone prophecy). And so he fled to Joppa (Jaffa in modern-day Israel), where he boarded a boat bound for Tarshish, probably in southern Spain.

> 'I CRIED OUT FROM THE BELLY OF HELL, AND THOU HAST HEARD MY VOICE. AND THOU HAST CAST ME FORTH INTO THE DEEP, IN THE HEART OF THE SEA, AND A FLOOD HAST COMPASSED ME: ALL THY BILLOWS, AND THY WAVES HAVE PASSED OVER ME.'

AN ACCURSED PASSENGER

Furious at having been disobeyed, the Lord sent a violent wind that threatened to break up the ship on which Jonah was sailing. This mighty tempest so terrified the crew that they threw their belongings overboard in hope of lightening the load; they also prayed for safe deliverance.

Jonah being disgorged from the belly of the whale, from a woodcut in the 16th-century German encyclopedist Conrad Lycothenes' Chronicle of Portents and Revelations *(1557).*

Refusing to join in their prayers, Jonah retired below deck and tried to sleep before he was awakened by the captain, who demanded that he too pray to his God for safe passage. As the tempest continued to rage, the sailors decided to draw lots to find out who had caused such a storm. When the lot fell upon Jonah, he was called upon to explain himself and it quickly became apparent that he was fleeing from the Lord. The sailors asked Jonah what they could do so that 'the sea may quiet down for us?' Jonah told them that the only way to appease God was for them to throw him overboard. At first the men refused, endeavouring in vain to row against the storm to try and reach land and safety. The tempest grew wilder until the desperate sailors were finally forced to do Jonah's bidding and throw their offending passenger into the sea. To this day, anyone who is thought to have brought bad luck to a ship is colloquially referred to as a 'Jonah'.

On the brink of drowning, Jonah was saved by a great fish (translated by William Tyndale in his English vernacular translation of the Bible in 1534 as a 'whale'), which God sent to swallow him whole. During his three days and nights inside its belly, the reluctant prophet had time to mull things over and, in doing so, devised a prayer of thanks to the Lord, promising to sacrifice himself and to become the Lord's servant. 'Those who pay regard to vain idols forsake their true loyalty,' he uttered in great sincerity, 'But I with the voice of thanksgiving will sacrifice to thee; what I have vowed I will pay.' On hearing this, God instructed the fish to vomit Jonah up onto dry land.

GAINSAYING THE LORD

Once Jonah was safe, the Lord again came to him and for a second time asked him to go to Nineveh and deliver His message among the wicked inhabitants. This time, Jonah readily agreed and set off on the three-day journey to the Assyrian city in order to pass on the warning of impending destruction. As soon as he arrived, Jonah informed its citizens that the Lord was angry with them and that in 40 days Nineveh would be toppled. He need not have worried about a hostile reception for his words. The people of Nineveh were shocked, readily accepting that Jonah's words were a direct threat from God. They were so afraid, in fact, that they proclaimed a fast and exchanged their opulent clothes for sackcloth. Even the king of Nineveh discarded his finery, decreeing: 'Let neither man nor beast, herd nor flock, taste anything; let them not feed, or drink water, but let man and beast be covered with sackcloth, and let them cry mightily to God.' Everyone hoped God would relent and show mercy, which He did, much to their jubilation.

Jonah, however, did not share their joy. He felt angry and humiliated that God had failed to carry out his dire prophecy, petulantly accusing God of sending him on a futile mission. The aggrieved prophet even went so far as to tell the Lord that, as he understood God's 'abounding steadfast love', he knew that He was bound to be merciful, and this was why, Jonah explained, he had not wanted to carry out the mission among the Ninevites in the first place. His pride damaged, Jonah begged the Lord to take his life: 'for it is better for me to die than to live.' The Lord ignored his request, and so Jonah left the city in a huff, making himself a shelter under a tree outside Nineveh to see if the Lord might after all change his mind and destroy it. But Jonah's prophecy was not to be fulfilled.

Jonah's story ends with a kind of parable. To save Jonah from the discomfort of the sun, the Lord caused a vine to grow over the shelter, providing a cool shade. On the following day, however, God sent a worm to eat the plant so that it withered and died. He then sent a 'hot and burning wind' that beat down on Jonah's head, causing him so much discomfort that the prophet lamented: 'It is better for me to die than to live.' This time God questioned Jonah's motives: 'Do you do well to be angry for the plant?' To which Jonah replied that he was 'angry enough to die'. God asked Jonah why he was concerned at the death of a plant and yet was angry because He had pardoned the lives of 120,000 people in Nineveh. Why, in other words, did he mourn the loss of the vine and lament his own discomfort when the entire population of Nineveh had been saved?

Prefiguring the Resurrection

Aside from the book that bears his name, the only other mention of Jonah in the Bible is in the New Testament, where Christ explicitly compared his fate to that of the Old Testament prophet. When the Pharisees question whether Christ's healings and other miracles are proof of his divinity, and demand a sign from heaven, Christ tells them that: 'there shall be no sign given to it, but the sign of Jonah the prophet. For as Jonah was in the whale's belly three days and three nights, so shall the Son of man be in the heart of the Earth three days and three nights.' Christ's prophecy was subsequently fulfilled with his interment in the sepulchre, his own 'belly of hell', from which, like Jonah, he emerged after three days and three nights.

delphic oracle
c.1400 BC–AD 392

Home of the Pythia

The Ancient Greeks, fearful of incurring divine wrath, were constantly concerned to discover the wishes and intentions of the capricious and often vengeful gods who ruled over them. One way in which they came to understand these desires was by means of oracles, sacred shrines where priests or seers interpreted the will of the gods. In the ancient world, many sites gained a reputation for dispensing oracular wisdom.

DELPHI
Timeline

*c.*1400 BC Earliest human occupation at the Delphi site

*c.*600 BC Delphi is established as an important oracle centre

548 BC Temple of Apollo at Delphi burnt down, then rebuilt

373 BC Second stone temple destroyed by earthquake and subsequently rebuilt

*c.*100 BC Delphi site in decline

AD 362 Last recorded oracular response at Delphi given to a question from Emperor Julian the Apostate

At Dodona, for example, in northwestern Greece, an oracle was established at the site of a holy oak tree among whose branches dwelt two goddesses, Diona and Dias. A seer who lived at this oracle (a man, according to Homer, with unwashed feet) would interpret the rustling of the leaves in order to explicate their wishes. Jason's ship, the *Argo*, supposedly had prophetic abilities because its prow had been carved by the goddess Athena from the wood of the holy oak at Dodona.

CENTRE OF THE WORLD

Yet by far the most famous oracle in ancient Greece was the one at Delphi, 610 metres (2000 ft) above sea level on the southern slopes of Mount Parnassus. The Greeks regarded Delphi as the centre of the Earth since, according to their mythology, after Zeus released two eagles, one from the east and another from the west, they met at Delphi. Here, during the Mycenaean Period (1600–1100 BC), a shrine was built to Gaia, the Earth Mother, and an oracle was constructed. The priestess sat on a rock and, guarded by a cave-dwelling she-dragon named Python, delivered her prophecies. However, Python began rampaging through the countryside, terrorizing the populace and killing their sheep, and the people of Delphi appealed for help to Apollo. He killed the dragon with his silver bow and golden arrows; thereafter the site, dedicated to Apollo, was called Pytho, after the dead dragon. The resident priestess duly became known as the Pythia.

The Pythia derived her inspiration quite literally from the spot in which she sat. Legend has it that intoxicating fumes rose from Python's decomposing body after it fell into the crevice housing the spring. Sitting over this fissure on a tripod, or three-legged chair, the Pythia would go into a trance triggered by the hallucinatory fumes. These vapours allowed Apollo to possess her spirit and to provide answers to the suppliants' questions. The

A Delphic priestess delivering a prophecy from behind a screen, as depicted in this circular painting (tondo) from a fifth-century BC drinking vessel.

Pythia herself had to undergo certain rites before venturing onto her tripod, including fasting, bathing in the Castalian Spring and drinking the waters from the Kassotis, a stream which ran through the cavern. Once seated on her tripod, the Pythia held laurel leaves in one hand and in the other a cauldron of Kassotis waters into which she gazed for her predictions.

THE ALL-POWERFUL PYTHIAE

The Pythiae played a vital role in shaping important political events. Each new Pythia was selected from a guild of priestesses on the death of her predecessor. Many of the women were married, but broke off contact with their families on assuming the role. In the early days, the Pythiae came from educated, aristocratic families; later on, they were often chosen from peasant stock. The Greek historian Diodorus Siculus (*c*.90–30 BC) says that the Pythiae were originally young virgins. However, after a supplicant from Thessaly kidnapped and raped one Pythia, the Delphians decreed that priestesses must in future be women of advancing years.

Supplicants came to Delphi for answers to all manner of problems, ranging from when a farmer should sow his crops to the best moment for a king to wage war. Only men were allowed to approach the Pythia, and were first vetted by the priests. If deemed suitable, they would then undergo many rituals before gaining entry to the oracle. They were taught how to frame questions correctly, and also had to offer gifts, sacrifice a ram to ensure its entrails showed favourable signs for a reading and undertake a ritual walk along the Sacred

> ‘ LOVE OF MONEY AND NOTHING ELSE WILL RUIN SPARTA. ’

Way leading to the temple. The larger the gift, the quicker the supplicant was allowed to see the Pythia. Excavations at Delphi have revealed more than 5000 such offerings.

GNOMIC UTTERANCES

The Pythia's pronouncements were notoriously cryptic and required interpretation by a priest, who composed the answers in verse. Over 500 of these utterances have survived. For instance, in 403 BC, the Spartan leader Lysander was warned to be aware of the 'serpent coming from the rear'. Eight years later he was killed by Neachorus, who attacked him from behind with a serpent painted upon his shield. In 359 BC, the Pythia informed Philip II of Macedon that whoever could ride his unbroken black horse, Bucephalus, would conquer the world. The only person to do so was his son, who became Alexander the Great. When Alexander himself consulted the oracle 20 years on, prior to his conquest of the Persian empire, the Pythia remained silent. He was then told to return later. Alexander went black with rage and dragged the priestess by the hair from her tripod. She screamed: 'Let me go; you're unbeatable.' This told the young warrior everything he needed to know.

When Emperor Nero visited the oracle in AD 67 he was told: 'Your presence here outrages the god you seek. Go back, matricide! The number 73 marks the hour of your downfall!' Angered by this condemnation of his recent murder of his mother, Nero ordered the Pythia to be buried alive. However, he also believed she was telling him that he would die at the age of 73 and, since he was only 30 at the time, he looked forward to what he thought would be a long reign. Nero died the following year, however, due to a revolt organized by Servius Sulpicius Galba, the governor of Hispania – who was 73 years old.

A PERILOUS PROFESSION

The reason why the Pythia spoke in such opaque riddles remains something of a mystery. The Greek historian Plutarch (c.AD 46–120), who was himself one of the priests at Delphi, claimed that the temple was filled with a sweet fragrance and that the Pythia's oracular powers were linked to the vapours that surrounded her. These fumes were no doubt key to her visions and prophecies. Tradition states that the deranged ravings of a goatherd, who tended his flocks on Mount Parnassus, first alerted the people of Delphi to the special powers attached to the vaporous fissure. Scientists have recently discovered that the Pythiae and the goatherd were all probably intoxicated by alcoholic fumes, as the oracle lay on a geological fault through which ethene gas escaped. Ethene gas has a sweet odour, and it can trigger trances, euphoria, amnesia and out-of-body experiences. Sometimes it also causes fits and spasms, and at least two Pythiae are known to have died from convulsions. Indeed, Plutarch himself noted that the life of a Pythia was shortened by serving Apollo.

The final reading at Delphi was given by a Pythia in AD 393, at which point the Roman emperor Theodosius I, a Christian, ordered that all pagan temples be closed. Her last words to the emperor were: 'Tell the king; the fair wrought house has fallen. No shelter has Apollo, nor sacred laurel leaves; the fountains are now silent; the voice is stilled. It is finished.' This prophecy was likewise fulfilled: within two decades, the Roman empire was invaded by Alaric the Visigoth.

The oracle at Delphi was found by French archaeologists in 1893. Now part of a UNESCO World Heritage Site, it has become one of Greece's most important archaeological treasures.

Toppled by a 'Mule'

One of the most famous oracular pronouncements by the priestess at Delphi, concerns Croesus, the famously wealthy king of Lydia (r. 560–c.547 BC), who at the start of his reign asked the oracle if he would rule for a long time. The Pythia's response was typically obscure. 'Nay,' came her reply, 'when a mule becometh king of Medes, flee, soft-soled Lydian, by pebbly Hermus, and stay not, nor feel shame to be a coward.' The king did not understand how a mule could become king of the Medes and so he sought advice about attacking Persia. 'After crossing the Halys,' he was told, 'Croesus will destroy a great empire.' The king was delighted, taking the Pythia's words to mean that he should attack the Persians and destroy their empire. Sadly for him, the great empire that fell was his own, as he was defeated by Cyrus, who was half-Mede and half-Persian, and hence a crossbreed, or 'mule'.

john the baptist

1st century AD

The Voice Crying in the Wilderness

Both the Hebrew Bible (Tanakh) and the prophetic books of the Old Testament make numerous references to the coming of a Messiah. The prophet Micah, for example, proclaimed that out of Bethlehem would come one who is 'to be the ruler in Israel', and who would be 'magnified even to the ends of the Earth' (Micah 5:2,4). Isaiah described a 'man of sorrows ... acquainted with grief' who would be 'led as a sheep to the slaughter' (Isaiah 53:3–7). This Saviour would be preceded, he prophesied, by a voice 'crying in the desert' that would prepare 'the way of the Lord' (Isaiah 40:3).

Many centuries later, during the reign of the second Roman emperor, Tiberius, a voice proclaiming the advent of the Kingdom of Heaven was indeed heard in the wilderness of Judaea. Biblical prophets, such as Elijah (see pages 21–24), who dressed in animal skins and lived in caves, often cut alarmingly ascetic figures. The hermit who appeared in the desert near the River Jordan in about the year AD 30 was no exception. Spurning fine garments, he was dressed in a leather girdle and humble clothes made from camel's hair, and his only food was locusts and wild honey. Preaching the need for baptism as a purification of the body and the soul, he soon attracted large crowds who flocked to the banks of the Jordan and gave him his name: 'John the Baptist'.

Good Tidings to Zion

Some listeners thought this charismatic preacher was possessed by a devil, others that he was himself the Messiah of whom he spoke. He himself was adamant that he was not the Messiah, but rather the prophet, spoken of by both Isaiah and Malachi, who had been sent to prepare the way for the Messiah. He was the messenger who would 'make straight' the paths of the Lord.

The exact date of his birth is uncertain, but John the Baptist was probably born about six months before Jesus. His father, Zacharias, was a priest at the Temple of Jerusalem and his mother Elizabeth the cousin (some sources say the aunt) of Mary, the mother of Jesus. Like Abraham and Sarah before them, Zacharias and his wife had been childless, with Elizabeth barren and past child-bearing age when the archangel Gabriel appeared to Zacharias, telling him that the Lord had heard his prayers for a child and would grant his wish. Gabriel continued: 'And you will have joy and gladness, as he will be filled with the Holy Spirit even in his mother's womb, and he will drink no wine or strong drink.' Amazed at what he had heard,

'I INDEED BAPTIZE YOU WITH WATER; BUT THERE SHALL COME ONE MIGHTIER THAN I, THE LATCHET OF WHOSE SHOES I AM NOT WORTHY TO LOOSE.'

John the Baptist anointing Jesus in the waters of the River Jordan; detail from a 19th-century engraving.

Zacharias refused to believe Gabriel's words, as a result of which the Lord caused him to lose the power of speech.

When Elizabeth was six months' pregnant, her kinswoman Mary, future mother of Jesus, was also visited by Gabriel, who told her that she would bear a son who would be known as the 'son of the Most High'. Mary immediately set off to be with her cousin, whom Gabriel had told her was also pregnant, and she remained with her for three months until the birth. When John, still in Elizabeth's womb, heard Mary's greeting, he kicked in joy and – as predicted by Gabriel – was filled with the Holy Spirit. According to Catholic belief, he was thereby cleansed of the stain of original sin. At John's circumcision, friends called the boy Zachary after his father, only to be reprimanded by Elizabeth, who informed them that his name was John. They turned to Zacharias, who, still unable to speak, wrote down on a tablet that the baby's name was indeed John, meaning 'God hath mercy'. Zacharias immediately regained the power of speech: 'His tongue loosed, and he spoke blessing God.' His astonished friends then exclaimed: 'What then will this child be?'

TRAILBLAZER FOR THE MESSIAH

There is no record of John's formative years or the date of his departure into the Judaean desert, where he led the austere life of a religious hermit. While meditating in the wilderness, John heard the Word of God instructing him to tell the multitudes that they must 'do penance; for the kingdom of heaven is at hand'. His ascetic lifestyle excited admiration and respect, and people flocked to hear his words and to be baptized. The Jews would have been familiar with the baptismal rite performed by John. Immersion in water was naturally associated with cleansing, and water purification rituals had a long history. The ancient Babylonians had used water in various cleansing rituals, while the Egyptians baptized their newborn infants as well as their dead, on whom they used the waters of the Nile, which they believed had powers of regeneration. The Jews themselves had used water to cleanse both physical and spiritual impurities, since the Torah called for immersion in the mikvah – a bath for ritual washing – for everyone from the high priest at Yom Kippur to menstruating women and those who had touched a corpse.

Whether Jesus and John the Baptist ever met as infants or children is unrecorded, but as an adult Jesus came to the River Jordan specifically to be baptized by John, in some respects an unnecessary ritual given that Jesus had no sins to wash away. John the Baptist protested that he was unworthy to baptize Jesus: 'I ought to be baptized by thee, and comest thou to me?' But

Jesus was insistent, and when he rose from the waters of the Jordan the heavens opened and the Holy Spirit descended upon him in the form of a dove. This baptism, according to Christian belief, marked the commencement of Jesus' ministry. Jesus later praised John the Baptist as someone who 'gave testimony to truth' but who had now been superseded by himself. 'He was a burning and a shining light,' Jesus told his followers, 'and you were willing for a time to rejoice in his light. But I have a greater testimony than that of John' (John 5:33-36).

A CRUEL FATE

John's fate was ultimately a tragic one. He continued to preach and to baptize on the banks of the River Jordan. His ministry included Galilee and Perea, which were ruled by Herod Antipas, son of the Jewish king Herod the Great. Herod Antipas had divorced his first wife in order to marry Herodias, wife of his half-brother Herod Philip II and daughter of another half-brother, Aristobulus. Having fallen in love with Herodias when visiting her home town of Rome, Herod persuaded her to come with him to Galilee. John openly chastised what he called Herod's adulterous relationship; as a result, egged on by Herodias, Herod imprisoned John in the fortress of Machaerus, 9 miles (14 km) east of the Dead Sea. However, according to the Romano-Jewish historian Josephus, John was imprisoned for political reasons, since Herod feared that his popularity might incite the people to rebellion.

Whatever the reasons for his incarceration, Herod had no wish to deal harshly with the Baptist, whom he believed a holy man. Yet his hand was forced when Salome, daughter of Herodias, danced before him at a banquet, delighting him so much that he offered to give her anything she desired. Consulting her mother, Herodias was persuaded to ask for John's head on a plate. Herod was forced to comply so as not to break his word, but apparently he was 'struck sad' by the request (Matthew 14:9). John was therefore executed in prison and his head delivered on a plate to Salome. The girl then gave the head to her mother, and John's body was claimed by his followers. Years later, Herod Antipas was defeated in battle by his former father-in-law, Aretas, and eventually he was banished to Lyon in France, a fate seen by many Christians as divine retribution for his having caused the death of John the Baptist.

WIDESPREAD RELICS

John's age when he died is unclear, but Christians believe that, like Christ, he was in his early thirties. His burial place was traditionally thought to be in Sebaste, Samaria; in AD 362 his tomb there was desecrated and the bones partly burned. Today, his head and other relics are reputed to be housed all over the world. Parts of the skull are said to be interred at diverse locations: the Umayyad Mosque in Damascus, in Amiens Cathedral in France, in a church in Halifax, Yorkshire, and in the church of San Silvestro in Capite, Rome. The hand with which John baptized Jesus is said to be in a Serbian Orthodox church in Cetinje monastery, while one of his arms and another fragment of his skull can allegedly be found at the Topkapi Palace in Istanbul.

A Prophet in Many Faiths

Like many biblical prophets, John the Baptist is an important figure not only in Christianity but also in other religions. Known in Islam as 'Yahya', he is described in the Qur'an as a righteous man and a prophet 'from among the good ones' who verifies the Word of Allah. He occupies an important position in Mormonism, since on 15 May 1829 he is said to have appeared in Pennsylvania to Joseph Smith (see pages 79-82), founder of the Latter-day Saints (the Mormon Church), and passed on to him the secrets of the Aaronic Priesthood. Meanwhile, the founder of the Bahá'í faith, Bahá'u'lláh (see pages 93-96), claimed that his predecessor, the Báb (see pages 86-89), was in fact an incarnation of John the Baptist, proclaiming the arrival of another Messiah.

jesus christ

c.6/5 BC–AD 30

Saviour of the World

The story of Jesus' life is told in the four Gospels of the New Testament – Matthew, Mark, Luke and John – but it was also foretold hundreds of years prior to his birth in the Old Testament books of Isaiah, Micah, the Psalms, Zechariah and Malachi. In Islam and the Bahá'í faith, Jesus is regarded as a prophet, though not as the Son of God, while in Judaism he is seen as a false prophet rather than the Messiah promised in the Hebrew scriptures. Christians believe that Jesus is the Son of God, and one of his prophecies – still holding true 2000 years later – was that his words would never be forgotten.

According to the Gospel of St Matthew, Jesus was descended from Abraham and King David through his father, Joseph. However, Christians also believe Jesus' conception to have been divine, since his mother Mary was visited by the archangel Gabriel who informed her that she had been chosen to bear the Son of God. The title 'Christ' comes from the Greek Christos, equivalent to the Hebrew Messias, meaning 'anointed one'.

THE VIRGIN BIRTH

The exact year and date of Jesus' birth have never been established. Most Christians celebrate the day on either 25 December (Western Church) or 6 January (Eastern Church), although some scholars consider a spring or summer birth to be more likely, due to the shepherds spending the night outdoors with their flocks when Jesus was born (Luke 2:8).

Although Joseph and Mary lived in Nazareth, Jesus was born some 70 miles (112 km) to the south, in Bethlehem, the home of Joseph's ancestors, to which the couple had travelled to comply with a census ordered by the Roman emperor, Caesar Augustus. As all of Bethlehem's inns were full, Mary gave birth to the child in a stable. Luke tells of an angel announcing Jesus' birth to a group of shepherds, who immediately hurried to see the newborn child (Luke 2: 8–19), whilst Matthew describes the three Magi, or wise men, who, realizing that the king of the Jews had been born, as foretold, followed the light of an unusually bright star to Bethlehem, where they too could pay their respects (Matthew 2:1–12).

Hearing rumours of the Messiah's birth, the Roman client king of Judaea, Herod the Great, feared a threat to his reign. He therefore ordered the killing in Bethlehem of all male babies up to two years of age, the episode known as the Massacre of the Innocents. An angel appeared to Joseph, commanding him to flee with his family to the safety of Egypt. The family remained in Egypt until Herod's death a few years later, after which they returned to Nazareth.

DESTINED TO SERVE THE LORD

Little is recorded of Jesus' childhood other than his visit to Jerusalem with his parents for the Jewish feast of Passover (Pesach) when he was 12. Thinking their son was in the party returning to Nazareth ahead of them, Joseph and Mary were alarmed to find that he had stayed

The captive Christ is mocked by Roman soldiers, in an engraving by Gustave Doré (1832–83).

c.6–5 BC Jesus, son of the Virgin Mary, is born in Bethlehem; massacre of the Innocents and the Flight to Egypt

c.AD **7–8** Jesus visits the Temple and discourses with the learned men of the Temple courtyard

c.AD **26** Jesus is tempted by the devil in the wilderness

c.AD **27** After being baptized by John, Jesus gathers disciples and begins his ministry

AD **28** John the Baptist is executed by the Roman client ruler of Judaea, Herod the Great; Jesus preaches the Sermon on the Mount

AD **29** Jesus reveals to his disciples his foreknowledge of his impending death

AD **30** Christ's triumphal entry into Jerusalem. Jesus Christ is tried by the Sanhedrin, condemned for sedition by the Roman procurator of Judaea, Pontius Pilate, and crucified on Golgotha, a hill outside Jerusalem

in Jerusalem. He was found in the Temple three days later, talking to teachers who were astonished at his wisdom and answers (Luke 2:47). His mother chastised him for his disappearance, to which he replied: 'Did you not know that I must be in my Father's house?', before accompanying his parents back to Nazareth. Here, it is believed, he trained and worked with his father as a carpenter, and all the while he 'advanced in wisdom and age' (Luke 2:52).

Jesus' ministry began after his public baptism in the River Jordan by his cousin, John the Baptist, when he was around 30 years old. According to Mark, at his baptism the heavens parted, the Spirit descended on him like a dove, and a heavenly voice cried: 'Thou art My beloved Son, with thee I am well pleased' (Mark 1:10-11). Filled with the Holy Spirit, Jesus was sent by God into the desert. There, after fasting for 40 days and nights, he was tempted three times by the devil, who urged him to turn stones to bread to relieve his hunger, to throw himself from the pinnacle of a temple, and to submit himself to him, the devil, in order to gain the glories of the kingdoms of the world. When Jesus refused to succumb to temptation, the devil departed and angels appeared, bringing him nourishment.

During his short ministry, when he attracted crowds often numbering in the thousands, Jesus preached mainly in Galilee (modern-day Israel) and Perea (modern-day Jordan). He spoke of the world ending catastrophically, saying that he would return to judge each man's sins. Repentance, he preached, was the only way to avoid damnation, while belief in him would lead to eternal life. Often speaking in parables to illustrate his point, he encouraged unconditional love for God, servitude and humility, and prayer for the forgiveness for one's own sins as well as for those of others. He was at pains to involve everyone in his teachings, including such undesirables as tax collectors, lepers and prostitutes. Although Jesus attracted many followers, he chose only 12 disciples to assist him with his mission. He then withdrew to a mountain in Galilee where he delivered his famous Sermon on the Mount, in which he declared that he had come to fulfil the utterances of the prophets.

MIRACLES AND PROPHESIES

According to the four Gospels, Jesus performed more than 40 miracles. Most of these involved healing, including the curing of fevers, leprosy, haemophilia, blindness, deafness, palsy, and even a withered hand, along with several cases where he successfully exorcised demons. He fed 5000 people with a few loaves of bread and a couple of fish, and he was able to turn water into wine at a wedding, calm a storm and walk on water across a lake. He even brought a number of people, most famously Lazarus, back from the dead.

Jesus also made many prophecies. The siege and destruction of Jerusalem in AD 70 by the Roman emperor Titus is believed by some to be the fulfilment of Jesus's prophecy made 40 years earlier on the Mount of Olives. Pointing to the magnificent temple with its vast platform and marble and limestone blocks, Jesus said to his disciples: 'You see all these, do you not? Truly, I say to you, there will not be left here one stone upon another, that will not be thrown down' (Matthew 24:2). Jesus also warned his disciples about impostors: 'Many will come in my name, saying "I am the Christ", and they will lead many astray.' This prophecy was also fulfilled; several historians attest that, in the first century after Jesus walked the Earth, some 60 other people claimed the title of Messiah.

Jesus likewise prophesied his own death. As he celebrated Passover with his 12 disciples at the feast later known as the Last Supper, he announced that one of them would betray him and that he would be killed. Caiaphas, the Jewish high priest, was behind the plot to put Jesus to death, but Judas Iscariot, one of his own disciples, identified him to the guards by kissing him on the cheek while he prayed in the Garden of Gethsemane immediately after the Last Supper. Once arrested, Jesus was brought before the Sanhedrin, the Jewish supreme court composed of high priests and the elders of the Sadducees and Pharisees. Asked by Caiaphas, head of the Sanhedrin, if he was the Son of God, Jesus refused to answer; he was nevertheless charged with blasphemy since he had said that the Son of Man should be seated

> ❛ THE SPIRIT OF THE LORD IS UPON ME, BECAUSE HE HAS ANOINTED ME TO PREACH GOOD NEWS TO THE POOR. ❜

at the right hand of God. He was then turned over to Pontius Pilate, the Roman procurator, on a charge of sedition for claiming to be the king of the Jews. Pilate did not believe Jesus guilty of any crime against Rome. Therefore, as it was custom for a prisoner to be freed at Passover, Pilate offered the crowd the choice of freeing either Jesus or another prisoner, a murderer named Barabbas. The crowd chose Barabbas.

THE RISEN CHRIST

Severely beaten and bruised, Jesus was crucified between two criminals at Golgotha (Mount Calvary), taking more than nine hours to die. A wealthy member of the Sanhedrin, Joseph of Arimathea, was given permission by Pilate to retrieve Jesus' body and to place it in his own tomb. Other members of the Sanhedrin approached Pilate, requesting that the tomb be sealed as Jesus had claimed – in another of his prophecies – that after three days he would rise again. Permission was granted, but the Gospels report that an earthquake shook the area, after which an angel rolled back the stone to reveal to Mary Magdalene and 'the other Mary' (usually understood as the mother of the disciple James) that the tomb was empty: Jesus had risen from the dead. Over the next 40 days, he was seen on 12 separate occasions by more than 500 people, including 'doubting' Thomas and the other disciples.

Today Christianity is the world's largest religion, with almost 2 billion followers. Christians believe that Jesus' death on the cross took away what St John called 'the sin of the world', and that his resurrection is proof of his divinity. His life provides an inspiring example to Christians, and it was one of the most undeniably important events in world history.

John of Patmos
c.AD 68–96

The Book of Revelation

The final book of the New Testament is known as the Book of Revelation, or sometimes as the Book of the Apocalypse. The word apocalypse comes from the Greek *apokalypto*, meaning 'to reveal', and the book deals with a series of visions received by its author while he was exiled on the Aegean island of Patmos in the latter half of the first century AD. The visionary was named John; he may have been John the Apostle, the beloved disciple of Christ, although grammatical errors in the Book of Revelation contrast with the Gospel According to St John, which was written in excellent Greek.

Whoever he was, John received visions of a divine drama in which Christians would be severely persecuted before receiving their reward in the New Jerusalem. Their chief adversaries are Satan and the Antichrist, the latter a heretical figure familiar to Jewish legend and mentioned in the Epistles of St John as a 'man of sin' who would usher in the end of the world. In the Book of Revelation, the Antichrist assumes the form of a seven-headed, ten-horned beast. As in the Epistles of St John, his appearance heralds great tribulations.

John's first vision was one of Christ in all his glory. It was given by 'one like unto the Son of Man,' a being with fiery eyes and dazzling clothing who stood among seven golden candlesticks and held seven stars in his hand (the number seven and its multiples recur throughout the text). He then was invited to enter a door opening into heaven. There he saw a magnificent being seated on a throne surrounded by a brilliant rainbow and 24 elders dressed in white and wearing golden crowns. In front of the throne burned seven lamps of fire, while at

'I WAS IN THE SPIRIT ON THE LORD'S DAY, AND HEARD BEHIND ME A GREAT VOICE AS OF A TRUMPET, SAYING, I AM ALPHA AND OMEGA, THE FIRST AND THE LAST: AND, WHAT THOU SEEST, WRITE IN A BOOK, AND SEND IT UNTO THE SEVEN CHURCHES WHICH ARE IN ASIA; UNTO EPHESUS, AND UNTO SMYRNA, AND UNTO PERGAMOS, AND UNTO THYATIRA, AND UNTO SARDIS, AND UNTO PHILADELPHIA, AND UNTO LAODICEA.'

REVELATION II; 10-11

its foot sat a lion, an ox, an eagle, and the face of a man, each with six wings and covered with eyes. These creatures kept repeating the words: 'Holy, holy, holy is the Lord God Almighty, who was, and is, and is to come.'

THE GREAT TRIBULATION

John was then shown how the figure on the throne held in his right hand a scroll with seven seals. These seals could only be opened by a seven-eyed, seven-horned lamb – the crucified Jesus – who would reveal what was to follow. As the 24 elders and four winged beasts fell down in adoration, the lamb began opening the seals. Interpretations of their meanings vary, though a common theme runs throughout. The first seal showed a white horse whose rider wore a crown and was bent on conquest. The second seal revealed a red horse whose rider carried a sword, representing a war caused by the Antichrist. A black horse, its rider holding scales, emerged from the third seal, indicating famine resulting from war. A 'pale horse' in the fourth seal was ridden by Death, who was to kill by the sword, pestilence, famine and wild beasts. The fifth seal showed John

John of Patmos receiving the Revelation, as portrayed in a 19th-century engraving.

the souls slain in the name of God calling for revenge, while the sixth revealed an earthquake that turned the sun black and the moon red. At this point John saw God mark with a seal the foreheads of His believers – 144,000 of them – from the tribes of Israel.

When the lamb opened the seventh seal, silence followed for half an hour. Then seven angels appeared, each bearing a trumpet which they sounded as a series of catastrophes – including hail, a mountain that toppled into the sea, and a falling star called Wormwood that turned the rivers to poison – struck the Earth. When the fifth angel blew his trumpet, he was given a key to open a 'bottomless pit' from which emerged a destroying angel named Apollyon and a swarm of armoured locusts with human faces. The sixth angel's trumpet released 200 million soldiers, mounted on fire-breathing horses, who would kill one person in three. The seventh angel then appeared, with a rainbow on his head and his feet on fire. He was carrying a small book that he commanded John to eat. When John ate the book, the angel informed him that he must now prophesy to many nations.

Another of John's visions concerned a woman 'clothed with the sun, and the moon under her feet, and on her head a crown of twelve stars' (12:1) – possibly a reference to either the Virgin Mary or the Church. As she struggled to give birth, a seven-headed dragon appeared, waiting to devour the newborn child, a boy who would rule the world. God snatched the child up to heaven and the woman fled into the wilderness for 1260 days. The dragon pursued the child to heaven, where Michael and his angels fought with him. The dragon – 'that old serpent, called the devil and Satan, which deceiveth the whole world' (12:9) – lost the battle and was hurled back down to earth, where he pursued the woman and made war on those of her offspring who obeyed God. Here he was assisted by two beasts, one a seven-headed monster that rose from the sea (a figure often interpreted as the Antichrist) and the other a leopard-like creature with the claws of a bear and the mouth of a lion. Everyone on Earth who followed the seven-headed monster was marked on his right hand or forehead with the number 666; anyone without the mark of the beast was killed.

THE WHORE OF BABYLON AND THE NEW JERUSALEM

As his vision continued, John saw a harlot – a woman clad in purple and scarlet holding a cup 'full of the abomination and filthiness of her fornication' (17:4) – astride the seven-headed beast. The word 'Babylon' was written on her forehead, for she was, the angel told John, a 'great city' (most likely Rome) that had power 'over the kings of the Earth' (17:18). Yet the great city would fall, the angel further explained, and then in another vision he showed John how the beasts would be captured and thrown into a bottomless pit where they would be joined by 'the old serpent'. There they would remain for the next 1000 years while the Messiah ruled the Earth. However, at the end of this 1000-year reign, Satan would be released, once again deceiving the nations and gathering their people into his army. God would then send fire from heaven, condemning Satan and his followers to an eternity in a bottomless lake of fire. Conversely, those who remained steadfast in their belief would have their names inscribed in the Book of Life and enter the New Jerusalem.

John's final vision was of this New Jerusalem. Here, in a city lit not by the sun but by the Lord's radiance, there would be, he learned, no sorrow, no darkness, no weeping and no death – a wonderful reward for those who had resisted temptation and suffered dreadful persecutions at the hands of Satan and the Antichrist. John then fell to his knees to give thanks to the angel for having revealed such things to him. The angel's reply suggested that the events of his visions were not far off: 'seal not the words of the prophecy of this book. For the time is at hand' (22:10).

OPEN TO INTERPRETATION

The Book of Revelation is a complex and many-layered work whose symbolism and ultimate meaning are the subject of much dispute. Some argue that John did not necessarily prophesy the end of the world but rather simply wished to warn Christians – subject at this time to much persecution by the Romans – not to be tempted away from their faith and to prepare themselves for further tribulations. In this view, his words were directed against the Romans, with the seven-headed beast symbolizing Rome, the city of seven hills that had been ruled by

---

Salvation for the Faithful

In the following passage from the Book of Revelation (Chapter 21, verses 5-10), St John of Patmos describes his vision of Christ revealing to him His great work of grace and promising that those who believe will be spared the Apocalypse:

And he that sat upon the throne said, 'Behold, I make all things new'. And he said unto me, 'Write: for these words are true and faithful'. And he said unto me, 'It is done. I am Alpha and Omega, the beginning and the end. I will give unto him that is athirst of the fountain of the water of life freely. He that overcometh shall inherit all things; and I will be his God, and he shall be my son. But the fearful, and unbelieving, and the abominable, and murderers, and whoremongers, and sorcerers, and idolaters, and all liars, shall have their part in the lake which burneth with fire and brimstone: which is the second death'. And there came unto me one of the seven angels which had the seven vials full of the seven last plagues, and talked with me, saying, 'Come hither, I will shew thee the bride, the Lamb's wife'. And he carried me away in the spirit to a great and high mountain and shewed me that great city, the holy Jerusalem, descending out of Heaven from God.

seven emperors. Some even claim that the events outlined in the Book of Revelation had already occurred at the end of the first century, during the reign of Emperor Domitian when he initiated the persecutions referred to in the book.

Others, however, believe that the events witnessed by John of Patmos are yet to come – and that they will occur shortly before the Second Coming of Christ. Believers in God, they claim, will be purified and strengthened through persecution before being transported into heaven. Prophets such as Hildegard of Bingen (pages 59–62), William Miller (pages 83–86), John Wroe (pages 89–92), Ellen Gould White (pages 105–108), Wovoka (pages 115–119) and Nontetha Nkwenkwe (pages 120–123) all have provided variations on this theme. Yet whatever the purpose and meaning behind the Book of Revelation, it will undoubtedly continue to frighten, baffle, inspire and excite the imagination of readers for many years to come.

The Roman Auguries

c.753 BC–c.AD 103

Birds of Ill Omen

The ancient Romans believed the gods communicated their wishes to humans by means of signs and omens. Almost every event, from flames appearing on the spears of soldiers marching into battle to such seemingly trivial episodes as sneezes or stumbles, could be interpreted as a divine message. No important action was ever taken, therefore, without the authorities first attempting to determine what these signs were, and whether or not they were favourable.

Elections, wars, marriages, the construction of new buildings or the passing of legislation – all required the services of an augur. The augur (pl. augures) was an ancient Roman priest or magistrate whose task was to interpret the will of the gods by studying signs from nature, in particular the behaviour of birds, which were regarded as messengers of Jupiter. As Livy (59 BC–AD 17) wrote in *The History of Rome*, these augures were held in such esteem that 'nothing was undertaken in peace or war without their sanction', and 'matters of the highest importance were suspended or broken up if the omen of the birds was unfavourable'. Anxious would-be bridegrooms and powerful senators alike had to await the augur's triumphant declaration: 'Aves admittunt' ('the birds allow it').

A TIME-HONOURED PRACTICE

Many ancient cultures, including the Greeks and the Etruscans, believed the behaviour of birds indicated the will of the gods. The Etruscans, for example, had interpreted certain bird calls as portents. But it was the Romans who established a complete science of augury. Rome had even received its name and location thanks to the practice. According to legend, Romulus and

> **'THE RAVENS, OF ALL OTHER FOWLS, SEEM TO HAVE
> A KNOWLEDGE OF THEIR OWN SIGNIFICATIONS IN
> PRESAGES AND FORETOKENS ... THE WORST TOKEN
> OF ILL LUCK THAT THEY GIVE, IS WHEN IN THEIR
> CRYING THEY SEEM TO SWALLOW IN THEIR VOICE
> AS THOUGH THEY WERE CHOKED.'**
>
> PLINY THE ELDER (AD 23–79), *NATURAL HISTORY*

Remus, the city's founders in *c*.753 BC, took the auspices in order to decide on which hill their city should be built: Romulus saw a dozen vultures on his chosen site, the Palatine, compared to Remus's six on the Aventine, and so the matter was settled. One of Romulus's first acts was to appoint three augures for the city.

The peculiar quality of the Roman auguries seems to have derived about 600 BC from a swineherd named Attus Navius. Having lost one of his pigs, Navius prayed to the Lares, the household gods who protected families and their property. He promised the gods that if the pig was returned he would sacrifice his choicest bunch of grapes to them. When the pig was found, Navius went about choosing the sacrificial grapes: he divided his vineyard into four equal sections, watched which quarter the birds favoured, then divided that section into quarters and once again watched the behaviour of the birds. Through this method of partition combined with birdwatching he eventually discovered an enormous bunch of grapes, which he duly sacrificed to the Lares. According to Livy, Navius subsequently became a celebrated augur, advising the king of Rome on matters such as whether or not the cavalry should be expanded.

Revenge of the Sacred Chickens

It was an unwise commander who ignored the warnings of the chickens kept for augury. In 249 BC, during the First Punic War, the Roman consul Publius Claudius Pulcher found himself confronting the Carthaginian fleet at Drepana, on the west coast of Sicily. The *pullarius* on board his ship informed Publius that the chickens had failed to eat their cake. Enraged to find his plans thwarted, the consul shouted *Bibant, quoniam esse nolunt!* ('If they won't eat, then at least they shall drink'), and summarily flung the unfortunate birds overboard. Soon after, he suffered an ignominious defeat. The consul survived, but was subsequently convicted of sacrilege and sent into exile, his political and military career in ruins.

COMPLEX RITUALS

By the time of the dictator Lucius Cornelius Sulla (138–78 BC), the three official augures appointed by Romulus had expanded to 15. They were distinguished by their special robes as well as by the instrument of their profession, a curved staff known as a *lituus*. Made from a tree branch, the *lituus* was a special wand used by the augures to mark out a templum, or sacred space, on the site (usually a hilltop) where the observations were taken. He also used the *lituus* to mark off divisions in the sky – north, east, south and west – according to astronomical calculations. In the middle of the templum he would erect the tabernaculum, a square tent whose opening always faced south. He would then position himself outside the tent, facing south, while his assistants began playing their flutes on the inside, possibly in hope of attracting birds but also, no doubt, to charm the gods.

The augur would next pour a libation of wine to Jupiter and state his question, asking

The emperor Augustus is seen seated with the lituus, *the augures' staff of office, on this cameo.*

for clear signs to be given within the boundaries of the templum. Certain rules were settled at this point. The augur would establish exactly what sort of signs he desired and which others he would ignore. As the flutes continued to play, he would watch the sky and await the signs. The most important signs were, of course, birds, and the augur would pay attention both to their singing and to their patterns of flight. The cawing of crows was interpreted as favourable, Cicero writes in *On Divination*, if the bird was to the augur's left, while a raven croaking to the right was also a good omen. In his *Natural History*, Pliny the Elder (AD 23–79) writes that the worst token of ill luck given by ravens 'is when in their crying they seem to swallow in their voice as though they were choked'. He seems to imply that certain birds, especially owls, almost always bode ill: the screech-owl he describes as 'most execrable and accursed', a 'monster of the night' that inevitably presages bad tidings. However, augures sometimes interpreted their cries as favourable omens if they came, like the cawing of a crow, from the left.

INTERPRETING THE EAGLE

Among the birds whose flight was scrutinized, the most important was the eagle, which was closely associated with Jupiter, followed by the vulture. Once again, the position of the bird in relation to the augur was all-important. Birds flying on the left of the augur – that is, in the east – were usually understood as favourable signs, as were those approaching from the south. Those arriving from the right or from behind, on the other hand, were birds of ill omen. The augur paid attention to other signs as well. Because thunder and lightning were associated with Jupiter, they were as valuable as eagles and ravens for determining the will of the gods. As in the case of birds, the location of the thunder and lightning in relation to the augur were crucial to the interpretation, with a flash of lightning on the left a sign of Jupiter's favour and assent, and a crash of thunder from behind an indication of his displeasure. The Romans probably derived these auspices from the Etruscans, whose *Libri Fulgurales* ('thunderbolt books') divided the heavens into 16 sections and described 11 different kinds of thunderbolts, each thrown by a different god. Pliny explains that Jupiter has three different types of thunderbolts in his power, while various of the other gods similarly wield special thunderbolts of their own. Besides these portents, other celestial phenomena, such as comets and eclipses, were likewise important auspices that required careful interpretation.

The auspices were by no means always clear, and an augur might receive conflicting messages. In the case of contrary indications from, say, a crow and an eagle, the evidence gleaned from the latter would always be given more weight. Furthermore, he had to decide when to cease his observations, and whether, in the face of unfavourable omens, to persist long enough to receive favourable ones. In any case, the observations usually lasted anything from one hour to a full day. Once the augur spoke or moved from his position in front of the tent, the ritual was at an end and the time for reckoning at hand. The augur would declare the results either as favourable or unfavourable; in the latter case he would announce *Alio die* ('another day'), leaving open the prospect of taking the auspices a second time and perhaps obtaining a more favourable result.

THE SACRED FOWL

Wild birds such as eagles and ravens were not the only fowl whose behaviour was studied by the Romans in order to establish their best course of action. It is a curious fact that the greatest military machine of the ancient world entrusted its fortunes to the appetites of chickens. Every Roman naval fleet had a collection of hens that were kept in cages in the care of officials called the *pullarii*, who were called upon to help with prognostications in times of doubt or crisis. Upon request by the authorities, a *pullarius* would open the cage and throw the chickens a special cake, then closely observe their actions. If these sacred fowl refused their food, uttering distressed cries and flapping their wings, the gods were clearly against the expedition. But if the birds greedily attacked the cake, then the legions could prepare to set off for victory. Their confidence would be further boosted if the *pullarius* witnessed crumbs of cake falling from the beaks of the chickens and striking the earth – table manners that the *pullarii* considered to be particularly auspicious.

The great statesman and orator Cicero (106–43 BC), who told the famous story of Publius Claudius Pulcher (see page 42), was himself an augur for the Roman state. By his time, however, the science of augury was in a steep decline. In the dialogue *On Divination* Cicero bemoans the neglect into which the practice has fallen. However, neither he nor many of his contemporaries seem to have placed much faith in it, regarding it as mere superstition. By the time of Pliny the Younger (c.AD 61–c.112), who was appointed an augur by the emperor Trajan (r. AD 98–117), the title was merely honorific and no longer denoted a seer.

mani
216–276

The Apostle of Light

Mani ('The Illustrious One') believed that God periodically revealed the truth to His chosen ones – Zoroaster, the Buddha and Christ – and that he himself was the chosen prophet for his own age. Born in the Persian empire, he was the founder of Manichaeism, a Persian religion combining elements of Christianity, Zoroastrianism and Buddhism with Greek philosophy and Indian Jainism. Claiming to be a synthesis of all religions, it stressed the duality of good and evil, light and dark, and spirit and matter.

by the sixth and seventh centuries AD, Manichaeism had developed into one of the most popular religions in the world, with followers in Mesopotamia, Babylonia, Europe, India, Tibet and China. It was later supplanted by Christianity and Islam, which appeared to offer easier paths to redemption, coupled with eternal hell for unbelievers.

A RELIGIOUS UPBRINGING

Mani, or Manichaeus, was an honorary title. Mani's Persian name was Shuriak and he was born near Baghdad, descended through his mother from the Arsacid dynasty of the kingdom of Armenia (then a client state of Persia). Mani's father Patek was a religious man who, when praying in the temple, heard a voice urging him to abstain from marriage, meat and wine. As a result, he joined a Gnostic Christian sect founded in AD 100 by the visionary leader Elkesai. The Elkesaites were noted for their vegetarianism and for ritual baptism to absolve them of their sins. Patek left his wife but took his son to grow up in this sect – of which Patek later became the Abbot – beside the River Tigris near al-'Amarah, Babylonia (modern Amarah, Iraq).

At the age of 12, Mani was visited by his 'celestial twin' El-taum (or At-taum), from whom he received his first revelation. El-taum told him to leave the Elkesaites and purify himself with ascetic practices until the time was right to proclaim himself a prophet. Mani was later to say of this experience that El-taum revealed to him the mysteries of the underworld and the heavens, light and darkness, and the apocalypse. 'The Holy Spirit disclosed to me all that has been and all that will be,' he declared. Twelve years later, El-taum visited Mani again and announced that the time had come: 'Peace be on you, Mani, from myself and from

A portrait of Mani, from a fresco in the Indian town of Kotcho.

the Lord who sent me to you and who has chosen you for His Message. He has now bidden you to invite to your truth, and to proclaim the good news of the Truth from before Him, and to persevere in that with all your zeal.' With this stamp of approval, Mani shared all that he had learnt of his new Gospel with his fellow Elkesaites, who responded unfavourably and beat him up. This beating prompted his rapid departure, accompanied by his father, who believed in his son's words.

A STRICT REGIMEN

Mani envisaged a dualistic world of spirit and matter, and of light and darkness. He preached that the world itself had been created by God from elements of light and spirit, but that it had been overcome by the demons of darkness. Ascension back to God – the ultimate goal of all humans – would be possible only when they were totally free from the dark matter. Mani believed his mission was to help people to free themselves, through abstinence, prayer, worship and the inspired preaching of a teacher such as himself. As attending to everyday affairs only promoted the darkness, Mani divided his religion into the Elect (the clergy) and the rest of the congregation, known as the Hearers. The Elect were forbidden to marry, work, slaughter animals or cut plants. The Hearers, meanwhile, attended to the Elect's earthly needs in return for hearing their teachings and gaining merit by serving them.

Life was not easy for the Manichaeans. The Elect, allowed only one vegetarian meal a day, were required to fast at regular intervals. They led a strict life of contemplation and study, praying seven times a day facing either the sun or moon; and they could not own property or engage in sexual relations. As animal products were believed to rouse the demon of darkness in man, the Elect could eat only vegetables provided to them by the Hearers. Certain foods, such as melons, cucumbers, wheat bread and fruit juices, were believed to possess a high content of light and so were consumed whenever possible. The Hearers were not so lucky as the Elect: their souls would inevitably be reborn, to pay the debt of having been part of the material world. In the meantime, they were expected to live by Mani's ten commandments, which, among other things, forbade fornication and required that they care for the Elect. In addition, they were expected to pray four times a day and to fast once a week.

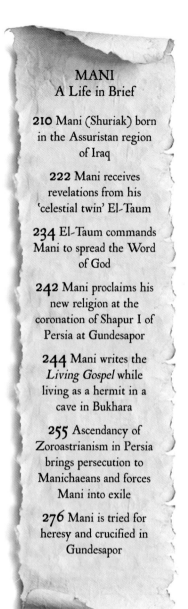

MANI
A Life in Brief

210 Mani (Shuriak) born in the Assuristan region of Iraq

222 Mani receives revelations from his 'celestial twin' El-Taum

234 El-Taum commands Mani to spread the Word of God

242 Mani proclaims his new religion at the coronation of Shapur I of Persia at Gundesapor

244 Mani writes the *Living Gospel* while living as a hermit in a cave in Bukhara

255 Ascendancy of Zoroastrianism in Persia brings persecution to Manichaeans and forces Mani into exile

276 Mani is tried for heresy and crucified in Gundesapor

TOLERATION AND PERSECUTION

Mani spent several years as a missionary, travelling through Persia and the Sindh (a province of present-day Pakistan) and spreading his new religion. As he had incorporated many local beliefs and customs into his teaching, Manichaeism soon gained in popularity. On 20 March 242, he proclaimed his new religion in the royal residence at Gundesapor, at the coronation of King Shapur I of Persia, announcing that he was Mani, the last of the great prophets. This claim was not well received in a land where Zoroastrianism (founded around 500 years earlier) was the prevailing religion, and he was forced to leave Gundesapor. Undeterred, Mani continued his missionary work, founding Manichaean communities in India and Turkestan. In 244, he spent a year in a cave in Bukhara, Uzbekistan, on the Silk Road, where he wrote his *Living Gospel* and illustrated – since he was also a talented artist – the *Ardahang*, a picture-book that encompassed his worldview. Inspired by the angel El-taum, Mani also composed numerous other sacred texts such as *The Treasure of Life* and *The Book of Mysteries*.

Eventually Mani returned to Persia, where he was able to convert King Shapur's brother, Peroz, who secured him an audience with the king. This time, the king was more receptive to the new religion, giving him royal sanction to spread his gospel throughout Persia. Mani continued to travel without fear of persecution, converting new followers as he went, until he was forced into exile in 255, when the Zoroastrian head priest Kartir persuaded Shapur to break his links with Mani and promote Zoroastrianism instead. Once again Mani fled, this time to central Asia, where he travelled in Tibet, Kashmir and western China, preaching with his usual zeal and picking up new converts on the way. Fortunately for Mani, Shapur's successor, Ormuzd I, proved sympathetic to Manichaeism and allowed him to preach freely. He even gave him a city in Khuzistan (western Iran) for his residence. But life rarely runs smoothly for a prophet: Ormuzd reigned for only a year, and was succeeded by his brother, Bahram I, who vehemently opposed Manichaeism and began persecuting non-Zoroastrian sects. Mani himself was arrested.

> 'AS ONCE BUDDHA CAME TO INDIA, ZOROASTER TO PERSIA, AND JESUS TO THE LANDS OF THE WEST, SO CAME IN THE PRESENT TIME, THIS PROPHECY THROUGH ME, THE MANI, TO THE LAND OF BABYLONIA.'

When questioned at his trial, Mani said: 'Ask all men about me; I have no master and no teacher from whom I have learnt this wisdom or from whom I have these things.' He explained that he received his teachings from God through His angel and that he was to preach to people because the world had fallen into error. 'But I have received from Him,' Mani continued, 'and revealed the way of Truth in the midst of the all, so that the souls of the many may be saved and escape punishment.' At 60 years of age, in the year 276, Mani was imprisoned at Gundesapor. He died 26 days later, having been crucified, his corpse flayed and the skin stuffed with straw. His body was then nailed to the city gate as a warning to his followers.

A Long History of Persecution

The persecution of Manichaeism, long practised in the Persian empire, was also enacted by the Roman emperor Diocletian in 296, in his bloody suppression of all non-pagan religious observance. Later, Christian Roman emperors were equally ill-disposed to the teachings of Mani: in 382, Theodosius I ordered all Manichaean monks to be put to death. However, the religion continued to flourish on the plains of Central Asia, and it became the state religion of Uighur in China until the Mongols wiped it out. Before converting to Catholicism at the age of 33 in 387, Augustine of Hippo was a Hearer (see text page 46) for nine years. He then became one of Manichaeism's deadliest enemies, writing a book condemning the religion; his denunciation added to its negative image and contributed to the decline of Manichaeism within the Christian world. In southern China, where Manichaeism was known as the Religion of the Venerable Light, it survived until the 17th century. The Bogomils of Bulgaria and the Cathars from the Languedoc region of southern France later followed many Manichaean precepts; they too were persecuted and wiped out for their heresy. Today the Oregon-based Order of Nazorean Essenes, also known as the Manichaean Orthodox Church, still adhere to some Manichaean beliefs.

merlin

c.500

Prophet of Camelot

The origins of Merlin are as misty as the island of the Britons that gave rise to the myth. According to legend he was a Druid priest, a wizard, a magician, a wild man of the woods, a prophet and diviner, the son of a demon – and founder of King Arthur's Camelot. He is said to have lived between the fifth and sixth centuries AD, his life a blend of Celtic myth and romantic history, yet in the early Middle Ages his fame was international and his prophecies have been compared to those of Nostradamus (see pages 73–76).

There were at least two Merlins. The Merlin of the North, known variously as Myrddin Sylvester (of the woods), Myrddin Celidonius (of Caledonia), or Lailoken, was a long-bearded sage living wild in the forests of southern Scotland, having been driven crazy by the death in battle of his lord Gwenddoleu. The Merlin of the South, namely Myrddin Emrys or Myrddin Ambrosius, was the prophet who foretold the kingdom of Arthur. The two were conflated by the 12th-century Welsh chronicler Geoffrey of Monmouth, who renamed them Merlin in his influential work *The History of the Kings of Britain* (1136).

MYRIAD MERLINS

This composite Merlin fits satisfactorily into the timescale of the legend of King Arthur as described by Geoffrey. But the historian also implies that Merlin was instrumental in the creation of the great stone circle at Stonehenge, the earliest part of which dates back to 3000 BC. Celtic Druids inhabited England from 2000 BC; with their considerable skills in engineering and the magic art of astronomy, they could well have been involved in the later stages of the building. It is possible, therefore, that there was a third, and much earlier Merlin, a descendant perhaps of the Greek sun god Apollo who is alleged to have once lived in Albion. Significantly, the name Myrddin means myriad, indicating that he may have been not one but many.

The Britain into which Geoffrey of Monmouth's Merlin was born was divided into numerous small kingdoms. After the fall of Troy, Brutus, a great-grandson of Aeneas, following a prophecy that he would found a race of kings in an empty island 'beyond the sun', had sailed westwards with his companions, landing at Totnes in southwest Albion. Although they did not find the island entirely empty, as it was already home to the Celts and Druids, the Trojans still flourished, renaming the land Britain, after their leader. Following the departure of the Romans in AD 410, Britain was constantly raided by Angles, Saxons and Jutes from across the North Sea. To escape the invaders, the Trojan Britons retreated west to Cornwall, Scotland and Wales.

Merlin was born in Wales in around 470. His mother, a daughter of the Welsh king of Demeter (or Dyfed), having renounced her vows as a vestal virgin – an act punishable by death – sought to protect herself by claiming that she had been impregnated by a spirit being and that the baby had been chosen by the gods. However, rumour also had it that the father was a demon – or even the devil himself. Realizing that the demon father had intended the child as

*A highly romanticized portrayal of Merlin (left)
by the painter Thomas Barlow (1829–89).*

Antichrist, his mother had him baptized at birth, thus foiling the devilish plot, although the boy retained his father's magical and prophetic powers. Named Ambrosius, meaning immortal, by his mother, he later he became known as Myrdin or Merlin.

ADVISER TO RULERS

Some 15 years after this unusual birth, the British king Vortigern, having invited the Saxons to help defend his kingdom, found himself tricked and threatened by his guests. His wizards advised him to build a stronghold to escape the marauders, the site chosen being at Dinas Emrys in North Wales. The builders of Vortigern's retreat were unable to prevent the tower of the stronghold from repeatedly collapsing; Vortigern was told by the Druids that in order to complete the building successfully, the blood of a fatherless boy must be spilt on the foundations – an old Druidical cure-all. The appropriately fatherless Merlin was discovered and brought to Vortigern. Undaunted, he informed the assembled Druids and magicians that the reason the tower kept falling was because it was built on top of a pool containing two fighting dragons, one red, one white – symbols of the wars between the Saxons and the Britons. The young Merlin predicted that Britain, represented by the red dragon, would at first lose and be overrun by the heathen conquerors, but that later, upon the arrival of King Arthur, the red dragon would rise again. And, sure enough, when the pool was drained, the dragons were found. Having succeeded in saving his own life, Merlin continued to make many obscure prophecies in the form of riddles. Meanwhile, the grateful Vortigern gave Dinas Emrys and the surrounding lands to the young seer – and there was no more talk of spilling his blood.

Over the years, fighting continued between the Saxons and the British. Geoffrey of Monmouth makes the spurious claim – in view of later dating – that Stonehenge was built as a memorial to British chieftains killed in battle. According to Geoffrey, the surviving king, Aurelius Ambrosius, summoned Merlin to design a suitable monument to the fallen. Merlin insisted that the Giants' Round, a circle of huge sarsen stones with medicinal properties, be brought from Ireland. Although too vast to be moved by normal means – for the stone ring had originally been assembled by a race of giants – Merlin used his magical powers to transport them to Salisbury Plain in order to complete the huge cosmic temple/observatory, much of which still stands today.

On the death of Aurelius Ambrosius, Merlin became bard to his successor, Uther Pendragon, advising him during the wars that continued to ravage the country in the sixth century. Later he provided the same service to Uther's son, the future King Arthur. Indeed, the magician is said to have been instrumental in the birth of Arthur in the following way: Uther had fallen in love with Ygerna, beautiful young wife of Gorlois, duke of Cornwall. In order to keep his wife safe during his absence, Gorlois locked Ygerna into the remote Cornish castle of Tintagel. Merlin, however, having inherited shape-shifting magic from his demonic father, caused Uther to change into the form of Gorlois, enabling him to enter the castle and impregnate the young woman. Later, Gorlois conveniently died in battle and Uther and Ygerna lived happily together – although Merlin took the baby into foster care for safety.

THE ONCE AND FUTURE KING

Following this escapade, little is heard of Merlin until the death of Uther Pendragon, after which an assortment of sub-kings squabbled over the leadership of Britain. Merlin clearly still retained his Druidical authority, for it was not until his protégé, Arthur, reached the age of 15 that he summoned the leaders to London, to choose the next king. The magician produced a stone into which a sword was fixed, stating that the contestant who could extract the sword would become the rightful king. All failed – until the boy appeared and withdrew the sword with the greatest of ease. Such was the beginning of the fabled reign of King Arthur.

Merlin remained as adviser to the young king, helping to lay the foundations of the kingdom of Camelot, creating the Round Table, and obtaining the magical sword Excalibur.

> '**OF MERLIN AND HIS SKILL WHAT REGION DOTH NOT HEAR?**
> **THE WORLD SHALL STILL BE FULL OF MERLIN EVERYWHERE.**
> **A THOUSAND LINGERING YEARS HIS PROPHECIES HAVE RUN,**
> **AND SCARCELY SHALL HAVE END TILL TIME ITSELF BE DONE.'**
>
> MICHAEL DRAYTON, *POLYOLBION* (1613)

The reign of Arthur is regarded to this day as a golden time of knightly valour, to which were later added Christian virtues.

Geoffrey of Monmouth wove together the stories of Merlin, Arthur and the Knights of the Round Table that he had garnered from an 'ancient book' and from other early chronicles. Being Welsh himself, he ensured that Wales featured prominently throughout. Later storytellers latched onto Geoffrey's tale, embroidering it with their own fertile imaginations. In 1160 Chrétien de Troyes established the genre of Arthurian romance throughout Europe, introducing Lancelot and the Quest for the Holy Grail, while around 1200 poet Robert de Boron revived the character of Merlin. Other notable writers who took up the Arthurian mantle were Sir Thomas Malory in his *Morte d'Arthur* (1469), Edmund Spenser in *The Faerie Queen* (1590), Alfred, Lord Tennyson in *Idylls of the King* (1855–6) and T. H. White in *The Once and Future King* (1958). Shakespeare, however, dismissed the tales of Merlin as 'skimble skamble stuff'.

AN UNCERTAIN FATE

There is a choice of three endings to the Merlin saga. Firstly, late in life, the magician falls in love with one of the Damsels of the Lake, Nimue or Viviane. The chosen one rejects his overtures but agrees to accompany him on a tour of Cornwall and Brittany, during which she learns much of his magic and, fed up with his importuning, uses this knowledge to confine him forever in a cave or tomb in the enchanted forest of Broceliande. The second version holds that, unable to prevent a war between Welsh and Scottish Britons, Merlin returns in despair to his mystical beginnings, living with nature spirits in the wilds of the Cornish forests and dying a hermit – a possible reversion to the tale of Merlin of the North.

Finally, and more attractively, Merlin is still alive. On Bardsey Island off the north coast of Wales, once the site of a Celtic monastery and for long a place of pilgrimage, he is said to inhabit an invisible glass house where he guards the Thirteen Treasures of the Island of Britain – waiting, perhaps, for the day when he will be called upon once again.

muhammaò
570–632

Founder of Islam

Muhammad, whose name means 'praiseworthy', was the founder of Islam, which today boasts up to 1.4 billion followers. Born into the Quraysh tribe in the northern Arabian town of Mecca (now in Saudi Arabia), Muhammad was a descendant of Ismail (Ish'mael), Abraham's son with Hajarah (Hagar). For 23 years from the age of 40, he received revelations from God via the angel Jibril (Gabriel). These revelations, which were recorded 20 years after his death, became known as the Qur'an.

Considered in Islam to be the last of a line of prophets comprising Adam, Noah, Abraham, Moses and Jesus, Muhammad believed that he was sent by Allah to restore the worship of one true God. He was born at a time when Arabia was governed by disparate nomadic tribes. As the terrain was harsh and barren, the search for food and water dominated all activities, causing constant strife and warfare. Loyalty towards one's tribe was absolute, and disputes were resolved on an 'eye for an eye' basis. Because of its water source, Mecca became the economic capital of the region, and nomads arrived to sell their goods and worship their gods in the Kabah, a cube-shaped, granite building constructed centuries earlier by Ismail and Ibrahim. When Muhammad was born, his tribe, the Quraysh, were in control of Mecca, having agreed with the nomadic Bedouins that a 20-mile (32-km) violence-free zone, known as the Haram, should be established around the Kabah.

A HARSH UPBRINGING

Muhammad's father, Abdullah, was a member of the Hashim, a poor clan within the Quraysh tribe. He died six months before his son's birth, and Muhammad, according to tribal custom, was sent by his mother Aminah to live with a Bedouin tribe until he was six. Aminah died soon after the boy returned to Mecca, and so he was adopted first by his grandfather and then, after his death, by his uncle Abu Talib, chief of the clan. When Muhammad was 25 and working as a merchant, he married his widowed cousin, Khadijah bint al-Khuwaylid. Then in her late thirties, she was a successful merchant in her own right, and she and Muhammad had six children together. Khadijah was a constant support to her husband, and he did not take another wife during her lifetime. After her death, Muhammad married a further 11 women, mostly widows. One of his wives was a Christian and another a Jew.

A MESSAGE OF PEACE AND CHARITY

Very little is known of Muhammad's life before the age of 40, but in 610 he experienced the 'Night of Destiny'. Every Ramadan, the annual period of fasting and contemplation (which, as *sura* [verse] 2:183 of the Qur'an makes clear, was observed even in pre-Islamic Arabia), Muhammad would retreat to a cave on Mount Hira to fast and meditate. On this particular occasion, he was visited by the angel Jibril (Gabriel), who commanded him to recite the words

The Dome of the Rock in Jerusalem stands on the spot where Muhammad is said to have ascended to heaven, accompanied by the angel Jibril.

of God (Allah). Allah then spoke to Muhammad, telling him that human beings had become greedy tyrants obsessed with material possessions. Allah stressed that He was the only God and that His subjects must bow before Him. Muhammad was terrified, but was reassured by his wife that the vision had indeed come from Allah himself, a fact later confirmed by Khadijah's cousin, who had studied the Old Testament.

For the next two years Muhammad preached to a small circle of close associates, stating that he was the prophet and messenger of Allah, that Allah was One, and that man must surrender completely to Him ('Islam' literally means 'peace and submission' [to the will of Allah]). In time, Allah – once again via Jibril – instructed him to take His message to the Quraysh and persuade them to change their acquisitive ways and help the less fortunate. Anyone who did so would be rewarded in Paradise, while those amassing selfish wealth would be punished in Jahim, a raging fire. This statement, which challenged the very fabric of Arabian

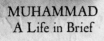
570 Birth of
Muhammad

578 Orphaned in 575,
Muhammad is assigned
to the care of his uncle
Abu Talib, head of the
Hashim clan

595 Muhammad marries
the wealthy
businesswoman Khadijah

610 The angel Jibril
appears to Muhammad
for the first time

620 Muhammad
undertakes the 'Night
Journey'

622 Muhammad and his
followers emigrate from
Mecca to Medina

630 The Muslims march
on Mecca, which they
take without bloodshed;
pagan idols are destroyed
and the Quraysh
pardoned

632 Death of
Muhammad in Medina

society, divided Muhammad's family. His uncle, Abu Talib, did not agree with the new religion; he did agree, however, to protect Muhammad as a kinsman. Initially, many of Muhammad's followers were women and slaves from the lower classes who stood to benefit from Allah's promises.

Between 612 and 620, Muhammad's preaching made him an increasing threat to his tribe. The wealth of Mecca rested on the Kabah, to which all tribes would come to pray; now Muhammad was threatening to destroy this way of life with his new ideas. In around 619 both his wife and his uncle died; another uncle, Abu Lahab, became head of the Hashim and guaranteed Muhammad protection. He therefore continued to proselytize in Mecca, while both his followers and enemies simultaneously increased.

FLIGHT TO MEDINA

After the death in 622 of his protector Abu Lahab, life in Mecca became ever more risky for Muhammad. And so, following a visit to Yathrib, a settlement near an oasis later known as Medina, where he had been invited to arbitrate in a dispute between clans, Muhammad decided to move himself and his followers there (the *hijra*, or 'emigration'). He built a house there for his wives, together with a place of worship where Muslims, Jews and Christians were welcomed equally.

Islam required Muslims to live peaceful lives and respect their neighbours, and never to fight other Muslims. But as the Muslims in Medina were poor, Muhammad reverted to the old Arab way of life, sending raiding parties to attack caravans passing Medina on the way to Mecca. As a result, the Muslims were barred by the Quraysh from making the annual pilgrimage to worship at the Kabah in Mecca. During this unsettling time, Muhammad experienced a revelation that condoned his followers' actions on the grounds that they had been driven from Mecca and were suffering hardship. After this latest revelation, he informed his congregation they should now pray facing towards Mecca rather than Jerusalem.

For ten years until his death in 632, Muhammad fought with Meccan tribes, fell out with some of the Jewish tribes and broke numerous treaties. Despite being outnumbered, his forces twice repelled the Meccans when they attacked Medina, in 625 and 627. During the Battle of the Trench in 627, he proved himself a clever tactician by gathering in the crops before the battle commenced and building a trench around the only accessible part of the city. The Quraysh ran out of supplies and were forced to lift the siege. On this occasion Muhammad abandoned his ethic of forgiveness and ordered the slaughter of 700 men from a disloyal Medinan tribe.

THE FINAL YEARS

In 628, after another revelation in which he saw himself praying at the Kabah, Muhammad announced to his followers that he planned to make a pilgrimage to Mecca. With a few companions he set off without weapons and, as was the custom, waited on the outskirts of the city for permission to enter. The Meccans refused him entry but agreed a truce. Muhammad

Muhammad's 'Night Journey'

In 620, while visiting his cousin near the Haram in Mecca, Muhammad prayed and slept near the tombs of Ismail and Hagar. Here he experienced the 'Night Journey', the first stage of which (the *Isra*) saw the angel Jibril appear to Muhammad and miraculously transport him on a winged horse called Buraq to Jerusalem, where he led other prophets in prayer. In the journey's second phase (the *Mi'raj*), Muhammad, still accompanied by Jibril, climbed a ladder to each of the seven heavens, finally ascending to the divine realm, where he met Allah. On the way he spoke with earlier prophets, including Adam, Abraham, Jesus, Enoch, Aaron, Moses and Joseph. Allah revealed that He was not the exclusive property of any one tradition, but that He had laid down a different law and way of life for different races. Both Christians and Jews had lived alongside Arabs for years, but Muhammad now gained a renewed respect for the 'People of the Book', as followers of these two other great monotheistic faiths were known.

As a result of this 'Night Journey', Muhammad introduced a number of new rules: Muslims ('those who submit to Allah') must pray five times a day facing in the direction of Jerusalem, hold special prayers on Friday afternoons, fast on the Jewish festival of Yom Kippur and observe certain dietary laws.

settled for the concession that he should be admitted the following year. Some in his camp dissented, but Muhammad was adamant he would not attack Mecca and set off for home. The next year he made the journey again, this time in the company of 2600 pilgrims. The Quraysh kept their word and the Muslims were permitted entry, remaining for the specified three days before returning peacefully to Medina. The following November, however, the Quraysh broke the treaty and attacked a tribe with close links to the Muslims. Muhammad responded by leading an army of 10,000 men to Mecca. When they reached the city, the Quraysh either fled or converted to Islam. After a night's rest, Muhammad rode his favourite camel to the Kabah, circling it seven times and calling out Allah's name. Then, after destroying all pagan idols around the Kabah and in the Haram, he announced an amnesty for the Quraysh.

After defeating tribes at nearby Ta'if, Muhammad returned to Medina. He continued to preach until, after suffering debilitating headaches, he died at the age of 63 on 8 June 632. He was buried at the Mosque of the Prophet in Medina. After Muhammad's death some Muslims thought that as only a relative of Muhammad was fit to lead, the title of caliph (religious leader) should go to Ali ibn Abi Talib, Muhammad's cousin and brother-in-law. Muslims with this view eventually became known as Shi'ites (from Shi'at Ali – 'the party of Ali'). The post, however, went to

> ‘ I AM GOD'S MESSENGER.
> I WILL NOT GO AGAINST HIS
> COMMANDMENTS AND HE WILL
> NOT MAKE ME THE LOSER. ’

Abu Bakr, a close friend of Muhammad's, and his followers became known as Sunnis (from Sunnah – 'example' [of the Prophet Muhammad]).

Muhammad brought to the attention of his people not a new religion, but an uncorrupted monotheistic version of the faith of Adam and Abraham. He was a remarkable person operating in a hostile environment where war and strife were a way of life. He was a man of peace who believed that all human life was sacred, and who wanted his people to live peaceably together, but who was forced by adverse circumstances into acts of war.

saint malachy
1094–1148

The Papal Prophecies

In the year 1140, Malachy, an Irish bishop, arrived in Rome with a party of monks. Exhausted after a lengthy journey, they rested on the Janiculum Hill outside Rome, gazing down on the city spread before them. The bishop is said to have fallen asleep – or maybe into a trance, for after a while his lips started moving and his scribe had to bend low to catch the whispered Latin words. It was dawn before Malachy finished speaking and awoke, whereupon he informed his companions that God had given him a vision of the identity of every pope until the end of time.

The document written by the scribe was passed to Pope Innocent II (d.1143) and was stored, forgotten, in the Vatican's archives until 1590, when it was unearthed by a Dominican historian. Unsurprisingly, its controversial contents raised concern amongst the Catholic authorities, for it was hardly in the interests of the Church to have such prophecies – including the forecast of an end to the papacy – becoming known to a wider world.

There has been much discussion as to the authenticity of Malachy's prophecies. Whether they did indeed result from the vision of an Irish monk or were cobbled together during the Renaissance (there is even a suggestion that they could have been based on prophecies by Nostradamus) is open to debate. The fact that they did not surface until 400 years after Malachy's death, and that they were not mentioned in St Bernard's biography of the saint, suggests that they may be later forgeries. Whatever their origin, however, many of the descriptions of future popes have turned out to be uncannily accurate.

CHURCH REFORMER

Malachy was born in Armagh in Northern Ireland in 1094, the son of an Irish nobleman. The boy Maelmhaedhoc (a name Latinized as Malachy) O'Morgair was brought up by his pious mother after the early death of his father. In his teens he was attracted to the hermit O'Haglan, who taught him the principles of self-denial, fasting and mortification of the flesh. At the age of 22, Malachy was ordained as a deacon and in 1123 appointed abbot of the dilapidated abbey of Bangor. He managed to restore the abbey with the help of just ten monks, an achievement later regarded as a miracle. It was here too that he experienced his first vision – being handed the crozier of Archbishop Cellach in a dream, and shortly afterwards receiving news of Cellach's death and his wish that Malachy

St Malachy, from a 14th-century woodcut.

should succeed him. Malachy continued to rise rapidly in the Church hierarchy, being consecrated bishop of Down and Connor in 1124, in the face of opposition from Cellach's relations. This proved a particularly tough assignment but one that he resolved with time and patience. Finally, in 1132, Malachy, despite his preference for poverty and simplicity, was appointed archbishop of Armagh, primate of the Church of Ireland. His influence on ecclesiastical affairs in Ireland was profound; like Boniface in Germany, he reorganized and reformed, restoring discipline and celibacy amongst the clergy, re-establishing Christian moral standards (which had declined severely following the Viking raids in the ninth century), and made the Irish church subservient to Rome.

CLAIRVOYANCE FROM CLAIRVAUX

Malachy resigned from Armagh in 1138 and returned to Connor, where he founded a priory of Austin Canons at Downpatrick. In 1139 he went to Rome via Scotland, England and France, in order to visit Pope Innocent II and to obtain papal approval for the reformed sees of Armagh and Cashel. En route he visited the Cistercian abbey of Clairvaux in France, where he met the future St Bernard, who was to become his most influential friend. He was so enthralled by the atmosphere of the abbey that he resolved to ask the pope for permission to resign his archbishopric and retire there. On his return from Rome he stopped again at Clairvaux, leaving some of his companions to learn the Cistercian way of life, and to collect five monks for a new foundation in Ireland that would become the great abbey of Mellifont.

In 1148, Malachy knew that death was approaching, but despite ill health, he determined to set out to deliver official documents relating to the sees of Armagh and Cashel to the latest pope, Eugenius III. Falling ill in France, he was welcomed once more by Abbot Bernard at Clairvaux and his last days there were amongst the happiest of his life. Promoted by Bernard, his cult spread and he was canonized in 1190.

A considerable number of miraculous cures were attributed to Malachy during his lifetime and after his death. Moreover, he foretold the persecution that Ireland would suffer at the hands of the English for seven centuries, from which she would eventually be delivered; and he prophesied that his country would be instrumental in restoring the true faith to England (thus implicitly foretelling the English Reformation more than three centuries before it took place).

THE PROPHECY OF THE POPES

Malachy is best remembered for his papal prophecies. Written in Latin in the form of two or three cryptic words for each future pope, the phrases supposedly give clues to their identity. These clues may derive from the coat of arms of their family or birthplace, their pre-papal names, their home town, province or previous posting, an important historical or notable event in their lifetime, or from a combination of any of the these. The 111 prophecies were first published in 1595 by the Benedictine historian who discovered them, Dom Arnold Wion.

ST MALACHY
A Life in Brief

1094 Malachy (Maelmhaedhoc) born in Armagh, Northern Ireland

1123 Appointed abbot of the monastery of Bangor, County Down, which he restores

1123 Promoted to bishop of Down and Connor

1132 Made archbishop of Armagh; reforms and disciplines the Church in Ireland

1139–40 Malachy journeys to Rome, where he receives his vision of the future popes

1148 Death of Malachy at the Cistercian abbey of Clairvaux

1190 Canonization of Malachy by the Roman Catholic Church

1595 Benedictine friar and historian Dom Arnold Wion publishes St Malachy's prophecies

Saint Malachy's predictions

Celestine II (Guido de Castello) 1143-4 Ex castro Tyberis - 'from a castle on the Tiber'. He was born in Città di Castello on the banks of the Tiber.

Adrian IV (Nicholas Breakspear) 1154-9 De rure albo - 'from the white field'. He was born in St Albans, England, land of white cliffs and snow.

Alexander III (Orlando Bandinelli Paparoni) 1179-81 Ex ansere custode - 'out of the guardian goose'. His family's coat of arms bore a goose.

Gregory X (Tebaldo Visconti) 1271-6 Anguinus vir - 'a snake-like man'. His coat of arms depicted a large serpent devouring a male child.

Nicholas III (Giovanni Gaetano Orsini) 1277-1280 Rosa composita - 'a compound rose'. A rose is emblazoned on his coat of arms.

The later predictions follow a similar pattern:

Boniface VIII (Benedetto Caetani) 1294-1303 Ex undarum benedictione - 'from a blessing of the waves'. His coat of arms bore waves.

Benedict XII (Jacques Fournier) 1334-42 Frigidus Abbas - 'the cold abbot'. He was abbot of Fontfroide (cold spring) in France.

Innocent VII (Cosmo Migliorati) 1404-06 De meliore sydere - 'from a better star'. A play on the pope's name; his coat of arms also included a star.

Sixtus IV (Francesco Della Rovere) 1471-1484 Piscator Minorita - 'Minorite fisherman'. He was a son of a fisherman and a member of the Minor Friars.

Gregory XV (Alessandro Ludovisi) 1621-3 In tribulatione pacis - 'in disturbance of peace'. The Thirty Years' War war broke out during his reign.

Innocent XII (Antonio Pignatelli del Rastrello) 1691-1700 Rastrum in porta - 'The rake at the door'. His surname Rastrello in Italian means rake.

Leo XII (Annibale Sermattei della Genga) 1823-9 Canis et coluber - the words 'dog' and 'snake' were insults applied to this disliked pope.

The last few mottoes relate to the more recent popes:

Benedict XV (Giacomo della Chiesa) 1914-22 Religio depopulata - 'religion laid waste'. During his reign the First World War killed 15 million people in Europe, and Russia established the atheist Soviet Union.

John XXIII (Angelo Giuseppe Roncalli) 1958-63 Pastor et Nauta - 'shepherd and sailor'. He had been patriarch of the maritime city of Venice. Prior to his election his rival, Cardinal Spellman, sailed a boat full of sheep up and down the Tiber, hoping to fit the bill!

John Paul II (Karol Wojtyla) 1978-2005 De labore solis - 'from the sun's labour', or 'from the sun's eclipse'. Various explanations: he was the first pope from Eastern Europe - and the sun rises in the east; he was the first pope to travel round the world - like the sun; he could be described as the sun or star of the workers, having lived under a communist regime. He was born during a solar eclipse and buried on the day of a partial eclipse. Some fundamentalists think the motto should read 'Eclipse of the Sun', believing the contemporary Church under John Paul to have deviated from true Catholic principles.

Benedict XVI (Joseph Ratzinger) 2005- De Gloria Olivae - 'from the glory of the olive'. The olive branch is a symbol of the Order of St Benedict, and Benedict is the name chosen by the current pope; an olive branch is also symbolic of world peace, to which he is dedicated.

Some say that the earlier prophecies are the most accurate; if they had been concocted immediately prior to their first publication, then of course they would have been written with the benefit of hindsight. However, the mottoes relating to the popes who came after that date seem equally significant and could clearly not have been known in advance.

Malachy's final motto prophesies the papacy of one Petrus Romanus – 'Peter the Roman' – destined to die a martyr, but he does not predict what is to follow. Nostradamus and others, however, have forecast many tribulations to come, including the persecution of the Holy Roman Church, the destruction of Rome, wars and earthquakes, climate change and famine, and the end of the world as we know it. More happily, prophets over the centuries have also spoken of these events as ushering in a new age of peace and calm, without judgement or fear.

hildegard of bingen
1098–1179

Sibyl of the Rhine

Hildegard of Bingen was ahead of her time. She communicated with popes, bishops and royalty and, unusually for a medieval woman, travelled widely, giving speeches about her visions. She wrote major works of theology as well as treatises on medicinal, botanical and geological themes; in addition, she even invented her own alphabet. Her music – she composed over 80 works – was a means, she once said, of capturing the beauty of paradise. Devised to be sung by nuns, it is still popular today.

Hildegard was born in Böckelheim, in the Rhineland. Her parents, Hildebert and Mathilda, whose surname is unknown, were members of the German aristocracy, her father having served as a soldier under Count Meinhard of Spanheim. They promised their sickly tenth child as a tithe to the Church, and so at the age of eight Hildegard was sent to live nearby with the Count's sister, the anchoress Jutta. When young, Jutta had decided to dedicate her life to God: she shut herself off from the world (the word 'anchorite' comes from the Greek *anachoreo*, 'I withdraw') and lived in a cell attached to the Benedictine monastery at Disibodenberg, devoting herself to prayer, meditation, the singing of psalms or embroidery.

A LIFE IN CHRIST
Along with other girls from noble families, Hildegard spent much of her time with Jutta, entering the anchoress's cell through a small door. When she was well enough – sometimes she was so infirm that she could barely walk or even see – she was taught to read and to sing psalms in Latin. She never grasped the art of writing, however, which is why in later years she

Hildegard – the Prophetissa Teutonica *('German Prophetess') – from a 16th-century woodcut.*

dictated her visions to a secretary. Hildegard had plenty of opportunity for contemplation, and resolved that she too would dedicate her life to God, and so joined a small nunnery next to the monastery that had grown on account of Jutta's popularity. Jutta died in 1136, and Hildegard, then aged 38, was chosen to replace her as abbess of the growing community of nuns.

UNSETTLING VISIONS

Hildegard claimed to have had visions from God since the age of three, though at first she shared them with only two people: Jutta and the monk Volmar, who was later to become one of her scribes. In 1141, however, a vision from God commanded her to write down what she saw. Yet despite being convinced of the divine origin of the inner voice, for a long time she refused this call to write, 'not out of stubbornness', she claimed, 'but from humility'. Finally, the burden of God's demand became too much, and she was forced to retire to her bed, mentally exhausted. The inner voice never ceased, so finally she spoke with senior members of her order, and it was agreed that whatever she saw in her visions was to be written down by a secretary. These writings were then sent to local church dignitaries, who confirmed their divine provenance. They were even sent to Bernard of Clairvaux (1090–1153), the renowned Cistercian abbot and instigator of the Second Crusade. Although not entirely convinced, Bernard brought them to the attention of Pope Eugenius (r. 1145–53) and also sent word that she must continue her writings. Such an important endorsement gave Hildegard the confidence to complete the work for which she is best known – the *Scivias* – and her popularity and fame began to spread.

Subsequently, Hildegard wrote two other visionary works. *Liber vitae Meritorum* ('Book of Life's Merits') gives a picturesque version of a life of virtue, as well as its opposite, to serve as a warning. *Liber divinorum operum* ('Book of Divine Works') tells how man fits into God's world, including his relationship to the elements, the planets and animals. One of the visions in this work greatly expands the theme of the 'five ferocious epochs' of world history, with Hildegard asserting that the world was fast approaching the 'end of time'.

FOUNT OF WISDOM

Music was very important to Hildegard, and she wrote scores of liturgical music and songs, all of them, she claimed, directly inspired by God. She also wrote a play, *Ordo Virtutum* ('Play of Virtues'), that was performed at her own convent. Two further books, *Physica* and *Causae et Curae*, known together as the *Liber subtilatum* ('The Book of Subtleties of the Diverse Nature of Things') presented her views on natural history and the use of plants and stones as cures. She claimed that only by using the correct plant or mineral could the human body be restored to its rightful balance.

Hildegard's fame spread quickly throughout Germany and Gaul, with crowds flocking to hear her words of wisdom. She addressed both men and women, and both commoners and people of high rank. Visitors of note included the archbishop Heinrich of Mainz, Archbishop Eberhard of Salzburg, and Saint Elizabeth of Schöna; and she was even invited to the palace of the Holy Roman Emperor, Frederick I Barbarossa, for a consultation. She corresponded with three popes – Anastasius IV, Adrian IV and Alexander III – as well as the German king Conrad III and ten archbishops, nine bishops, 49 abbots, 23 abbesses and countless priests, teachers, monks and nuns. She also undertook four extensive preaching tours around Germany.

A year before completing the *Scivias*, Hildegard was told by God to move her growing convent from Disibodenberg to Rupertsberg, near Bingen, some 19 miles (30 km) away on the left bank of the Rhine. There was much opposition from the abbot and monks, since pilgrims seeking Hildegard brought alms to the monastery. When she fell ill again, however, the abbot, fearing that her illness was caused by her being prevented from following God's plan, reluctantly allowed her to leave, along with about 20 nuns. When her new monastery was filled to capacity she opened another a few miles away at Eibingen, on the right bank of the Rhine. She travelled between the two, overseeing the nuns and composing her music, as well as her theological and medical works. However, despite her celebrity, a year before she died the ecclesiastical authorities in Mainz sentenced her convent to an interdict that prohibited it from participating in certain holy matters of the church. This interdict arose from a dispute over the burial of a man in the churchyard next to Hildegard's convent. As the man had been excommunicated, the church requested that his body be removed from holy ground. However, as the young man had received the sacraments, Hildegard judged him to have been reconciled with the church and so refused the authorities' request. The resulting conflict caused her much distress, and only after lengthy correspondence was the interdict removed.

Despite chronic infirmity, Hildegard lived to the ripe age of 81. She was buried in the church at Rupertsberg; when both convent and church burnt down in 1632 her relics were transferred to Eibingen, where a special shrine was built to house them. A remarkable and talented woman, she commanded respect from bishops, popes and kings at a time when most women played very much a secondary role in a man's world.

The *Scivias*

The work known as the *Scivias* (short for *Scito vias Domini*, 'Know the Ways of the Lord'), which took Hildegard ten years to complete, records her visions in great detail. It is a prophetic text that recalls, in its harsh admonitions and denunciations, the utterances of some of the most visionary Old Testament prophets. The opening describes how she has been called by the Lord and granted insight into His mysteries and intentions. She then goes on to recount 26 of her visions, beginning with the Fall of Man (which, intriguingly, she blames on Satan rather than, as was usual in the Middle Ages, on Eve). One of her most unsettling visions involves 'a monster shaped like a worm, wondrously large and long ... black and bristly, covered with ulcers and pustules', with fire and arrows shooting from its mouth 'and the uncleanness of frogs issuing from its bowels'. This terrible creature lies chained on its back beside a marketplace selling 'worldly delights'. Hildegard helpfully offers a 'key' to the vision, explaining that the evil worm represents the devil, the chain how his power has been curtailed by the Son of God, and the marketplace 'pride and vainglory in corruptible riches, licentiousness and lust for transitory pleasures'.

Hildegard's most famous vision, recounted near the end of the book, was of the Apocalypse. In it, she foresees the 'five ferocious epochs' to come and portrays in graphic detail the rape of the Church by the Antichrist. The Church will emerge triumphant, however, and her last vision in the *Scivias* is of the Last Judgement, when the dead arise, the good are rewarded, and the unbelievers punished to eternal damnation with no right of appeal. She foresees a 'black skin' peeling back from all of Creation as a new sun and new moon appear in the heavens. 'And so there was no night, but day,' she concludes, 'and it was finished.'

JOAN OF ARC
1412–31

French Prophetess

On 30 May 1431 a 19-year-old illiterate French peasant girl was burned at the stake in Rouen. Her crimes were allegedly heresy and sorcery. And her name was Jehanne la Pucelle – or, more famously, Jeanne d'Arc, rendered in English as Joan of Arc.

A portrait (c.1485) of Joan of Arc, the 'Maid of Orléans', by an unknown artist.

The story of the transformation of a teenager from a humble rural background into the leader of an army is an extraordinary one, made more so by the fact that she claimed to be guided by voices coming directly from God. Joan burst onto the scene at the age of 17 and in just two years succeeded in routing the combined English and Burgundian forces and in having Charles, duke of Orléans, crowned king of France. Such heights of success could only lead to a fall; Joan made enemies on her military campaigns, and in the end they conspired to bring about her downfall.

VISITED BY ANGELS
Joan was born in the village of Domrémy, in the Meuse Valley, where her mother owned a few hectares of land and her father, Jacques d'Arc, was prominent in village affairs. Joan was said to be physically strong as a result of helping on the farm along with her siblings, but as she grew older, she became increasingly pious. The secret that she kept to herself, not even confiding in her priest, was that she had begun, from the age of 12 or 13, to hear voices and see blinding lights; she came to believe that she was being visited by angels.

Joan also saw saintly visions – although sceptical psychologists have suggested that these may have been adolescent delusions, schizophrenic episodes, or the result of conflict within her family. Nevertheless Joan insisted that she had been visited by Saints Michael, Catherine and Margaret. When questioned later she was unable to give clear descriptions of their appearances, but explained that she saw them 'with the eyes of my body'. Furthermore, she claimed that the saints and angelic voices had instructed her to go to the aid of the king of France and that they had told her she would lift the siege of Orléans.

At the time of Joan's birth in 1412, the French economy was in a precarious state. Over the previous 90 years, France and England had been fighting what was to become known as the

Hundred Years' War. The insanity of the French king Charles VI ('Charles the Mad') had led to civil unrest and resulted in his brother, the dauphin Charles, duke of Orléans, and his cousin, the duke of Burgundy, clashing over the regency. The English, who had earlier ruled most of southwestern and northern France, had entered into an alliance with the Burgundians, with the aim of establishing a dual monarchy; by 1429 most of northern France was under their control. With the English holding Paris and the Burgundians the important city of Reims, things did not augur well for the followers of the duke of Orléans; although they still held Orléans itself, the last remaining city north of the Loire still loyal to France – it was now under siege.

GAINING THE DAUPHIN'S EAR

In 1428, Joan's voices told her to leave her father's house and ask her uncle, Durand Laxois, to take her to the town of Vaucouleurs to meet the garrison commander Robert de Baudricourt – the man with the power to commend her to the duke of Orléans. She informed Baudricourt that she was destined to raise the siege of Orléans, that her Lord wanted the dauphin to become king, and that she would be instrumental in his coronation. Asked for the name of her Lord, Joan replied confidently that he was the King of Heaven. Unsurprisingly, her initial overtures were rejected, but Joan persevered, gradually gathering a number of supporters to her cause. In addition to spending much time in prayer, she took – rather surprisingly – to wearing costly men's clothing. She also acquired the ability to ride skilfully on a knight's war saddle.

Baudricourt's resistance was finally worn down by Joan's tenacity and in February 1429 he despatched her with a party of six companions to the king at the royal castle of Chinon. En route the group escaped an enemy ambush in which the ambushers were apparently unable to move; whether this was a trick played on Joan or whether God protected His own is unclear.

AN INSPIRED LEADER

On meeting her, the dauphin and his advisers were initially sceptical about the young peasant girl who claimed divine guidance. But Joan soon began to make a favourable impression on the duke, bringing him a private message that could only have come from God. Furthermore, she told Charles of things to come: that she had been sent by the King of Heaven, firstly to raise the siege of Orléans and then to lead him to Reims for his coronation. In despair following a series of humiliating defeats, Charles was ready to grasp at straws. Accepting Joan's claim that she was instructed by voices from God to lead her country to victory, and by her prophecy of a military reversal at Orléans, he agreed to equip her for war and to place her at the head of his army. Before this could happen, however, Joan had to undergo a theological interrogation lasting for some three weeks, in order to check on her morality, and also a physical examination to ensure she was truly a maid.

It may be asked how a simple peasant girl could so suddenly metamorphose into a skilful military strategist. Was she more morale-raiser

A Medieval Show Trial

The trial of Joan of Arc was purely political. The duke of Bedford had claimed the throne of France for the young King Henry VI of England, while Joan had been responsible for the coronation of his rival. Getting rid of this troublemaker would facilitate English plans for dominance over France. And so, although the clerical notary Nicholas Bailly could not find any real evidence against Joan, legal proceedings began at Rouen. The prisoner was denied a legal adviser and complained that all those present at the trial were against her. Asked if she was in God's grace, Joan subtly replied: 'If I am not, may God put me there; and if I am, may God so keep me.' Had she answered yes, she would have convicted herself of heresy; if no, she would have confessed her guilt. Such was her skill under questioning that an Englishman at the trial commented: 'Really, this is a fine woman. If only she was English.' Although Pope Calixtus III declared Joan innocent of the heresy charges brought against her, the judge, Bishop Cauchon was nevertheless determined to find her guilty, not only of heresy but also of blasphemy, sorcery, apostasy and lies.

than soldier, more inspiring figurehead than commander? Certainly she had extraordinary self-confidence, attacking where the French army had hitherto taken a fatally cautious approach. On 5 May 1429, disregarding the French leadership, she insisted on mounting an assault on the main English strongholds outside Orléans, leading a charge that resulted in victory, and riding alongside her men despite an arrow wound to the shoulder. She followed this up with a series of stunning strategic successes against the enemy, routing the English at the Battle of Patay. As the triumphant French army set out for Reims, towns along the way returned to French allegiance. The gates of Reims were opened and the coronation of Charles VII took place on 17 July.

CAPTURED, TRIED AND EXECUTED

For the next few months, Joan continued her involvement with the French army as they pursued the remaining English and Burgundians. On 23 May 1430, after a skirmish, Joan left the field last, in the position of honour – and was captured by the Burgundians. She was imprisoned in Rouen, the seat of the occupying English; at one point she was held in a 21-metre (70-ft)-high tower from which she leapt in an attempt to escape her captors. No ransom was forthcoming from King Charles VII. Joan, the saviour of France, was abandoned to face trial for heresy by her captors, the Burgundians and the English.

During the trial, Joan was held in a secular prison rather than under the supervision of nuns. The wearing of men's clothes was regarded as heresy; to repeat this offence was a capital crime. Joan agreed to wear female clothing while imprisoned, but either because of molestation by her male guards or because her female clothes were stolen, she reverted to male attire. This offence sealed her fate.

Joan was sentenced to death for witchcraft and heresy. Her voices had promised her that she would escape; at the end she admitted that they had deceived her. As she was tied to the stake, she repeatedly invoked the holy name of Jesus and asked for the help of the saints in paradise. When she was dead, the English exposed her naked body and then burned it twice more to prevent the collection of her ashes (which were thrown in the Seine). Her executioner later said: 'I greatly fear that I am damned, for I have burned a holy woman.'

Joan's actions, whether divinely inspired or not, succeeded in turning a squabble between the French and English into a war of liberation. Following a retrial in 1456, Joan was declared an innocent martyr. In 1920, she became a canonized saint.

JOAN OF ARC
A Life in Brief

1412 Joan born in the village of Domrémy to a peasant family; she begins to hear voices at the age of 12 or 13

1420 English military successes force French king Charles VI to sign the humiliating Treaty of Troyes, disinheriting his son (the dauphin) in favour of King Henry V

1429 (February) Joan travels to Chinon to persuade the French dauphin Charles to resist; her rallying of French forces compels the English to withdraw from the key city of Orléans

1429 (June–July) The French defeat the English at the Battle of Patay; Charles VII is crowned in Reims

1430 Joan of Arc is captured by Burgundian allies of the English

1431 Tried and found guilty of heresy and witchcraft, Joan is burned at the stake in the marketplace in Rouen

1920 The Catholic Church canonizes Joan of Arc

' EVERYTHING I HAVE DONE THAT WAS GOOD I DID BY COMMAND OF MY VOICES. '

GiRolamo savonarola
1452–98
Prophet of Florence

In May 1498 three Dominican priests were hanged and burned in Florence. The execution brought to an end the career of one of history's most charismatic preachers, Girolamo Savonarola, whose drastic prophecies had terrified the audiences that flocked in their thousands to hear him speak. Born in the same year as Leonardo da Vinci, he preached in Florence – the city that nourished both Leonardo and Michelangelo – at the height of the Italian Renaissance.

Savonarola's oratorical power, personal piety and reputation as a prophet were such that he dominated political life in Florence throughout the 1490s, when he opposed the study and influence of the classics and became a fierce scourge of moral corruption and the instigator of the 'Bonfire of the Vanities'.

Savonarola was born in Ferrara, where his grandfather had been a distinguished physician at the court of the duke of Ferrara and an expert on spa waters. As a young man he studied at the city's university, where he composed a gloomy poem entitled 'The Ruin of the World'. This work was worthy of an Old Testament prophet in its lament that:

> *not a single righteous man is left ... The good*
> *are oppressed, and the people of Italy*
> *become like unto the Egyptians who held*
> *God's people in bondage ... Divide,*
> *O Lord, divide once again the waters*
> *of the Red Sea, and let the impious*
> *perish in the flood of Thy wrath!*

In 1475, unable to bear the vice and corruption around him any longer, he entered the Dominican Order in Bologna, only to find the Roman Catholic Church equally corrupt. This discovery gave rise to his next poem, 'The Ruin of the Church', in which he denounced the Vatican as a 'false, proud harlot'. He remained in the Church, however, finding solace in prayer and fasting, and

A portrait of Savonarola by the Renaissance painter Fra Bartolommeo (1472–1517).

resolving to combat wickedness and reform morals. A close study of the Book of Revelation (see John of Patmos, pages 38–41), on which he preached sermons in 1486, excited his interest in prophecy and the Apocalypse. Thus armed, he arrived in Florence in 1489 to serve as prior of the Dominican monastery of San Marco.

A HOTBED OF HUMANISM

Savonarola was appalled by what he witnessed in Florence. In the 1480s the city was ruled by Lorenzo de' Medici ('The Magnificent'), a member of a wealthy dynasty and a great patron of the arts. For much of the previous century Florence had been at the heart of a vibrant cultural revival, a rebirth of painting, sculpture and architecture that owed much of its inspiration to the example of the ancient Greeks and Romans. The city's artists and writers turned for wisdom and inspiration not to the Bible but to the writings of the ancients: preachers quoted Ovid from the pulpit, Plato and Virgil were taught at the university, and artists and sculptors such as Sandro Botticelli and Michelangelo depicted scenes and subjects from classical mythology. 'They tickle men's ears with talk of Aristotle and Plato, Virgil and Petrarch,' Savonarola complained in a sermon, 'and take no concern in the salvation of souls.'

Savonarola found such 'paganism' dangerously misguided because the ancients, living before the time of Christ, had lacked what he called 'the supernatural light of faith'. He wished to turn Florence from 'a new Rome' or 'new Athens' into a 'new Jerusalem', and for the Florentines to be inspired not by pagan writers but by the Bible and the Early Christian martyrs. He objected not only to the study of classics but also to the opulent attire of the Florentines, their love of gambling, cosmetics, mirrors, and even their paintings and musical instruments. 'You fill your churches with your own vanities,' he protested with regard to the beautiful frescoes and altarpieces that had been painted for Florence's churches.

FIRE AND BRIMSTONE

At first the Florentines were impervious to Savonarola's rebukes. However, in the spring of 1492 he preached a series of sermons which described in horrifying detail visions that he claimed were divinely inspired. The night before one sermon he had seen a hand bearing a dagger descend from the sky above Florence, after which the sky darkened and then arrows and swords rained down in the city; war, famine and pestilence followed. In another vision, revealed to him on Good Friday in 1492, a black cross rose into the sky above Rome while a golden cross appeared above Jerusalem: anyone failing to worship the golden cross would be slain, he prophesied, by invaders that he graphically described as 'barbers armed with giant razors'. 'O Florence,' he declaimed

SAVONAROLA
A Life in Brief

1452 Girolamo Savonarola born in Ferrara, northern Italy

1469 Lorenzo de' Medici becomes ruler of the Florentine Republic, promoting Renaissance literature and art in the city

1475 Savonarola joins the Dominican Order

1492 Death of Lorenzo de' Medici; Savonarola preaches the first of his sermons prophesying death and destruction to Florence

1494 In an apparent fulfilment of one of Savonarola's apocalyptic visions, Charles VIII of France invades Italy, capturing Florence and allowing Florentine republicans to overthrow the ruling Medici

1497 The first Bonfire of the Vanities: Savonarola and his supporters burn 'immoral' worldly goods, including works of art and literature; Savonarola is excommunicated

1498 Public execution of Savonarola on the Piazza della Signoria in Florence

from the pulpit, 'for your sins, for your brutality, your avarice, your lust, your ambition, there will befall you many trials and tribulations!' His words unleashed mass hysteria in the cathedral; even the scribe recording his words broke down in tears, while his followers, who staggered through the city wailing and crying, became known as the *Piagnoni*, or 'snivellers'.

THE BONFIRE OF THE VANITIES

Savonarola's reputation as a prophet and divinely inspired messenger of the Lord was dramatically enhanced when his prophecy about an invasion of Florence was fulfilled. In September 1494 the king of France, Charles VIII, invaded Italy with an army of 30,000 men in order to press his claim to the throne of Naples. Crushing all opposing armies, he entered Florence in triumph in the middle of November, causing the Medici to flee the city. When the French departed 11 days later for Rome and Naples, Savonarola found himself more powerful than ever. He even wrote a treatise called *Dialogue on Prophetic Truth* in which he asserted that God still gave men the gift of prophecy, and that he himself was one of these persons. Even as shrewd and cynical an observer as Niccolò Machiavelli, then a young man, believed Savonarola to be possessed of the gift of prophecy: 'Everybody knows,' he later wrote, 'how the descent into Italy of Charles VIII, King of France, was predicted by Brother Girolamo Savonarola.'

> ❛O FLORENCE, FOR YOUR SINS, FOR YOUR BRUTALITY, YOUR AVARICE, YOUR LUST, YOUR AMBITION, THERE WILL BEFALL YOU MANY TRIALS AND TRIBULATIONS!❜

In the years that followed, Savonarola exerted massive influence over the city's moral and political life. He preached moral regeneration from his pulpit (including the stoning to death of homosexuals) and ordered the people to fast for three days a week on bread and water (as a result of which the butchers suffered financially). He rid the church of San Marco of its illuminated manuscripts and gold crucifixes, then urged the Florentines to follow suit in their own homes. The result was a Bonfire of the Vanities on the Piazza della Signoria in 1497, at which playing cards, bottles of perfume, carnival masks, musical instruments, and even books and paintings were heaped into a 60-foot-high pile in the middle of the city's public square and set alight.

SAVONAROLA'S STAR WANES

Savonarola's fall was as dramatic as his rise. In the summer of 1497 he was excommunicated by Pope Alexander VI (né Rodrigo Borgia) for promoting dangerous doctrines. Decrying the excommunication as invalid, Savonarola continued to preach and celebrate Mass, even holding a second bonfire in 1498. Many in the city, however, had begun to turn against him. In the spring of 1498 a Franciscan friar denounced him as a heretic and a false prophet, challenging him to prove the truth of his claims by means of an ordeal by fire. Savonarola declined the opportunity, though one of his followers, Brother Domenico, took up the challenge. On 7 April a fire was lit in Florence's public square and Brother Domenico was invited to pass through it. The ordeal fizzled out when he insisted on carrying the Blessed Sacrament with him into the flames – a gesture deemed tantamount to blasphemy. The ordeal was called off, but the unsatisfactory episode cost Savonarola much of his support. The following day, Palm Sunday, a mob stormed San Marco and seized the friar. He was taken to prison and, under torture, confessed that his prophecies had been based on what his Dominican spies had learned in the confessional. In mid-May two papal commissioners arrived from Rome. As the people greeting them chanted 'Death to the friar!' one commissioner confidently informed them: 'He shall die without fail.'

On 23 May Savonarola and two of his followers, including Brother Domenico, were led to a scaffold on the Piazza della Signoria with their hands bound. Brother Domenico believed in Savonarola to the last: 'Keep this well in mind,' he proclaimed, 'that the prophecies of Brother Girolamo will all be fulfilled, and that we die innocent.' Savonarola's companions were hanged first; then, as the executioner turned to the friar, a voice in the crowd shouted: 'O prophet, now is the time for a miracle!' But none occurred. Savonarola was hanged, then the scaffold was set alight and the bodies burned. Though the authorities tried to dispose of the friar's remains by throwing them into the River Arno, his devotees claimed to have recovered some of them, including his heart, which was said to have miraculous powers of healing and exorcism.

In the decades after his death, many of Savonarola's doom-laden prophecies appeared to fulfil themselves, especially when another scourge of clerical corruption, Martin Luther, set the Reformation in motion in 1517. In the turbulence that followed, the *Piagnoni* saw in each bloody battle or invasion a chastisement from the Lord that fulfilled another of the friar's terrible prognostications.

(Ursula Sontheil)
Mother Shipton
1488–1561

English Wisewoman

In 1488, according to legend, an illegitimate child was born to a 15-year-old orphan, Agatha, in a cave beside the River Nidd at Knaresborough in North Yorkshire, England. The birth was said to have been accompanied by a crack of thunder and the smell of sulphur, and the baby was huge and ugly. Rumoured to be a daughter of the devil, the child was nevertheless rather surprisingly baptized by the abbot of Beverley and given the name Ursula Sontheil.

When Ursula was two years old, Agatha retired to a convent in Nottingham, leaving her child in the care of a foster mother. This woman blamed Ursula's mischievous exploits on the devil, thus fuelling gossip that she was indeed Satan's daughter. Ursula is said to have shown signs of remarkable abilities when quite young; not only did she have the power to foretell the future, but from an early age she would also play tricks on anyone who behaved unkindly towards her.

A HIDEOUS SOOTHSAYER
Though Ursula had a deformity, possibly the hunchback proverbially common among witches, she was also very intelligent. Despite her appearance – bulging eyes, a huge nose and a face adorned with red and blue pimples – at the age of 24 she managed to find herself a husband. He was a local carpenter, Toby Shipton, hence the name 'Mother Shipton' by which she has

A woodcut of c.1488–1560 depicts Mother Shipton,
Cardinal Wolsey and the city of York.

been known throughout the centuries. The fact that such an unprepossessing woman still found a love match inevitably gave rise to rumours that she had used charms or potions to ensnare the simple man, although the pair were said to be 'very comfortable' together.

Early on, when she forecast that 'Water shall come over Ouze Bridge; and a windmill shall be set upon a tower, and an Elm tree shall lie at every man's door,' her words became fact, as a piped water system was set up in York, a windmill drawing up water from the river, which then crossed the bridge to people's houses through pipes made of elm wood. She further prophesied that: 'Before Ouze Bridge and Trinity Church meet, what is built in the day shall fall in the night, till the highest stone of the Church be the lowest stone of the Bridge.' Following a great storm one night, York's Trinity Church did indeed collapse; part of the steeple was swept away into the river and, when the bridge was rebuilt, stone from the top of the steeple was used in the foundations. Rather more alarming was her prophecy about the Lord Mayor of York: 'When there is a Lord Mayor living in Minster-yard, let him beware of a stab,' she warned. Later a Lord Mayor living in Minster Yard did indeed die of stab wounds.

Mother Shipton's ability to foretell the future caused people to treat her with a somewhat fearful respect; as she became more confident, so her predictions covered matters of wider significance and her reputation spread throughout the country. Her prophecies, like those of Nostradamus (see pages 73–76), were given in obscure verse form and many meanings can be read into them. Even so, many of her predictions came to pass within her own lifetime, and others in later centuries.

PROPHECY IN AN AGE OF TURMOIL

Prophets have a habit of making their mystical utterances at times when people have a particular need for clarification or comfort. In the 16th century, England was in a state of havoc and change, caused by Henry VIII's wars in France and his divorce that occasioned the split from Rome. Mother Shipton predicted that the 'English Lion' (Henry VIII) – would 'set his paw on the Gallic shore' and that the 'Lilies' (the French) 'would begin to droop for fear'. And sure enough, with the help of Emperor Maximilian of Austria, Henry's invasion of France was successful. Later she forecast the Dissolution of the Monasteries and the fall of Henry's Lord Chancellor, Cardinal Thomas Wolsey. Scathingly calling him 'the Mitred Peacock,' she stated that: 'his Train shall make a great show in the World – for a time; but shall afterwards vanish away, and his great Honour come to nothing.' Cardinal Wolsey heard this troubling prophecy, together with an additional forecast that he would see – but never reach – York.

So great was the reputation of Mother Shipton that the cardinal sent three noble lords in disguise to Knaresborough to try to gather further, and hopefully more promising, information. The prophetess was unable to oblige, but when told that Wolsey would have her burned at the stake as a witch on reaching York, she threw her shawl into the fire, followed by her stick, neither of which would burn – thus confirming her visitors' fear of her powers of sorcery.

Soon after this episode, Wolsey did indeed set out for York. Spending the night at a castle nearby, he climbed the tower to try to make out the city in the distance. But the next day, before he could continue his journey, he was met by Lord Percy who had come to escort him back to London to face a charge of high treason; en route he fell ill and never regained consciousness.

Mother Shipton made many prophecies in the years that followed, concerning Edward VI, Lady Jane Grey, the prosecution of Protestants by Queen Mary and the death of Mary Queen of Scots. The old prophetess of Knaresborough died in 1561, but her predictions resonated long after her death, covering, for example, events such as the Plague of 1665 and the Great Fire of London the following year:

> *Triumphant death rides London through*
> *And men on tops of houses go.*

FORETELLING THE MODERN WORLD

Mother Shipton's prophecies did not stop with the Tudors and Stuarts; many of her rhyming couplets appear to predict all manner of technological innovations, such as cars and trains: 'A carriage without horse will go'; iron ships: 'In water iron then shall float / as easy as a wooden

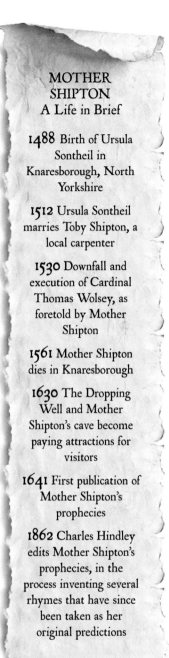

MOTHER SHIPTON
A Life in Brief

1488 Birth of Ursula Sontheil in Knaresborough, North Yorkshire

1512 Ursula Sontheil marries Toby Shipton, a local carpenter

1530 Downfall and execution of Cardinal Thomas Wolsey, as foretold by Mother Shipton

1561 Mother Shipton dies in Knaresborough

1630 The Dropping Well and Mother Shipton's cave become paying attractions for visitors

1641 First publication of Mother Shipton's prophecies

1862 Charles Hindley edits Mother Shipton's prophecies, in the process inventing several rhymes that have since been taken as her original predictions

boat'; aeroplanes: 'And men shall fly as birds do now'; submarines: 'Beneath the water, men shall walk / shall ride, shall sleep, shall even talk'; telephones, radio or perhaps even the internet: 'Around the world thoughts shall fly / in the twinkling of an eye'; combine harvesters (or maybe tanks): 'And roaring monsters with men atop / shall seem to eat the verdant crop'.

Mother Shipton made several apocalyptic forecasts concerning wars and strife, murder and other dastardly deeds, volcanoes, earthquakes, disease, floods and famine. One prophecy that fortunately did not come true was the ending of the world in 1881. Despite the fact that it was over 300 years since her death, fear of this prognostication caused many people to spend sleepless nights at prayer throughout that year.

CRANK OR WISEWOMAN?

Was Mother Shipton a genuine seer or just an eccentric recluse whose reputation grew with time? Her prophecies first appeared in print in 1641; however, since very few people could read, stories were passed on by word of mouth, giving ample scope for confusion and embellishment. The tales of her deeds and sayings must therefore be taken with a large pinch of salt – although some of these prophecies certainly can be interpreted as having forecast later events. Numerous books have been written recounting her life and prophetic verses: Charles Hindley, who edited her rhymes in 1862, later admitted to making most of them up – although it is possible that he may be referring only to the later verses, which seem to be written in a more modern style. But there is no doubt some people used the fear generated by Mother Shipton's words for their own ends.

The cave in Knaresborough where Mother Shipton is said to have been born still exists, beside the so-called Petrifying or Dropping Well. Local people believed the well to be magic and kept their distance, having seen small objects, such as leaves or a dead bird, turned to stone in its falling waters. Later it became a place to which many came to drink or wash in its waters, which were reputed to have healing powers. By 1630 the well's fame led to it becoming the earliest paying visitor attraction in England. The high mineral content gives the water a calcifying effect: objects left there to become petrified include a shoe belonging to Queen Mary, who visited in 1923 and, more recently, items from the cast of various TV soap operas, plus a number of teddy bears and soft toys.

Spain's 'Wooden Horses'

Three years before the death of Mother Shipton, Queen Elizabeth I came to the throne. The prophetess of Knaresborough accurately predicted many of the events of the long reign of England's 'Virgin Queen', including a clear allusion to the defeat of the Spanish Armada in 1588:

> The maiden Queen full many a year
> Shall England's warlike sceptre bear.
> Those who sighed, then shall sing
> And the bells shall changes ring.
> The Papal power shall bear no sway
> And Rome's trash shall hence be swept away.
> The locusts from the Seven Hills
> This English Rose shall seek to kill -
> And the Western monarch's wooden horses
> Shall be destroyed by Drake's forces.

Nostradamus
1503–66

French Seer and Astrologer

During his lifetime, Nostradamus, born Michel de Nostredame in Saint-Rémy-de-Provence in southern France, made over 6000 prophesies. They have rarely been out of print since his death in 1566. He has been credited with predicting such diverse events as the Plague of London (1665), the Great Fire of London (1666), the rise of both Napoleon and Adolf Hitler, the two world wars, and even the terrorist attacks of 11 September 2001.

Nostradamus, in a 17th-century portrait by Jean Boulanger (1608–80).

Little is known of Michel's childhood years other than that he was one of eight children born to grain dealer Jaume de Nostredame. Nostradamus's grandfather, Guy Gassonet, was a Jew who converted to Catholicism and changed his name to Pierre Nostredame. His grandson was to Latinize the family name to Nostradamus in 1550, when he published his first almanac.

FROM MEDICINE TO MAGIC

Nostradamus entered the University of Avignon at the age of 15, but his time there was short as an outbreak of plague forced its closure. Nostradamus then worked as an apothecary until 1529, when he enrolled at the University of Montpellier to study medicine; however, when it was discovered he had engaged in a manual trade – which disbarred him from university entry – he was promptly expelled.

Further misfortunes followed. Nostradamus married young, but his wife and two children were carried off by the plague in 1534. After their deaths he travelled in France and Italy for ten years, working as an apothecary in Marseilles, Salon-de-Provence and Aix-en-Provence and

'ALTHOUGH, MY SON, I HAVE USED THE WORD PROPHET, I WOULD NOT ATTRIBUTE TO MYSELF A TITLE OF SUCH LOFTY SUBLIMITY.'

using his medical knowledge to help combat the plague (although he admitted later that his remedies, notably the 'Rose Pill', were ineffective). In 1547 he settled in Salon-de-Provence and married Anne Ponsarde, a widow who bore him six children. Around this time, Nostradamus's interest drifted away from medicine and towards the occult, and in 1550 he wrote his first almanac. These almanacs included weather forecasts, planting and social calendars with some general predictions and military events added for good measure. They were extremely popular, being published annually – and sometimes several times a year – until his death.

READING THE STARS

In 1555 Nostradamus began compiling a collection of 1000 long-term predictions, stretching as far ahead as the year 3797. Written in batches of 100, known as 'Centuries', and following no particular logical or sequential order, these verses form part of his famous work *The Prophecies*. The second collection was published in 1557 and the third in 1568, two years after his death. His quatrains – four-line verses in a mixture of French, Latin, Greek and Italian – were made deliberately obscure in order to avoid (some people argue) accusations of heresy. Century IV:55 is typical of his allusive style:

> *When the crow on a tower made of brick*
> *will do nothing but croak for seven hours;*
> *it foretells death, a statue stained with blood,*
> *a tyrant murdered, people praying to their Gods.*

Nostradamus claimed his system of prediction was based on judicial astrology, a means of forecasting future events by calculating the movements of planetary and stellar bodies and their relationship to the Earth. His method was heavily criticized by his fellow astrologers, who considered it impossible to predict the future in this way. His almanacs were so popular with the general public, however, that requests came to him from far and wide to compile personal horoscopes.

Nostradamus eventually gained a powerful devotee. After reading his 1550 almanac, Queen Catherine de' Medici, wife of King Henri II of France, invited him to Paris to write horoscopes for her children. In 1555, he was summoned to court again, allegedly to discuss a prophecy that seemed to suggest that her husband would be killed in a duel:

> *The young lion will overcome the older one,*
> *in a field of combat in single fight;*
> *He will pierce his eyes in their golden cage;*
> *two wounds in one, then he dies a cruel death.*

The duel nonetheless went ahead. In honour of the marriages of the king's sister and daughter, tournaments were

---

NOSTRADAMUS
A Life in Brief

1503 Nostradamus born in Saint-Rémy-de-Provence on 14 December

1518 Enters the University of Avignon

1531 Travels to Agen, where he marries

1534 Nostradamus's wife and children die from the plague

1545 Returns to France after travelling first in France and later in Italy

1547 Nostradamus settles in Salon-de-Provence, where he marries Anne Ponsarde, who bears him six children

1550 Writes the first of his yearly almanacs, Latinizing his name from Nostredame to Nostradamus

1555 After reading his almanacs for 1555, which hint at unnamed threats to the royal family, Catherine de'Medici, the queen consort of King Henri II of France, summons Nostradamus to Paris to explain them

1561 Nostradamus is imprisoned for publishing his almanac without the prior permission of a bishop

1566 Dies of dropsy on 1 July, having foretold his own death

held with King Henri jousting against Gabriel, comte de Montgomery, captain of the king's Scottish guards. In an apparent confirmation of Nostradamus's prophecy, the king was fatally wounded when splinters from Montgomery's lance pierced his helmet and entered his eye. King Henri died in agony ten days later. However, there is no evidence that Nostradamus actually composed this quatrain, which was not printed until 55 years after his own death.

OPAQUE PREDICTIONS

In the 20th century Nostradamus's prophecies were interpreted as anticipating major events such the Spanish influenza epidemic of 1918–19; he wrote of a 'horrible war prepared by the West that is followed by pestilence' (Century IX:55). The assassinations of John F. Kennedy and Robert Kennedy are apparently foretold in Century I:26: 'The great man will be struck down by a thunderbolt in the day and another falls at nightime.' An interpretation of another verse suggests that the Antichrist whom Nostradamus claims will start a Third World War will come from beyond the 'great Tartary' – evidently China. As no specific names or dates are mentioned in any of these quatrains, however, they are open to many interpretations.

There is much disagreement as to whether Nostradamus was indeed a seer or merely a clever entrepreneur who earned a good living from his predictions. Closer inspection of his verses has revealed allusions to the works of classical historians and chroniclers such as Plutarch, Suetonius, Livy, Villehardouin and Froissart. His apocalyptic prophecies, moreover, resemble both biblical passages and the *Mirabilis Liber*, a collection of prophecies printed in 1522. Even those who believe he was a true prophet rarely agree on what he predicted, and many of his prophecies require a certain amount of semantic violence to reach their 'fulfilment'. For example, his supposed prediction of the rise of Hitler (Century II:24) has been translated thus by Erika Cheetham:

> *Beasts wild with hunger will cross the rivers,*
> *the greater part of the battlefield will be*
>   *against Hitler.*
> *He will drag the leader in a cage of iron,*
> *when the child of Germany observes no*
>   *law.*

In his original text, however, Nostradamus wrote not of 'Hitler' but of 'Hister', a probable reference to a name by which the Lower Danube was formerly known. Another of Nostradamus's prophecies, Century VI:97, is claimed by some commentators to anticipate the terrorist attacks of 11 September 2001:

> *Five and forty degrees, the sky shall burn:*
> *To great 'New City' shall the fire draw*
>   *nigh.*
> *With vehemence the flames shall spread and*
>   *churn,*
> *when with the Normans they conclusions*
>   *try.*

However, New York's latitude is, technically speaking, 40°47', not 45 or even 40.5 degrees, while the term 'New City' appears frequently in Nostradamus's quatrains, where it literally denotes a new city.

Claim and Counterclaim

In 1939, after reading the works of Nostradamus, Magda Goebbels, wife of Nazi propaganda minister Josef Goebbels, excitedly passed them on to her husband. He immediately spotted their potential, writing in his diary:

> *The Americans and English fall easily to this kind of propaganda. We are therefore pressing into service all star witnesses of occult prophecy. Nostradamus must once again submit to being quoted.*

Indeed, so impressed was Goebbels by the power of this medieval Frenchman's predictions that he ordered verses to be forged predicting that Hitler would win the Second World War. Printed copies were dropped from aeroplanes all over France. The British retaliated by dropping their own Nostradamus leaflets, which confidently forecast Hitler's defeat.

In later years, Nostradamus was troubled with gout and arthritis, which restricted his movements and eventually developed into oedema. In June 1566, sensing the end was near, he made a will bequeathing his worldly goods to his wife, with trusts for his children, since by this time he was quite a wealthy man. On the evening of 1 July, he told his secretary, Jean de Chavigny: 'You will not find me alive at sunrise.' This prophecy, at least, proved accurate: the following day he was found dead beside his bed. Nostradamus was buried in a Franciscan chapel that is now part of the restaurant La Brocherie in Rue d'Hozier, in Salon-de-Provence, southern France. His body was exhumed by superstitious soldiers during the French Revolution but later re-interred in the Collégiale St-Laurent in Salon after the town's mayor placated the soldiers by assuring them that Nostradamus, in Century 1:3, had predicted the successful outcome of the Revolution.

Nostradamus's predictions have exerted a powerful influence on the public imagination for over 400 years. And, if the 9 million website addresses on the Internet linked to him are anything to judge by, this influence shows no signs of waning.

COINNEACH ODHAR
c.1600–c.1675

The Brahan Seer

In 1851, great crowds flocked by both carriage and railway to Fairburn Tower, near Dingwall in northern Scotland. The attraction was a cow that had given birth on the top floor of a ruined tower that once belonged to the Mackenzies of Fairburn, lairds of the Seaforth estate. The animal had entered the abandoned building and climbed the winding stairs to the top, where the tenant farmer stored fodder. After eating her fill, she was unable to descend. But what lent this curious local event real drawing power was the fact that it had been precisely forecast by a Highland seer two centuries earlier.

The seer in question was a man named Coinneach Odhar ('Kenneth the Sallow'), known to folklore as the Brahan Seer. Little is known of his life, but he was supposedly born at the beginning of the 17th century in the Outer Hebrides, in the village of Baile-na-Cille, on the remote Isle of Benbecula, 35 miles (56 km) south of the Isle of Lewis.

COINNEACH'S SECOND SIGHT

Several stories exist as to how Coinneach received his prophetic gift. The least credible involves his mother meeting the ghost of a Norwegian princess who had drowned while bathing in the sea and then been buried in the churchyard at Baile-na-Cille. The princess directed Coinneach's mother to a lake where she found a small blue stone with a hole in the centre that allowed her son to see future events. Other versions of the story claim that Coinneach himself found the stone while cutting peat near Dingwall, on the estate of the Kenneth Mor Mackenzie, third earl of Seaforth, a wealthy clansman for whom he worked as a labourer. The stone saved his life in these tales, since he woke up from an afternoon nap on a hillside to find the mysterious stone tucked inside his waistcoat. Peering through the hole, he saw how the earl's wife – or, in one version, his own wife – has poisoned the lunch that sat temptingly beside him. Wisely, he spurned the meal and went on to find fame as a seer.

The Brahan Seer had bad news for the Mackenzies. As the last of their line sank into his grave, he claimed: 'the remnant of his possessions shall be inherited by a white-hooded lassie from the East, and she is to kill her sister.' These events duly unfolded. The death of Francis Mackenzie and his four sons meant the Seaforth estate passed to his eldest daughter, Lady Mary, who was stationed for several years in the East Indies as the wife of Vice-Admiral Sir Samuel Hood. Following Sir Samuel's death in Madras in 1814, she returned to England dressed in the traditional Indian white hood of morning. Nine years later, in 1823, this 'white-hooded lassie from the East' took her unmarried sister for a ride in a pony carriage near Brahan Castle. Lady Mary lost control of the vehicle, which overturned and – as the Brahan Seer had foretold – killed her sister.

Highland legend attributes numerous other prophecies to the Brahan Seer. Some involved minor events, such as 'a black hornless cow' giving birth to a two-headed calf, or a fox rearing a litter of cubs on the hearthstone of Castle Downie. Another concerned Strathpeffer, a village some 15 miles (24 km) northwest of Inverness. One of its attractions is an ancient monument known as the Eagle Stone, a rock carved with the image of an eagle, the symbol of the Munro clan. Coinneach claimed that if the stone fell over three times, then the valley would flood. The Eagle Stone is reputed to have been toppled twice already in its history; in the 1930s, after another of Coinneach's forecasts was fulfilled

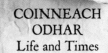

COINNEACH ODHAR
Life and Times

c.1600 Coinneach Odhar, the Brahan Seer, born in Baile-na-Cille on the Outer Hebridean island of Benbecula

c.1675 The Brahan Seer is executed at Chanonry Point on the Moray Firth, allegedly for insulting his master, the third earl of Seaforth

1746 Devastating defeat of the Jacobite army at the Battle of Culloden, an event foretold by Coinneach

1769 First mention in print of the Brahan Seer, in Thomas Pennant's *A Tour in Scotland*

1877 Alexander Mackenzie publishes his bestselling *The Prophecies of the Brahan Seer*, the first collection of Coinneach's prognostications

(see box feature, page 78), the authorities there took the precaution of cementing the rock firmly in place.

BEARER OF BAD TIDINGS

Other prophecies of Coinneach dealt with less parochial matters, such as the Battle of Culloden. While passing by what would later become the notorious battlefield that claimed the lives of more than 1200 Scottish clansmen in April 1746, the Brahan Seer is said to have exclaimed:

A carved stone in Ross, northern Scotland, associated with the Brahan Seer.

'Thy bleak moor shall, ere many generations have passed away, be stained with the best blood of the Highlands.' Another of his prognostications – 'the clans will become so effeminate as to flee from their native country before an army of sheep' – may anticipate the Highland clearances (the enclosure of farmland and forcible eviction of tenant farmers by wealthy landowners in the late 18th and early 19th centuries).

> ' GLAD AM I THAT I WILL NOT SEE THAT DAY [OF THE BATTLE OF CULLODEN], FOR IT WILL BE A FEARFUL PERIOD; HEADS WILL BE LOPPED OFF BY THE SCORE AND NO MERCY SHALL BE SHOWN … ON EITHER SIDE. '

The Brahan Seer met the untimely end that often awaits a prophet. One version holds that his knowledge of Lord Seaforth's adultery in Paris, unwisely related to Lady Seaforth, brought about his death. In another version he died resulting from a snide comment at a dinner party, when he remarked that the Seaforths' aristocratic young guests looked more like 'the children of footmen and grooms'. In both versions he was arrested on Lady Seaforth's orders, accused of witchcraft, and thrown headfirst into a barrel of burning tar. Even so, there was still time for one last prophecy. As he was arrested he threw his magic stone into boggy ground outside the castle, proclaiming that it would be found inside the belly of a pike by a child born with two navels, who would then inherit his powers. To date, despite much searching of the bog in the years after Coinneach's death, this prophecy has yet to be fulfilled.

Trains, Gas Mains and Flying Machines

Like his more famous Provençal predecessor, the 'Nostradamus of the North' apparently foretold the advent of new technologies. For example, he predicted a time would come 'when full-rigged ships will be seen sailing eastward and westward by the back of Tomnahurich', a wooded hill on the outskirts of Inverness. The forecast seemed absurd to his contemporaries, but 150 years later, in 1822, the Caledonian Canal opened and ships did indeed sail behind Tomnahurich Hill. He also predicted the appearance of 'a chariot without horse or bridle' (variously interpreted as a train or an automobile) and streams of fire and water flowing beneath the streets of Glasgow (fulfilled two centuries later when gas mains and water pipes were laid beneath the city's streets). One of his stranger prophecies was that a ship would come from the sky and moor itself on a church steeple in Strathpeffer. This seemingly unlikely event came to pass in 1932, when the mooring ropes of an airship taking off from a nearby fair became entangled with the spire of St Anne's Church in the town.

SHROUDED IN MYTH

Did Coinneach Odhar truly exist? No mention of him appears in print until 1769, and the only written sources for his prophecies are 19th-century collections and commentaries by historians and folklorists. Nor is there any reliable record of his life. Like Merlin, King Arthur and Robin Hood, he remains a highly elusive figure. Intriguingly, scholars have discovered that in 1577 an 'enchanter' known as Keanoch Owir was prosecuted for 'diabolical, inquitious and odious crimes of the art of magic' by the authorities in Ross-shire, the county where the Brahan Seer is said to have lived. Oral tradition in the Highlands may have built the myth of Coinneach Odhar on the distant memory of Keanoch the enchanter. Whatever the truth, the 'Nostradamus of the North' has exerted a strong fascination for several centuries, especially in Scotland, and the novelist Sir Walter Scott and the scientist Sir Humphry Davy both reputedly set great store by his prophecies.

JOSEPH SMITH JR
1805–44

Founder of the Mormons

In 1830, Joseph Smith Jr founded the Church of Jesus Christ of Latter-Day Saints, better known as the Mormons. Determined to take Christianity back to its origins, he built temples, revised the Bible, experienced visions and uttered a series of prophecies and revelations. Ultimately, his unorthodox teachings and his views on polygamy led to his murder by an Illinois mob, and he still remains a deeply controversial figure. Yet his church today boasts a worldwide membership of over 12.5 million.

Soon after Joseph Smith's birth, his family moved from Vermont and settled on a farm near Palmyra, in western New York State. Poor, ill-educated and unaffiliated to any particular religious denomination, Smith's parents believed in heavenly voices, direct revelations and miraculous cures. His father used a divining rod to search for wells and hidden treasure, and young Joseph, inspired by a local magician, began to use a seer stone for the same purpose. As a child he suffered from 'falling fits' – probably epileptic seizures – and it was after one such episode that he started to experience visions.

Many new religious sects were flourishing in New York State in the early 19th century. At the age of 14, Smith went alone into the woods to pray for guidance on which to join. God and Jesus appeared to him, warning him that all churches were corrupt and telling him to await their further instructions.

HEAVENLY VISITATIONS

Four years later, in 1823, Smith claimed that God sent the angel Moroni to him to tell him about the 'Bible of the Western Continent', a supplement to the New Testament that explained the history of an ancient Hebrew tribe. According to Moroni, a small band of Israelites had landed on the coast of Chile in 600 BC; their descendants had split into two groups, the Nephites and the Lamanites, who proceeded to fight each other until the former were virtually exterminated. Moroni, who had once lived among the Nephites, had recorded the history of the tribes on golden plates which he hid, awaiting the arrival of his Chosen One.

In 1827, Smith claimed that Moroni had shown him their hiding place – at a drumlin called Cumorah, near Rochester, New York. Here, on the site where the Lamanites and Nephites had fought their final battle, Smith unearthed a stone box containing a set of golden plates, 20 by 15 centimetres (8 in x 6 in), fastened with three gold rings. The plates were inscribed with hieroglyphics, their Egyptian origin being confirmed, according to the Mormons, in 1828 by Dr Charles Anthon, Professor of Latin and Greek at Colombia College, New York. The professor later denied the claim, however, stating that the writing was 'anything else but Egyptian hieroglyphics'.

As well as the golden plates, Smith also found a pair of spectacles, known as Urim and Thummin – names referring to special divination tools (possibly stones or crystals) that had

The Prophet Joseph Smith Preaching to the Indians:
engraving by Charles Mettais (1860).

been used by Aaron and other high priests to discover the will of the Lord. The spectacles
consisted of crystal eye-glasses that enabled Smith to translate the hieroglyphics on the plates.
Barely literate himself, he employed a succession of scribes – his wife Emma, a farmer named
Martin Harris, and two friends, Oliver Chowdry and David Whitmer. Over a period of 21
months, they recorded Smith's dictation – almost 300,000 words of it – as he sat behind a
curtain studying the plates with the help of Urim and Thummin.

Smith was able to translate only the first 116 pages of the golden plates before the angel
Moroni removed them, along with the spectacles, as a punishment for having allowed Harris
to borrow the translated pages to show his wife. Later, Moroni returned the plates but not the
spectacles. Thereafter Smith was reduced to translating with his seer stone, which he placed
in a hat into which he buried his face. This technique, which he had learnt as a youngster,
apparently enabled him to read the script. However, the process had already landed Smith in
trouble with the law; he had been found guilty in 1826 of fraudulent interpretation following
an attempt to locate buried treasure for a group of investors, and released from gaol only on
condition that he left the area.

In 1830, with Harris's financial backing, 5000 copies of the Book of Mormon – an allusion
to the angel Moroni – were printed and Smith declared to be God's prophet, entitled to power
and obedience from his followers. To prove the validity of the golden plates, 11 witnesses
including Smith, his father and two brothers, Hyrum and Samuel, signed affidavits confirming
they had either seen them or witnessed Joseph translating them using the seer stone. Not long
afterwards, Moroni again removed the plates, since when they have never reappeared.

MOUNTING OPPOSITION

The first Mormon Church, known as the Church of Christ, was founded in 1830, Smith and Chowdry having baptized each other in Lake Seneca, on instruction from John the Baptist. They in turn baptized their followers and sent them out to spread the message. From this point on, Smith started to attract serious opposition from what the Mormons referred to as 'gentiles'. As a result, Smith was forced to move from Pennsylvania to Kirtland, Ohio, home of a recent Mormon convert, Sidney Rigdon.

Smith soon became unpopular in Kirtland, however, and a year after establishing his headquarters there, he was dragged from his bed, tarred and feathered. Following one of his revelations, he and his colleagues had set up the Kirtland Safety Society Bank, which promptly collapsed, leaving large debts. Accused of unethical banking, Smith faced civil law suits and was arrested for fraud. Many of his followers lost money, causing a schism within the Church of Christ, and in 1838 Smith and Rigdon fled to Missouri, Smith informing his remaining followers that Jesus Christ would return – to the town of Independence.

Mormons from other states started to descend on Missouri, causing violent skirmishes with the locals. Following Rigdon's sermon urging followers to wage a 'war of extermination' on anyone who disturbed the Mormons, their fate was sealed. Governor Liburn W. Boggs issued an 'Extermination Order', stating that Mormons be treated as enemies and driven from Missouri, for the sake of public peace. Smith and his church leaders were jailed, charged with treason and the attempted murder of Governor Boggs.

TURMOIL IN NAUVOO

Released from prison several months later, Smith fled to Illinois, accompanied by 15,000 followers. Here, he established himself in the small town of Commerce, which he renamed Nauvoo – Hebrew for 'pleasant land'. Somehow he managed to acquire a charter from the State of Illinois giving independent status to the Mormons and allowing them to run their own municipal courts, a university and a 5000-strong military unit known as the Nauvoo Legion. Smith also brought with him his own private army, the Danites, to protect him and to coerce his followers either to conform to his rule or leave the church. For Smith still had many enemies within as well as outside the church; he had thwarted an attempt to depose him as early as 1836, but matters came to a head in 1844 when Hyrum Smith read out his brother's latest revelation – concerning polygamy – to the church council.

Despite the fact that the Book of Mormon forbade polygamy, Smith now stated that the practice, rife in the Old Testament, from Abraham to Solomon with his 700 wives, was again acceptable. Many Mormons opposed this, but between 1833 and 1844, and against the wish of his wife Emma, Smith took 33 further wives, including Emma's sister; 11 of his new wives were already married to his followers. But Smith really overstepped the mark when he took as concubine the wife of Dr R. D. Foster. Foster and another prominent Mormon leader, William Law, set up a newspaper, the *Nauvoo Expositor*. Announcing that Smith had too much power

---

JOSEPH SMITH JR
Life and Times

1805 Joseph Smith born in Sharon, Vermont

1823 Smith receives his first revelation from the angel Moroni

1830 Smith founds the Mormon Church at Fayette, NY

1838 Smith and his followers are forcibly expelled from Missouri

1839 Mormons settle at Nauvoo, Illinois

1844 After sanctioning polygamy, Joseph Smith is murdered: Brigham Young becomes leader of the church

1846 Mormons begin their 'Great Migration' to the west

1847 Young founds Salt Lake City, Utah

1904 The Mormon Church officially renounces polygamy

and that the revelation on polygamy was not sanctioned by God, they demanded that the city's charter be rescinded. Smith responded by shutting down the newspaper, an attack on press freedom that contravened the First Amendment of the United States Constitution. Nauvoo erupted in violence; Smith proclaimed martial law, but was unable to secure the city now that the State of Illinois had become involved. He and his brother Hyrum were arrested and imprisoned, pending trial in nearby Carthage.

Although the governor of Illinois, Thomas Ford, had promised Smith and his associates a fair trial, he was unable to protect the prisoners. In June 1844, a mob of 200 men, their faces blackened to hide their identities, stormed the jail. Shots were fired, killing Hyrum immediately; Smith returned fire, wounding several of his attackers, before he too was shot. He fell to his death from a second-floor window and was buried later in Nauvoo.

SMITH'S LEGACY

Throughout his turbulent life, Joseph Smith made numerous unfulfilled prophecies. He predicted that Jesus Christ would return in 1891; that New York, Albany and Boston would be destroyed if they rejected his Gospel; that the Kirtland Safety Society Bank would prosper; and that the US government would fall if it failed to compensate the Mormons for their mistreatment in Missouri. On his death, he left a wife, three children and 33 women to whom he was 'spiritually' married. He also left the Church of Christ in crisis.

In August 1844, after much turmoil, Brigham Young, a 43-year-old follower, was elected to take up Smith's mantle as leader. As the Mormons continued to be persecuted in Nauvoo, Young led the Latter-Day Saints on an exodus into Utah, where their headquarters remain today. Polygamy was officially banned in 1904, although in the 21st century it is still practised by perhaps as many as 30,000 fundamentalist Mormons.

'I RETIRED TO A SECRET PLACE IN A GROVE, AND BEGAN TO CALL UPON THE LORD; WHILE FERVENTLY ENGAGED IN SUPPLICATION, MY MIND WAS TAKEN AWAY FROM THE OBJECTS WITH WHICH I WAS SURROUNDED, AND I WAS ENWRAPPED IN A HEAVENLY VISION, AND SAW TWO GLORIOUS PERSONAGES, WHO EXACTLY RESEMBLED EACH OTHER IN FEATURES AND LIKENESS, SURROUNDED WITH BRILLIANT LIGHT WHICH ECLIPSED THE SUN AT NOON DAY.'

william miller
1782–1849

The Great Disappointment

On the morning of 22 October 1844, as crowds of people in the northeastern United States waited for the sun to rise and Jesus Christ to appear, the man whose prophecies had drawn them there was apprehensive. For this was the third occasion when followers of William Miller had gathered to witness Christ's return, and although Miller was adamant the Messiah would make an appearance, he was not entirely sure of the precise date.

This uncertainty did not deter the Millerites, as his followers were called. No one knows how many believers gathered together on that day, or on the previous occasions, but estimates vary between 50,000 and 500,000 people. Many had even sold their farms and possessions in anticipation of the promised new Millennium. Some of them, according to newspaper reports, wore white Ascension robes. Like his acolytes, Miller yearned for Christ's return: 'How tedious and lonesome the hours,' he had written a few months earlier, 'while Jesus, my Saviour, delays.' But the delay continued. As the sun breasted the horizon on that chilly autumn morning, the crowds were to be disappointed once again.

William Miller had been raised a Baptist. Born in Pittsfield, Massachusetts, the eldest of 16 siblings, he moved with his family at the age of four to the hamlet of Low Hampton, in upstate New York, on the edge of the Adirondack Mountains. Both his grandfather and father were

William Miller, from a lithograph published in c.1841.

farmers and, although a studious child and voracious reader, William seemed destined to follow in their footsteps. His life's direction changed in 1803 when he married Lucy Smith and moved a few miles to her hometown, Poultney, across the state border in Vermont. While continuing at first to farm, he became increasingly involved in civic life, becoming Constable, Deputy Sheriff and Justice of the Peace. Besides producing ten children, Miller served as a lieutenant in the Vermont militia, while records show that he was also an active Freemason.

A RATIONAL OR REVELATORY GOD?

Shortly after moving to Poultney, Miller renounced his Baptist faith. He had come under the influence of a group of local free thinkers who introduced him to the sceptical thought of the 18th-century British philosophers known as the Deists. The Deists' confidence in the powers of science, combined with their concerns about religious persecution, had brought them to the conviction that reason should be applied to religion, and that nothing in the Bible should be beyond the scrutiny of science. Accordingly, they rejected miracles, prophecy and divine revelation. They believed that God did exist, but

'I AM FULLY CONVINCED THAT SOMEWHERE BETWEEN MARCH 21ST 1843 AND MARCH 21ST 1844, ACCORDING TO THE JEWISH MODE OF COMPUTATION OF TIME, CHRIST WILL COME, AND BRING ALL HIS SAINTS WITH HIM; AND THAT THEN HE WILL REWARD EVERY MAN AS HIS WORK SHALL BE.'

that He did not actively involve Himself with man's life on Earth.

Events, however, ultimately forced Miller to question his religious scepticism. He reversed his beliefs for a second time after taking part in the Battle of Plattsburg in New York state in 1814, during the War of 1812 between Britain and the United States. At Plattsburg, the American contingent of 5000 was outnumbered three to one by an army of seasoned British troops. However, to everyone's amazement, the Americans prevailed, an outcome that Miller saw as miraculous. 'So surprising a result, against such odds,' he wrote in his memoirs, 'did seem to me like the work of a mightier power than man.' This view of divine intervention in human affairs was clearly at odds with his Deist beliefs.

After the war, Miller was discharged from the army and returned first to Poultney before moving with his family to a farm back in Low Hampton. His experiences in the war had unsettled him spiritually, and although he had not entirely abandoned his Deist convictions, he once again began attending Baptist services. On one occasion, when asked to read a sermon on 'The Duty of Parents to Their Children', he was so overcome with emotion that he was unable to finish. Overwhelmed with the love of God, he later wrote in his Apology and Defence: 'I immediately felt how lovely such a Being must be; and imagined that I could cast myself into the arms of, and trust in the mercy of, such an One.'

FORETELLING THE SECOND COMING

Miller's Deist friends challenged his new beliefs, asking how he could be so sure the Bible was the Word of God. Miller responded by studying its contents in detail, and by 1818 he was convinced he had found the answer. Through detailed analysis of the Book of Genesis and other biblical accounts, he declared that it was possible to decipher the

Why 1843?

In working out the date of Christ's return, Miller used the 'Day-Year Principle' first set out in AD 380 by the Christian commentator Tichonius, according to whom the 'three and a half days' mentioned in Revelation (see John of Patmos pages 38-41) as the time elapsing between the deaths of the prophets Elijah and Moses and their resurrection on Judgement Day should be read as three and a half years. Furthermore, Miller interpreted the statement in Daniel 8:14 that in 2300 days 'the sanctuary shall be cleansed' as an allusion to the Earth's purification by the fire of Christ's Second Coming. And so, converting the 2300 days into years, and beginning his count at 457 BC, when Artaxerxes I of Persia had authorized the rebuilding of Jerusalem, Miller arrived at 1843 as the date of the Messiah's return. He would later describe this Second Coming as 'The Advent.'

messages contained within the Bible. Having studied the prophetic numbering systems mentioned in the books of Daniel, Ezekiel and the Book of Revelation, he became convinced that these systems foretold, among several other significant events, the birth of Jesus and the fall of Jerusalem.

In 1822, Miller published his findings to the world at large in a 20-point document. 'I believe that the Second Coming of Jesus Christ is near,' he dramatically proclaimed, 'even at the door, even within twenty-one years – on or before 1843.' Before embarking on a round of public lectures in 1831, which sometimes attracted thousands, Miller continued to hone his hypothesis. After submitting a series of articles to his local Baptist newspaper, he was inundated with requests for more information. In response he published *Evidence from Scripture and History of the Second Coming of Christ, about the Year 1843: Exhibited in a Course of Lectures.* By 1840 Miller had become so popular that Joshua Vaughan Himes, a pastor in Boston, founded a newspaper especially to promote his ideas. Himes also became Miller's publicity manager, helping him to achieve nationwide prominence.

UNQUENCHED FAITH

Miller never wanted to set a specific date for Christ's return, but he was strongly encouraged to do so by his followers, some of whom, his *Memoirs* ruefully state, showed a 'tendency to fanaticism' and 'wild and foolish extremes and vain delusions' that he was anxious to refute. When his original timespan – sometime between 21 March 1843 and 21 March 1844 – came and went without Christ's reappearance, Miller adjusted his calculations to comply with the Jewish calendar. The new date was set for 18 April 1844. Once again, Christ did not appear, and Miller somewhat sheepishly told the world: 'I confess my error, and acknowledge my disappointment; yet I still believe that the day of the Lord is near, even at the door.' One of Miller's followers, Samuel S. Snow, presented a paper at a Millerite meeting in Exeter, New Hampshire, in August of that year, claiming that by using Miller's calculations he had arrived at the date of 21 October 1844. The failure of Christ, once again, to arrive on the appointed date ('the expectation of the Advent at that time,' William Miller's *Memoirs* report, 'was proved to be premature') became known as the Great Disappointment.

In 1845, Miller's ever-faithful followers convened in Albany, New York, to profess their continued belief that the Son of God would return. However, many people were disillusioned by the Great Disappointment. Some returned to their original faiths, while the remaining Millerites split into the Evangelical Adventists – the original believers – and the Seventh-day Adventists. To this day there remain around a half-dozen Protestant sects who still believe that Christ will return in person and that the wicked will be judged and destroyed.

WILLIAM MILLER
A Life in Brief

1782 William Miller born in Pittsfield, Massachusetts

1804 Miller abandons Baptism and becomes a Deist

1814 Fighting in the Battle of Plattsburg, Miller hails the American victory as the sign of a miracle and questions his Deism

1822 Miller sets out his Millenarian beliefs in a 20-point document

1840 Joshua Vaughan Himes begins publishing the fortnightly Millerite newspaper *Sign of the Times*

1843-4 Miller predicts Christ's Second Coming as falling within this timespan

1844 (21–22 October) Christ's failure to appear occasions the Great Disappointment

1849 Death of William Miller

1863 Formal establishment of the Seventh-day Adventist Church

The largest of these groups, the Seventh-day Adventists, originally led by Mrs Ellen Gould White – who claimed to have received visions from God supporting Miller's premise – was formed shortly after the Great Disappointment.

Despite the Great Disappointment, Miller never gave up on his belief that one day Christ would return: 'I am not yet cast down or discouraged,' he wrote to Himes on 10 November 1844. Did he think of himself as a prophet? There is no evidence to suggest that he did, or indeed that he believed that God had revealed special knowledge exclusively to him. Rather, he regarded himself as a student of the Bible, believing that careful analysis of the texts would make possible a system to reveal the date when Christ would return to save the righteous. Miller died in 1849 and was buried in Low Hampton, New York, where his white clapboard farmhouse has been preserved as a museum.

siyyid 'ali muhammad
1819-50
The Báb

A few weeks after thousands of Millerites in America waited for the return of Christ in April 1844, in Persia a 25-year-old named Siyyid 'Ali Muhammad likewise announced the imminent arrival of a messenger from God. According to 'Ali Muhammad, this messenger would be the Promised One – 'He Whom God Shall Make Manifest' – foretold in the Shi'a Islamic tradition. His mission would be to transform the spiritual life of the human race. After making this announcement, the young 'Ali Muhammad took the name of Báb – 'the Gate' – indicating he was the portal through which this divine revelation would flow.

'Ali Muhammad was born in 1819 in Shiraz, an ancient city in what is now southwestern Iran. Raised by his uncle after the death of his father, he worked in the family business as a cloth merchant, but from a young age he was also interested in religion. In Shi'a Islam there was at this time a religious movement, the Shaykhi, which had been founded by Shaykh Ahmad al-Ahs'i (d.1826). The Shaykhi believed in the imminent reappearance of the Mahdi, a messianic figure, descended from Muhammad, whose name means 'Guided One'. He was believed to be in a state of 'occultation', or spiritual hiding, in the mysterious city of Jábulká, from which he would one day return alongside Jesus to restore religion in a faithless world.

A SPECIAL CALLING

As a young man, 'Ali Muhammad was so captivated by these ideas that he took a sabbatical from his business in order to study at the school of the Shaykhi in Karbala, in modern-day Iraq. The leader of the Shaykhi at that time was Ahmad's successor, Siyyid Kázim, who, before his death in 1843, urged his followers to search for the Promised One. One follower, Mullá Husayn-i-Bushru'i of Khorasan, prayed and fasted for 40 days before setting out for Shiraz on his quest. As he walked the streets of the town, he was approached by a young man wearing a green turban, an item of clothing which, like the name Siyyid, indicated him to be a descendant of the prophet Muhammad. Recognizing him as none other than 'Ali Muhammad, a studious young man whose piety had earlier impressed him, Husayn explained that he was searching for the Mahdi. 'Ali Muhammad replied that he was this very redeemer. When 'Ali Muhammad then began composing a commentary on the Surah of Joseph from the Qur'an (one of Shaykh Ahmad's requirements to prove the credentials of the Mahdi) Husayn knew his search had ended.

A few months after his encounter with Husayn, when he travelled to Mecca and Medina in Arabia, 'Ali Muhammad repeated his claim, this time at the Kabah, the holiest of Islamic shrines in Mecca. He wrote to the sharif, or governor, of Mecca, to tell him he was the Mahdi, but the authorities did not take his declaration seriously (five other people had made the same claim) and he soon returned to Persia.

The Báb later revised his claim, stating that after him an even greater Manifestation of God would appear, one who was far superior to himself. In this way he likened himself to the forerunner of Christ, John the Baptist (see pages 31–33). It is unclear whether he called himself the Báb in order to avoid attracting the death sentence that a claim to be the Mahdi might bring, or whether he had genuinely changed his view of his own destiny. Whatever 'Ali Muhammad's reasoning, Husayn continued to believe him to be special, becoming his first disciple. Seventeen

The shrine of the Báb on Mount Carmel near Haifa, Israel.

SIYYID 'ALI MUHAMMAD
A Life in Brief

1819 Birth of Siyyid 'Ali Muhammad in Shiraz, Persia

1844 'Ali Muhammad announces the imminent coming of the Promised One and names himself the Báb

1848 During his trial for blasphemy, the Báb proclaims himself the Mahdi; persecution and murder of Bábis in Persia

1850 The Báb is executed by firing squad

1852 Attempted assassination of the shah brings the imprisonment of many Bábis in Tehran, including Bahá'u'lláh, founder of the Bahá'í faith

1863 Bahá'u'lláh declares himself the Promised One foretold by the Báb

1899 Followers of the Báb inter his body near Mt Carmel in Palestine; the site becomes the headquarters of the Bahá'í faith

'WHAT YOU SEE IN THE QUR'AN, YOU WILL FIND IN THE BAYÁN, AND WHATEVER YOU WILL NOT FIND IN THE QUR'AN, LOOK FOR IT IN THE BAYÁN. MY BAYÁN HAS ABROGATED QUR'AN AND ISLAM! OBEY ME BEFORE THE SWORD COMES OUT OF THE SHEATH!'

of Kázim's disciples also recognized 'Ali Muhammad as the Báb, and they too joined the movement.

ON COLLISION COURSE WITH ISLAM

The Báb issued many new decrees, in an attempt to supplant Islamic Shar'ia law with his own. For example, he suggested that the *Qibla* – the direction in which people prayed – should be changed from Mecca to his house in Shiraz. He changed to a solar calendar that was based on 19 months and 19 days. He advocated many other new rituals and practices, including 'erasing all the books from the face of the Earth except those written about Bábism'. He stated that believers should be prohibited from marrying non-believers, further declaring that 'Allah has made obligatory on every Bábi king that he should not let a single person remain alive in his kingdom who does not accept Bábism'. In addition, according to the *Bayán* – one of the Báb's key religious texts – it was permissible for believers to 'loot and plunder the properties of those who do not accept Bábism', and to destroy the holy places of other religions. On a more enlightened note, he promoted education and did not see the need for women to wear the veil.

Traditional religious scholars regarded Bábism as incompatible with Islam. As the Báb's disciples continued to spread the word, the Islamic authorities felt increasingly threatened. Consequently, between 1845 and 1850, the Báb spent much of his time in prison in Persia, while in 1848 thousands of his followers were massacred. In 1847, the shah of Persia, Muhammad Shah Qajar, who was not unsympathetic to the cause, summoned the Báb – who was then enjoying a brief spell of freedom in Isfahan – for an audience in Tehran. However, the shah's prime minister, Hajji Mirza Aqazi, intervened, imprisoning the Báb first in Tabriz and then in the fortress of Máh-Kú in Azerbaijan. It was here the Báb composed the *Bayán*, in which he mentioned for the first time that another Messiah would come after him.

Successors to the Báb

Bábism as a political and religious force did not long survive the death of the Báb. A failed attempt on the life of the shah in 1852 led to further persecutions and massacres of the Bábis. Those who survived these reprisals were exiled to Baghdad. The Báb had appointed as his successor 17-year-old Mirzá Yahya, known as Subh-i Azal ('Morn of Eternity'), who at the time was living with his elder half-brother, Mirzá Husayn-'Ali Núrí. The Báb gave strict instructions that the young man must obey the Promised One when he appeared. Lacking in confidence, the boy looked to his brother for advice - who, in 1863, sensationally announced that he was the Promised One foretold by the Báb. Styling himself Baha'u'llah (see pages 93-96), he would become the founder of the Baha'i faith.

Azal died in Cyprus in 1912, leaving behind a dwindling band of followers. Today the Azali-Bábis, as they are known, are thought to number in the low thousands. Very much a secretive minority with no apparent leader or central organization, they are found mainly in Cyprus and Iran.

TRIAL AND EXECUTION

In 1848 the Báb was tried for blasphemy and apostasy. At this trial – which was presided over by the 17-year-old Crown Prince Násiri'd-Dín, who was to become shah upon the death of his father three months later – he dramatically announced that he was the Mahdi. This claim seriously challenged Persia's religious, social and political order, for if the Báb truly was the Mahdi, then no secular government could legitimately rule without his agreement. The mullahs sought the death penalty, and violent conflict between Bábis and Muslims seemed inevitable. However the government, worried about further uprisings, asked medical experts to declare the Báb insane. The Báb thus avoided execution, instead receiving 20 lashes to the soles of his feet, after which he was incarcerated in the fortress of Chihríq, in what is now northern Iran.

When Amir Kabir became prime minister in 1850, he rejected the verdict of insanity and ordered the Báb's execution in Tabríz by firing squad. The night before, a young man, Muhammad 'Alíy-i-Zunúzí, demanded to die alongside the Báb, a wish the authorities were only too happy to grant. Thousands of people gathered on the morning of 9 July to witness the execution. Rows of Christian soldiers aimed their guns at the two prisoners, who were secured with rope to a wall. The crack of the muskets was followed by clouds of smoke, and when it cleared the Báb's companion stood alive, released from his bindings, while the Báb himself was nowhere to be seen, leading his followers to rejoice that he had ascended into heaven. However, he was later found in his cell and executed the following day, along with his companion. He was only 31 years old. His body, left outside the city gates to be eaten by wild animals, was retrieved by his followers, hidden, and eventually buried in 1899 near Mount Carmel in Palestine. In the early 20th century a domed shrine was built to commemorate his name.

JOHN WROE
1782–1863
The Society of Christian Israelites

As the sun set on the evening of 12 July 1827, anyone abroad in the Yorkshire city of Bradford, England, would have seen wandering through the streets a hunchbacked man with long, unkempt hair and a wild beard. Perhaps the strangest of his eccentricities was that he was wearing rags that deliberately revealed his bare buttocks. 'And every market town that thou enters in thy travel,' he had enjoined his followers, 'thou shalt put on those old rags and old shoes, without hat, with thy buttocks uncovered, and drop letters.'

That particular day, acting on a vision from God, Wroe was intent on informing the people of Yorkshire more widely of his prophecies. And so he put up posters around two busy Bradford markets, before setting off for Leeds, Tadcaster and York to do the same. These actions were typical of the bizarre and controversial practices performed by Wroe in his 45-year career as self-proclaimed messenger of God and leader of the Society of Christian Israelites.

Wroe was born near Bradford on 19 September 1782, to Joseph and Susanna Wroe. The Wroes were comfortably off as Joseph, a farmer, had made successful investments in the coal and wool-weaving industries that had recently brought prosperity to the area. However, he mercilessly bullied his son; Wroe was later to claim his hunchback had been caused by his father, who forced him as a child to carry heavy loads. At the age of 24, Wroe escaped his father's clutches and started up his own business locally as a wool-comber; in 1816, he married Mary Appleby, who eventually bore him seven children.

SEARCHING FOR FOLLOWERS

In 1819, Wroe fell seriously ill, suffering six days of fever, blindness and loss of speech, and experiencing visions that he believed were of divine origin. In lucid moments between fever and trances, Wroe scribbled down the details of his visions. He claimed to have been shown Christ on the cross, Moses, Aaron, the 12 patriarchs, and even the throne of God, which he noted was encrusted with precious gems. John Wroe believed that, after a struggle between good and evil, Christ would return to reign over the Earth for 1000 years, until the Day of Judgement foretold in the Book of Revelation.

Recovered from his illness, Wroe published his prophecies in 1820 as *Visions of an Angel*. After praying for guidance in understanding the messages, Wroe became convinced he should inform Jews of what he had seen, and in June 1820 he set off to testify at a Liverpool synagogue. The Jews did not embrace him as he had hoped, and by October Wroe had changed tack, attaching himself to the Southcottians.

A contemporary sketch of the prophet John Wroe.

The Southcottians

The Southcottians were followers of the Devonshire prophet Joanna Southcott (1750–1814) who claimed that, even though she was a 64-year-old virgin, she would give birth to a Messiah known as the Shiloh. When she died without her prophesy having been fulfilled, a man named George Turner took up the mantle, claiming that the Shiloh would make an appearance as a six-year-old boy in London on 14 October 1820. Wroe first came to prominence among this group when he spoke at a Southcottian meeting in Bradford a month before, warning that the event would not come to pass. When Wroe was proved correct, his stock rose among the Southcottians, who by now were riven with divisions and ripe for takeover by a dynamic new leader.

BUILDING THE NEW JERUSALEM

In 1822 Wroe announced to the Southcottians that he had been told in a vision to act as a prophet. Not everyone accepted his claim, but so persuasive and charismatic was he that he eventually won many of them over. He duly renamed the Southcottians the 'Society of Christian Israelites' and introduced Mosiac laws – his own peculiar tests of faith combined with corporal punishment administered by the women. These included a 'Cleansing Process' in which – according to ex-members of the sect – a woman held a man's genitals in one hand and, with the other, beat him with wet lint. Drinking spirits, smoking tobacco, shaving or cutting the hair, possessing portraits, and wearing the colours red, yellow and black – all these were forbidden. Women mainly wore blue and green garments, covering their faces with veils in their everyday life, while men sported hats with green felt under the rim.

Soon after organizing his new religion, Wroe travelled around England and Wales spreading his message, especially targeting the Jews. In 1823 he set off on the first of his two European tours of that year, to Gibraltar, Spain, France, Germany and Italy, where he visited synagogues and Roman Catholic churches. In a foretaste of things to come, Wroe was not well received, experiencing intimidation throughout his tour. Back in England, he introduced circumcision, undergoing a public circumcision ceremony on 17 April 1824, an event that became known as the 'Baptism of Blood'. Also in 1824, at Idle Thorpe in Yorkshire, he was baptized in the River Aire before a reported crowd of 30,000 people. He also tried unsuccessfully to part the waters of the river – a failure that seems not to have dented his reputation among his followers.

On three separate occasions, Wroe spent 40 days wandering the countryside, sustaining himself on the local vegetation. On one such trip, in 1826, he had a vision that a place of worship called the Sanctuary should be built in Ashton-under-Lyne, Lancashire; this city would become the New Jerusalem, where 144,000 of his brethren would gather on the Day of Judgement. The Sanctuary was duly opened the following year. Another vision, in 1854, was responsible for the construction of Melbourne House, 3 miles (5 km) outside Wakefield in Yorkshire. The Lord had apparently declared that, in order to finance the building, each follower should purchase from Wroe a gold ring priced at £1 3s 6d (approximately £93 or $186). Wroe later demanded that members donate 10 per cent of their earnings to him – a decree that, according to Edward Green, author of *Prophet John Wroe*, put many of them in the workhouse.

DOGGED BY CONTROVERSY

Throughout his ministry Wroe was dogged by scandals, many of a sexual nature. In 1823, although already married to Mary Appleby, he was 'spiritually' married in the Christian Israelites' Chapel to Sarah Lees; and shortly after these nuptials he announced that Sarah would give birth to the promised Shiloh the following year. Despite the sect's eager preparations for this event, including the manufacture of a silk-lined cradle, a baby girl was born.

Life became even more difficult for Wroe when he was accused of sexual misconduct by three of his 'virgins'. In 1829 he had announced that the 'Spirit of the Lord' had commanded him to take seven virgins 'to cherish and comfort him' but not to know him carnally. However, it was not long before three of these virgins made allegations that Wroe had told each of them confidentially that the Shiloh was to make an appearance and that he was to be the instrument. One named Sarah Pile claimed that Wroe 'used to suck on her breasts' and that she stayed with him only to satisfy his

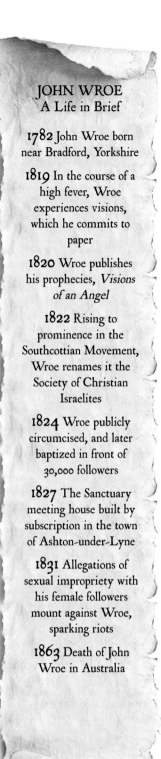

JOHN WROE
A Life in Brief

1782 John Wroe born near Bradford, Yorkshire

1819 In the course of a high fever, Wroe experiences visions, which he commits to paper

1820 Wroe publishes his prophecies, *Visions of an Angel*

1822 Rising to prominence in the Southcottian Movement, Wroe renames it the Society of Christian Israelites

1824 Wroe publicly circumcised, and later baptized in front of 30,000 followers

1827 The Sanctuary meeting house built by subscription in the town of Ashton-under-Lyne

1831 Allegations of sexual impropriety with his female followers mount against Wroe, sparking riots

1863 Death of John Wroe in Australia

'lustful inclinations'. He was summoned to Ashton-under-Lyne to answer these charges but was not convicted, as the majority of his supporters dismissed the allegations. Two members, however, were so irate that they posted notices of the supposed misconduct around the town. The tide began to turn. When Wroe arrived at the Sanctuary to preach, he was heckled so loudly and continuously that he was forced to escape through a secret passage. Supporters and opponents, fighting among themselves, destroyed the building. By 1831 riots followed Wroe wherever he went. In Bradford he was dragged through the streets by his hair; he was also thrown down three flights of stairs.

PROPHECY AND LEGACY

Wroe travelled to Europe and America throughout his ministry, and he went five times to Australia. During this period he made many prophecies that he published in *The Life of John Wroe with Divine Communications Revealed to Him.*

> **' THE PARLIAMENT SHALL GO TO BED, AND IN THE MORNING THEIR HOUSES SHALL BE ASHES. '**

In June 1828 Wroe claimed that God would send storms to many nations, and to England in particular, because of its lack of faith; a month later, England experienced exceptionally heavy rains. In May 1831 he predicted that the Houses of Parliament would burn down, a prophecy fulfilled in the autumn of 1834, when the Palace of Westminster burned to the ground. One of his other prophecies was less accurate, since he announced that he would never taste death but, like Elijah, would be translated straight into heaven. However, he died in Australia on 5 February 1863, at the age of 81.

The Christian Israelites continued after Wroe's death. Wroe's grandson inherited the majority of the prophet's estate, including Melbourne House as well as The Old Whim, a public house owned by Wroe despite his official strictures on alcohol consumption. For many years after his death, a room was set aside at Melbourne House with his slippers and a suit carefully laid out for when he returned. Today the Christian Israelite Church no longer exists in Britain, though it still maintains congregations in Australia, the United States, Poland and Russia.

Damning Evidence

On 5 March 1831, the Manchester newspaper *The Voice of the People* published sensational and damaging allegations by one of John Wroe's 'virgins' of gross sexual misconduct by the millenarian preacher:

> *In her evidence she declared that he came at night, and got into bed to her, and lay beside her; that he frequently kissed her, and required her to kiss him; he declared how great his love was for her, and that spiritual love far exceeded temporal; and such would be the love in the kingdom of heaven; and that his love for her by far exceeded the love which he had for his own wife. (It is then stated that he caused her to commit the most revolting and unnatural act of indecency which can be conceived, with the mention of which we will not defile our columns.) These acts, it appears, were committed frequently, even in the day-time, and became so common, that she had no doubt that it was right. He used to sleep with her during her illness, contrary to his own laws.*

A month later, on 10 April, Wroe suffered three broken ribs and barely escaped with his life when a mob ransacked his meeting-house in Bradford.

baha'u'llah
1817–92
Founder of the Baha'í Faith

As Baha'u'llah lay chained to his fellow prisoners in a foul-smelling underground dungeon in Tehran – the Siyáh Chál, or Black Pit – he experienced a powerful vision that would change his life. He and his brother Bábis (followers of the Báb, Siyyid 'Ali Muhammad; see pages 86–89) had been imprisoned in 1852 for the alleged crime of attempting to assassinate Násiri'd'-Dín, the shah of Persia.

For four months Baha'u'llah remained incarcerated for a crime that neither he nor his companions had committed. It was, however, in these squalid conditions, with his health failing, that he felt light washing over his body, and the Maiden of God appeared before him, telling him that he was the Promised One prophesied by the Báb. Baha'u'llah understood what this meant: he was to be the Messenger of God, who would usher in a new age of spiritual unity. He decided, however, to keep his visit from the Maiden and mission from God a secret for a further 11 years.

Born Mirzá Husayn-'Alí Núrí in Tehran in 1817, he would later change his name to Baha'u'llah ('The Glory Of God'). He was the son of Mirzá Buzurg of Núr, a province of the district of Mazandaran in northern Persia. His father had risen through the ranks of the civil service, eventually becoming a tax collector and governor of two provinces. When Muhammad Shah came to power, however, a government purge saw Mirzá Buzurg stripped of his assets and he died a broken man in 1839. His son, a devout Muslim, married his first wife Asiyih Kahanum at the age of 18; in 1848 he took the widow Katimih as his second wife, and in 1862 married his third wife, Gawhar Kahnum of Kashan. He would father a total of 14 children, of whom only seven survived, due to the physical hardships his family was later to experience.

In 1844, Baha'u'llah, then aged 25, first heard about the Báb and his claim to be the promised Mahdi of Shi'a Islam. Though he never met the Báb, he was so impressed that he quickly joined in the spreading of his controversial teachings. Following the Báb's execution by firing squad in 1850, three angry renegade Bábis attempted to assassinate the shah; as a consequence, the entire Bábi community were subjected to reprisals. Thousands were slaughtered, and many others, including Baha'u'llah, incarcerated. He managed to avoid execution only because his sister was married to the Persian Secretary to the Russian embassy, who intervened on his behalf. The terms of his release, however, stipulated that he must leave the country.

DISPOSSESSED AND EXILED

Stripped of his wealth and possessions, Baha'u'llah left Persia with his family for Baghdad, in Ottoman Iraq, where the Bábis had already established themselves. Baha'u'llah's half-brother Subh-i Azal, the person chosen by the Báb to lead the Bábis, joined Baha'u'llah in Baghdad. Azal was not a natural leader and indeed was only an adolescent when he was appointed leader. The Bábi community therefore turned for spiritual guidance to his more charismatic

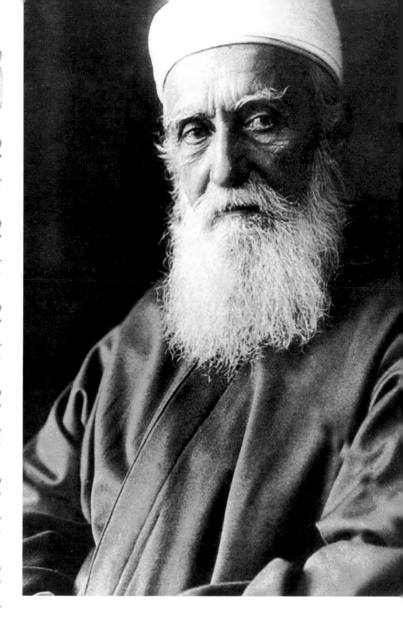

Abdu'l Bahá, Baha'u'llah's son, leader of the faith from 1892 until his death in 1921.

sibling. Azal quickly became jealous of his half-brother and began attempting to discredit him. As a result, and without confiding even in his family, Baha'u'llah and a companion left Baghdad for the mountains of Kurdistan near Sulaymaniyah, where he remained for two years. He lived as a hermit and spent some of this time in a Sufi retreat where he wrote two of his religious works, *The Seven Valleys* and *The Four Valleys*. Meanwhile the Bábi community in Baghdad began disintegrating under Azal's weak leadership (the young man had further alienated his followers by taking one of the Báb's widows as his wife, a violation of the Báb's teachings). Search parties were despatched to find Baha'u'llah and to urge him to return.

RETURN OF THE PROPHET

In 1856 Baha'u'llah agreed to return to Baghdad. He had still told no one of the earlier vision in which he was proclaimed as the Promised One, and for a further seven years he spent his time teaching the Bábi faith and writing two more major works, *Hidden Words* and the *Book of Certitude*. He was to call this period the 'Days of Concealment', during which he continued to experience visions from the Maid of Heaven but remained silent regarding their import. Pressure from Persian officials in Baghdad culminated in the Ottoman government exiling Baha'u'llah to Constantinople (present-day Istanbul) in 1863. Before setting off for this exile with his family and 25 Bábis, Baha'u'llah was offered, for a few days, the use of a private garden outside Baghdad. Here he was able to bid farewell to his fellow Bábis, who were looking to him as their leader instead of Azal. It was in this spot, now known as the Garden of Ridván (Paradise), that he told a select few that he was the messianic figure promised by the Báb. The Baha'í today commemorate this event as the Festival of Ridván.

Baha'u'llah spent only four months in Constantinople before, following the Persian Ambassador's campaign against him, he was asked to leave. This time he was sent to Adrianople (Edirne in Turkey), where he remained for four and a half years. It was here that in 1866 he openly proclaimed himself the Promised One foretold by the Báb. He wrote to the leaders of the world, among them Pope Pius X, Queen Victoria, Czar Alexander II of Russia, Emperor Napoleon III of France, King Wilhelm I of Prussia, Násiri'd-Dín Shah of Persia and Sultan 'Abdu'l-'Azíz of the Ottoman empire. He informed them that he was the Messiah whose coming was foretold in both the Christian and the Muslim scriptures, and requested that they accept him as such. He also asked them to renounce their material possessions, care for the poor, settle disputes, and help make the world peaceful and secure.

While in Adrianople, Baha'u'llah challenged his half-brother Azal to accept his claim to be the Promised One. A trial of divine will was arranged at a mosque in 1867, with God supposed to strike down the impostor, though the issue remained unresolved when Azal failed to appear. Azal is also said to have poisoned Baha'u'llah, who was left with a permanent trembling in his hand. Azal then sent inflammatory reports about his half-brother to the Ottoman government, ensuring that Baha'u'llah once again found himself exiled. This antagonism between Azal and Baha'u'llah instigated a split within the Bábi community – the followers of Azal becoming known as the Azalis, and the followers of Baha'u'llah as the Baha'í.

Praise for a Just Ruler

In 1871 Baha'u'llah wrote a letter to Queen Victoria, praising the abolition of slavery in the British empire:

O Queen in London! Incline thine ear unto the voice of thy Lord, the Lord of all mankind, calling from the Divine Lote-Tree: Verily, no God is there but Me, the Almighty, the All-Wise! Cast away all that is on Earth, and attire the head of thy kingdom with the crown of the remembrance of thy Lord, the all-Glorious. He, in truth, hath come unto the world in His most great glory, and all that hath been mentioned in the gospel hath been fulfilled. The land of Syria hath been honoured by the footsteps of its lord, the Lord of all men, and north and south are both inebriated with the wind of His presence.

We have been informed that thou hast forbidden the trading in slaves, both men and women. This, verily, is what God hath enjoined in this wondrous Revelation. God hath, truly, destined a reward for thee, because of this. He, verily will pay the doer of good his due recompense . . .

Baha'u'llah was also a great admirer of British parliamentary democracy, and called repeatedly for a constitutional monarchy and an elective government to be established in the Ottoman empire.

Continuing Persecution

In August 1868, at the age of 51, Baha´u´llah was forced by the authorities to leave Adrianople for the fortress of Akko, on the coast of what is now Israel. Azal, meanwhile, was sent to Cyprus. Baha´u´llah never wavered from his faith or his ideals in these harsh conditions, and it was in this prison that he wrote the Most Holy Book, which outlined the religious laws of the Baha´í. The Baha´í faith includes a number of important tenets, the most fundamental of which is the underlying unity of the world's religions. Prophets, from many major religions, including Adam, Abraham, Moses, Zoroaster, Jesus Christ and Muhammad, are all regarded as manifestations of one God. The Baha´í hold, moreover, that the Báb and Baha´u´llah are not the last of these manifestations. Finally, in an age of nationalism and state conflict, Baha´u´llah taught that love of humanity was greater than the love of country.

Over time, Baha´u´llah gained the respect of the Ottoman as well as the local Syrian authorities, and eventually his prison-like conditions were relaxed. Although remaining in custody, he was allowed to move outside the fortress, later taking residence in the mansion of Bahjí ('Small Garden'), where he died of a fever in 1892, at the age of 75. Baha´u´llah was buried in a shrine next to the mansion of Bahjí, in present-day Israel. He was succeeded by his eldest son, Abdu'l-Bahá, who would recognize Buddha and Krishna as true prophets. There are estimated to be 5 million Baha´ís in the world today. One of the largest communities, numbering 300,000, is found in Iran. Here the Baha´ís are still, according to the United Nations, victims of discrimination and human rights violations.

> ❛ WHILE ENGULFED IN TRIBULATIONS I HEARD A MOST WONDROUS, A MOST SWEET VOICE, CALLING ABOVE MY HEAD. TURNING MY FACE, I BEHELD A MAIDEN – THE EMBODIMENT OF THE REMEMBRANCE OF THE NAME OF MY LORD – SUSPENDED IN THE AIR BEFORE ME. ❜

Louis Riel
1844–85

Métis Prophet

On 31 July 1885, Mr Justice Hugh Richardson, magistrate for the North-West Territories in Canada, addressed the prisoner standing before him in the packed courtroom. Louis Riel had been found guilty of 'a crime the most pernicious and greatest that man can commit'. Having 'let loose the flood gates of rapine and bloodshed', Riel must expect the harshest punishment. The judge ignored the jury's plea for clemency and sentenced the prisoner to death by hanging.

Thus ended the messianic career of the man whom another judge, hearing the appeal, called 'a man of more than ordinary intelligence, who could have been of great service to those of his race in this country'. Louis Riel was born in the Red River Colony, in present-day Manitoba, the eldest in a family of 11 children. His parents were Métis, people of mixed French and Indian blood. Red River was an isolated community of white settlers, English-speaking mixed-bloods (known as the 'country-born'), and French-speaking Métis. Though most of the white settlers farmed the land, many Métis, who formed the majority, were involved in the fur trade, and the settlement was administered by the enormous fur-trading corporation, the Hudson's Bay Company.

EDUCATED AND ARTICULATE

Riel studied at Catholic schools in Red River before being sent to a seminary in Montreal at the age of 14 to train for the priesthood. There, he impressed the priests with his piety and studious application, as well as his charm, though he was also introverted, moody and depressive. The death of his father in 1864 traumatized him so much that he withdrew from his studies and for several years worked as a law clerk in a Montreal firm before returning to the Red River Colony in 1868.

Red River had changed during Riel's absence. In 1868 jurisdiction over it was about to be transferred from the Hudson's Bay Company to the government of Canada. The Dominion of Canada had been founded a year earlier, and many Canadians were eager to absorb the colony into their domains, especially since the Americans had designs of their own on it. As French speakers, the Métis faced an uncertain future in Canada, which was predominantly white and, with the exception of Quebec, English-speaking and Protestant. Their fears mounted when a member of the party charged with surveying the lands – an operation that many Métis feared would deprive them of their property – turned out to be Thomas Scott, a Protestant Irishman with an open contempt for the Métis.

Well-educated and fluent in both French and English, Riel stepped forward as a leader of his community. In the summer of 1869 he declared the survey a menace and demanded that any union with Canada must have the assent of the Métis. Direct action was quickly taken. In November, in what became known as the Red River Rebellion, he and 400 followers seized a fort in Red River; he then prepared a 'List of Rights' and declared himself head of a

Louis Riel (centre), the Métis leader who launched two armed struggles against the Canadian government in 1869 and 1885.

'provisional government'. Negotiations with the Canadians proceeded, with Riel eventually securing language rights and a grant of 5,700 square kilometres (1.4 million acres) for the Métis in what became, in the summer of 1870, the new province of Manitoba. Hatred of Riel by Protestants was deepened by his politically unwise sanction of the execution of the hostile and boisterous Scott. When a Canadian military force arrived in Manitoba in 1870 as part of an 'errand of peace', Riel found it expedient to cross the border into the United States.

MENTAL INSTABILITY

Three years later, after returning to Manitoba, Riel was elected to Parliament. However, his political aspirations were frustrated by both a $5000 bounty placed on his head by Ontario Protestants for the 'murder' of Scott and his expulsion from Parliament on a motion introduced by the MP Mackenzie Bowell, a prominent Orangeman (and future prime minister of Canada). Ousted from politics, the deeply devout Riel turned to religion. He became obsessed with what he regarded as his mission to guard the spiritual well-being of the Métis, and to establish a new Roman Catholic religion in North America, with the bishop of Montreal, Ignace Bourget, as its pope. He experienced his first vision in 1874, and by 1875 his emotional outbursts and continual weeping alarmed the household of the priest with whom he was staying. In 1876, after causing a scene during Mass, he was admitted to a mental asylum in Montreal under the name 'Louis R. David'. He was soon transferred to another asylum at Beauport, near Quebec City.

Here, under another assumed name, 'Louis La Rochelle', Riel impressed his doctor with his knowledge of philosophy and theology. Yet he also declared himself a prophet, called himself Louis 'David' Riel, and spent many hours in prayer, often enlisting the help of the staff to hold his arms in the shape of a cross. The doctor remained unconvinced by some of these displays, wondering whether his patient was truly hallucinating or whether he was merely acting a part. Riel was released from the asylum after 18 months and told to pursue an outdoor life – an ironic piece of advice given that the bison on which the Métis had depended were swiftly vanishing from the plains.

Like many Métis who had left Red River after 1870, Riel moved farther west. He relocated to the Montana Territory and in 1881 married a Métis woman. Involving himself in local politics, he joined the Republican Party in an attempt to curtail the whiskey trade that was wreaking such havoc with his people. He also became a naturalized American citizen and took a job teaching at a Jesuit mission on the Sun River in Montana. And there he might have remained had he not received a visit, in June 1884, from a delegation of Métis led by Gabriel Dumont.

CATALYST TO CATASTROPHE

A legendary horseman and buffalo-hunter, the 46-year-old Dumont was born in Red River but moved west and in 1873 became the leader of the Métis who had settled along the South Saskatchewan river in the North-West Territories. Within a decade of his arrival it was clear that the buffalo on which the Métis depended were gone from the prairies, and so Dumont petitioned the Canadian government for farming assistance, schools and confirmation of Métis ownership of the land on which they had settled. Increasingly frustrated with government inaction, he became convinced that only Louis Riel was capable of bringing the necessary pressure to bear.

LOUIS RIEL
A Life in Brief

1844 Louis Riel born in Red River, Manitoba

1858 Riel sent to Montreal to study for the priesthood

1867 Foundation of the Dominion of Canada within the British empire

1869 Red River Rebellion breaks out, led by Riel

1873 Riel is elected to the Canadian parliament, but is expelled soon after

1876 Imbued with messianic visions, Riel is admitted to a mental hospital

1881 Riel becomes a schoolmaster in Montana

1885 (March) The Métis begin an armed rebellion against Canadian forces

1885 (16 September) After a failed appeal, Riel is executed in Regina

Riel returned to Canada almost immediately after Dumont's visit. He and his family went to Batoche, the main Métis settlement on the South Saskatchewan. Matters initially looked encouraging as the long petition composed by Riel and sent to Ottawa resulted in promises of a government commission to examine the grievances. By early 1885, however, with no sign of this being implemented, Riel began to hatch grandiose plans for the creation of a homeland for the Métis in preparation for the Last Judgement. Believing himself the emissary of God, he began preaching his own idiosyncratic brand of religion. He renamed the days of the week, changed the Lord's Day to Saturday in accordance with Mosaic law, and declared Bishop Bourget the new pope. The small settlement of Batoche became the 'City of God'.

An Unequal Struggle

Riel's pronouncements enthused the militant element among the Métis, who began arming themselves for battle. In March, hearing a rumour that 500 North-West Mounted Police were headed for Batoche, Riel declared that 'Rome has fallen' and formed a provisional government. The first skirmish was fought with the NWMP at the end of the month, leaving 12 policemen and five Métis dead. The Canadian Prime Minister, John A. Macdonald, ordered the militia, garrisoned 150 miles (240 km) away at Fort Qu'Appelle, to march across the prairie to Batoche. Dumont favoured a guerrilla campaign against the troops, who vastly outnumbered the Métis fighters, but Riel – in what proved a strategic blunder – elected to concentrate their forces in Batoche. Unsurprisingly, the Canadian troops swiftly crushed the insurrection. Dumont escaped to Montana, but Riel, looking 'careworn and haggard', with long hair and a beard, was captured and taken south to Regina, capital of the North-West Territories. Here, charged with treason, he was shackled with ball and chain in a tiny cell in the NWMP barracks.

Riel's trial before a jury of English-speaking Protestants began in Regina on 20 July. Two priests testified that Riel was insane, as did the superintendent of the asylum in Beauport. Riel's own dignified and articulate defence of his position seemed to belie a diagnosis of madness, and the jury found him guilty after only a half hour's deliberation. The death sentence was confirmed on appeal, and the execution was carried out on 16 November.

Prophet, statesman, hero, patriot, martyr, traitor, madman – Louis Riel is still the most complex and controversial figure in Canadian history. In recent decades several attempts have been made in the Parliament of Canada to revoke his conviction and recognize him as a Father of Confederation. Thus far, none has succeeded.

'I AM A PROPHET, I HAVE BEEN ORDAINED NOT AS A PRIEST, BUT AS A PROPHET OF THE NEW WORLD TO PREACH A REFORMATION TO YOU … AND I WILL CONTINUE TO FULFILL MY MISSION UNTIL I MOUNT THE SCAFFOLD.'

helena petrovna blavatsky

1831–91

The Theosophical Society

In 1889 a two-volume work was published in London purporting to reveal 'a few fundamental truths from the Secret Doctrine of the Archaic ages'. These mysterious verities would now be permitted to see the light, the author declared, 'after long millenniums of the most profound silence and secrecy'. In her preface, the author expressed apprehensions about how such a work might be received: 'It is more than probable that the book will be regarded by a large section of the public as a romance of the wildest kind.' Some critics have treated the book with scepticism, but it would ultimately generate a large following.

The book was *The Secret Doctrine: The Synthesis of Science, Religion and Philosophy*, and its author was Helena Petrovna Blavatsky, the co-founder of the Theosophical Society. Madame Blavatsky, as she became known, was born in the Ukraine in 1831. Descended from a well-connected Russian family (her mother was a novelist of some distinction) she had apparently been difficult and demanding as a child, ordering about the family servants and terrorizing the local peasantry with claims of supernatural powers. At the age of 17 she married General Nikifor Blavatsky, the middle-aged vice-governor of Yerevan in Armenia. The marriage was unhappy and apparently still unconsummated when, three months after the wedding, the spirited young bride stole a horse and made her way back across Russia to her family.

Her marriage behind her, Madame Blavatsky embarked on a series of travels and remarkable adventures. By her own account she worked as a concert pianist, a circus performer and a fortune-teller in Cairo (a career that ended when – not for the last time – she was accused of fraud). She even claimed to have fought alongside Giuseppe Garibaldi at the Battle of Mentana in 1867, suffering injuries from musketballs as well as 'a stiletto wound in the heart'. Besides Egypt and Italy, her travels took her to England, France, Canada, Mexico, Ceylon and India. In London in 1851 she met, in Hyde Park, a teacher of Tibetan Buddhism about whom she had dreamed since her childhood. Finally travelling to Tibet in the late 1860s she was initiated into Buddhism after disguising herself and then watching secret rites performed by 'Ascended Masters'.

PROMOTING UNIVERSAL BROTHERHOOD

By the early 1870s Madame Blavatsky had moved to New York City, where she worked as a seamstress and then as a medium, performing feats such as levitation, clairvoyance and telepathy. In 1874 she so impressed one of the journalists writing articles on the Spiritualist movement, Henry Steel Olcott of the *New York Tribune*, that the next year (following a failed venture called the Miracle Club) the two of them founded the Theosophical Society. The aims of the Theosophical Society, whose name derived from the Neoplatonist term Theosophia,

1831 Helena Petrovna
Blavatsky born in
Yekaterinoslav, Ukraine

1875 Blavatsky and
Henry Steel Olcott
found the Theosophical
Society

1877 Publication of *Isis
Unveiled*

1882 Headquarters of
the Theosophical
Society moved to Adyar,
India

1888 Blavatsky
publishes *The Secret
Doctrine*

1891 Death of Madame
Blavatsky in London; a
portion of her ashes is
buried in India

1907 Henry Olcott
dies; Annie Besant takes
over leadership of the
Theosophical Society

meaning 'knowledge of the divine', were to create a 'Universal Brotherhood of Humanity', to encourage the comparative study of religion, and to investigate the unexplained laws of nature.

In 1877, several years after the founding of the Theosophical Society, Madame Blavatsky wrote her first book on the occult. Entitled *Isis Unveiled: A Master-Key to the Mysteries of Ancient and Modern Science and Theology*, it was billed as 'a brief summary of the religions, philosophies, and universal traditions of human kind, and the exegesis of the same, in the spirit of those secret doctrines, of which none – thanks to prejudice and bigotry – have reached Christendom in so unmutilated a form, as to secure it a fair judgement'. She claimed the works had been channelled to her through spiritual masters whom she called the 'Brothers' – teachers who had reached a higher plane of existence than other mortals. Like theosophy as a whole, the book can be seen as a reaction against the organized religion and scientific materialism of the 19th century. The work rejected the dogmas of science and religion in favour of the wisdom of the 'ancient sages' (everyone from Plato to what she called 'the abstruse systems of old India') whose writings revealed the doctrines of a 'universal religion'. The publication of *Isis Unveiled* was greeted not so much by scepticism towards her philosophical claims as by incredulity that a woman could have written such a work.

THE GLOBETROTTING 'INGENIOUS IMPOSTOR'

Madame Blavatsky became a naturalized American citizen, but in 1879, after another brief and unsuccessful marriage, she departed with Olcott for India, eventually basing herself at Adyar, near Chennai (Madras). Five years later she left Adyar under a cloud after an investigator from the Society for Psychical Research (an organization founded in 1882 and headed by Henry Sidgwick, Professor of Moral Philosophy at Cambridge University) was summoned to investigate allegations of fraud. The investigator, Dr Richard Hodgson, discovered suspicious paraphernalia at the headquarters, including trapdoors, sliding panels, a mannequin and spring-loaded apertures in the ceiling. In a report (whose accuracy and impartiality have been disputed by the Theosophical Society) he declared Madame Blavatsky 'one of the most accomplished, ingenious, and interesting impostors in history'.

After leaving India, Madame Blavatsky settled in Germany and then Belgium before moving permanently to London. In 1888 she published *The Secret Doctrine*, whose purpose was 'to assign to man his rightful place in the scheme of the Universe' and to uncover the fundamental unity from which all religions spring. This time she was careful to state that her knowledge did not come from 'Brothers' on a higher plane but from ancient books and manuscripts: 'For what is contained in this work is to be found scattered throughout thousands of volumes embodying the scriptures of the great Asiatic and early European religions, hidden under glyph and symbol, and hitherto left unnoticed because of this veil.' *The Secret Doctrine* marked the attempt, she wrote, 'to gather the oldest tenets together and to make of them one harmonious and unbroken whole'.

Helena Petrovna, in a portrait by Gordon Wain (dates unknown), pictured with the symbol of the Theosophical Society above her head.

One of her most important arguments was an optimistic appraisal of the human condition. She argued that human consciousness was evolving in the same way that – as Darwin had recently demonstrated – *Homo sapiens* had evolved from apes. Evolution continued, that is, in the realm of human consciousness as individuals, born and reborn through reincarnation, worked their way towards spiritual perfection and a union with the cosmos.

The following year, 1889, Madame Blavatsky published two further books, *The Key to Theosophy* and *The Voice of Silence*. The former stated that a true theosophist must pursue the highest moral ideals, work ceaselessly for others and strive for oneness with the whole of

The Impact of Theosophy

Theosophy has made its influence felt in the arts, politics and education. After the great Irish poet W. B. Yeats (1865-1939) met Madame Blavatsky in London in 1887, he joined the Theosophical Society and became one of her private pupils. Painters such as Paul Gauguin (1848-1903), Wassily Kandinsky (1866-1944) and Piet Mondrian (1872-1944) were likewise influenced by Theosophy. Kandinsky wrote a treatise called *Concerning the Spiritual in Art* (1910) while Mondrian kept a portrait of Madame Blavatsky in his studio. Another member of the Theosophical Society, A. O. Hume (1829-1912), a British civil servant and political reformer, was one of the founders of the Indian National Congress, while Annie Besant founded the Indian Home Rule League in 1816. It is appropriate, then, that a handful of Madame Blavatsky's ashes has been interred under her statue in Adyar.

humanity. Its teachings would influence Mahatma Gandhi (1869–1948), who met Blavatsky in 1890 while he was studying law in London. Though he declined to join the Theosophical Society, he later remarked that *The Key to Theosophy* had opened his eyes to the ancient wisdom of his homeland.

WIDE-RANGING INFLUENCE

Madame Blavatsky suffered ill health through many of her last years, her infirmities possibly exacerbated by a fondness for cigarettes. Weakened by kidney and heart problems, she succumbed to influenza in London on 8 May 1891, several months shy of her 60th birthday. The Theosophical Society continued to thrive after her death, with the women's rights and labour activist Annie Besant (1847–1933), famous for leading the London Match Girls' Strike of 1888, taking over the leadership following the death of Olcott in 1907.

Controversy dogged Madame Blavatsky throughout her career, and after her death critics would claim that far from being communicated by higher beings on an astral plane, her books were actually cobbled together from various uncredited sources.

Nonetheless, her convictions about the underlying unity of all religion found a wide and appreciative audience in the decades that followed, as did her insistence on a deeper spiritual reality beyond the material world of nature and her appeal for a universal brotherhood without distinctions of race, creed, sex or colour.

'THE WORK NOW SUBMITTED TO PUBLIC JUDGEMENT IS THE FRUIT OF A SOMEWHAT INTIMATE ACQUAINTANCE WITH EASTERN ADEPTS AND STUDY OF THEIR SCIENCE. IT IS OFFERED TO SUCH AS ARE WILLING TO ACCEPT TRUTH WHEREVER IT MAY BE FOUND, AND TO DEFEND IT, EVEN LOOKING POPULAR PREJUDICE STRAIGHT IN THE FACE. IT IS AN ATTEMPT TO AID THE STUDENT TO DETECT THE VITAL PRINCIPLES WHICH UNDERLIE THE PHILOSOPHICAL SYSTEMS OF OLD.'

ellen gould white

1827–1915

Founder of the Seventh-Day Adventist Church

'Glory be to God!' 17-year-old Ellen Harmon suddenly gasped. She was praying with five other women in the home of a Mrs Haines in Portland, Maine, two months after the Great Disappointment of 1844 (see pages 83–86). The room went quiet. The young woman seemed to stop breathing, and her dark eyes remained fixed glassily on something in front of her. She was experiencing her first vision, one in which she saw the Adventists being led to Heaven by Jesus.

To her friends, Ellen seemed to be oblivious to her immediate surroundings, while she felt as though she was enveloped in a dazzling light. When she regained her senses, her breathing resumed and, according to witnesses, the

Ellen Gould White, the founder of the Seventh-Day Adventist Church.

sparkle returned to her eyes. This was just the first of many such events. Over the next 70 years, Ellen would receive more than 2000 dreams and visions – varying in length from a minute to nearly four hours – which she described in some 40 books and 5000 articles.

FROM METHODISM TO MILLENARIANISM

Ellen and her twin sister Elizabeth were born in Gorham, Maine, on 26 November 1827, to a farmer named Robert Harmon and his wife Eunice. Robert soon gave up his farm and moved with his family, which had swelled to eight children, to work as a hat maker in Portland. At the age of nine, Ellen was injured when a stone thrown by a playmate struck her on the nose and left her unconscious for three weeks. The accident caused her much physical discomfort, and for the next two years she could not breathe through her nose, her hands trembled, and she often felt dizzy. Her education was affected by the accident, but she later claimed it had been:

'... a blessing in disguise. The cruel blow, which blighted the joys of Earth, was the means of turning my eyes to Heaven.' While Ellen's family attended the Methodist Church, they also accepted the views of William Miller and eagerly awaited the return of Christ. From the age of 12, Ellen, who was especially influenced by the Millerite movement, became particularly fearful of the Judgement Day. She and her family were eventually expelled from the Methodist Church because of their support for the Millerites.

After receiving her first vision in December 1844, Ellen felt impelled to pass on the message to Millerites disillusioned by the failure of Christ to return. At first she was reluctant to share her vision, but her friends encouraged her. These were difficult times for the Adventists, but Ellen persevered in her attempts to reignite their enthusiasm for Christ's eventual return by convincing them that she was God's messenger. In 1846 she married James White, a young Adventist preacher with whom she would eventually have four sons. Soon after their marriage, the Whites became convinced of the sanctity of the seventh day of Creation and, following a vision experienced by Ellen on 3 April 1847, began observing Saturday as the Sabbath. For the next ten years, both the Whites continued to preach. James, who worked part-time on the railroad to support the family, published his wife's prophetic views on the future of the church. Among these were *A Sketch of the Christian Experience* and *Views of Ellen G. White*, printed in 1851, along with numerous articles in the Adventist newspaper *Review and Herald*. On 14 March 1858, while attending a funeral service in the Lovett's Grove (now Bowling Green) public school in Ohio, Ellen received one of her most important visions, in which she witnessed the conflict between Christ and Satan. She published details of the vision that same year, in *Spiritual Gifts, Volume 1: The Great Controversy Between Christ and His Angels and Satan and His Angels*.

A HEALTHY MIND IN A HEALTHY BODY

There was a growing need for the new group of Adventists to be properly organized, and so in 1863, under the direction of James White, the Seventh-day Adventist Church was established. A few months later, Ellen experienced a vision of the relationship between spirituality and physical health. As before, she began by exclaiming 'Glory be to God' before entering a trance-like state. On this occasion she was shown the importance to spiritual health of a good diet, pure water, clean air, sunshine and exercise. She subsequently published six pamphlets on the subject, inspired, perhaps, by the fact that a number of the preachers, including her husband, had become ill through poor diet and overwork. Following a vision on Christmas Day in 1865, she established the Western Health Reform Institute in Battle Creek, Michigan, where vegetarianism came to be accepted by Seventh-day Adventists.

Ellen travelled widely throughout the United States, preaching and lecturing. On 1 April 1874, while in California, she received a vision urging the Seventh-day Adventists to broaden their horizons and spread their message overseas, as a result of which missions were founded all over the world. James White died in 1881, and in 1885 Ellen first travelled abroad, spending two years visiting missions in Europe. She also travelled in the American South, involving herself in the foundation of Oakwood Industrial School (now Oakwood College), which educated African-Americans. By the 1890s, however, her influence within some sectors of the church had begun to wane. She had never held any church office, nor was she a member of conference committees or on the boards of institutions, always claiming that she was merely the Lord's messenger. However, some church leaders resented her counsel, and at the General Conference of 1891 she was asked to travel to Australia, at the age of 64, to assist in church work there. She remained there for nine years, effectively sidelined, until in 1900 she received another vision urging her to return to the United States.

'I KNOW THAT MANY HAVE CALLED ME A PROPHET, BUT I HAVE MADE NO CLAIM TO THIS TITLE. MY SAVIOUR DECLARED ME TO BE HIS MESSENGER. "YOUR WORK," HE INSTRUCTED ME, "IS TO BEAR MY WORD".'

AN INSPIRATIONAL ORGANIZER

Ellen continued to write during her last years and she was instrumental in calling in 1901 for a reorganization of the Seventh-day Adventist General Conference to provide for the expanding interests of the church. She remained active until, in February 1915, she tripped and broke her hip. Confined to bed, she died five months later at the age of 87, and was buried beside her husband in Battle Creek, Michigan.

Today, although there is disagreement about the extent of her gift of prophecy, most Seventh-day Adventists believe that Ellen Gould White was inspired by the Holy Spirit. However, they regard her writings, significant as they are, to be of secondary importance to the Bible, and to have been influenced both by ideas from other authors and by her own cultural milieu. Ellen herself never stopped believing that she was a messenger of God or hoping – like William Miller – that Christ would return in her lifetime. Yet she wisely avoided Miller's error

Wayward Predictions

Many of Ellen Gould White's prophecies failed to materialize. In 1851 she predicted that the Old City of Jerusalem would never be rebuilt; however, Jerusalem was rebuilt when the State of Israel was carved out of Palestine in 1947. Later, during the American Civil War, she predicted that England would declare war on the United States, causing 'general war, general confusion'. Perhaps one of her most conspicuous prophetic failures was her announcement in 1856 that some people alive in that year would witness the return of Christ: 'I was shown the company present at the conference. Said the angel, "Some food for worms, some subjects of the seven last plagues, some will be alive and remain upon the Earth to be translated at the coming of Jesus".' Throughout her career, she was also given to making some extremely contentious statements, claiming for example that masturbation can cause serious illnesses, the Flood was caused by the amalgamation of man and beast, and that Jupiter was inhabited by tall, majestic people.

of setting a specific date for His return. Learning from the Great Disappointment, she said: 'Again and again have I been warned in regard to time setting. There will never again be a message for the people of God that will be based on time.'

Ellen was a remarkable and charismatic woman whose publications covered religion, education, social relationships, prophecy, evangelism and nutrition. She used her visions to make important administrative decisions, and played a major role in the doctrinal development of the church. Today, the Seventh-day Adventist Church boasts a membership of over 14 million worldwide and continues to prepare for Christ's Second Coming.

FÁTIMA PROPHECIES 1917

Messengers of the Virgin Mary

On 13 October 1917, 50,000 people gathered at Cova da Iria, scrubland owned by the Santos family for pasturing their sheep, just a few kilometres from Fátima in Portugal. The huge crowd was there to witness an apparition of the Virgin Mary. Yet although many of the assembled faithful reported that the sun changed colour and turned on its axis – a phenomenon that became known as 'the Miracle of the Sun' – only Lúcia dos Santos, aged ten, and her cousins Francisco, nine, and Jacinta, seven, saw a vision of the Holy Mother.

Lúcia, Francisco and Jacinta had already seen the Virgin Mary five times in the previous six months. Lúcia, a deeply religious child, was born on 7 March 1907, the youngest of seven children of Antonio and Maria Rosa dos Santos, who lived in the hamlet of Aljustrel, several miles from Fátima. At the age of eight, Lúcia was given the job of tending her family's flock of sheep. Her cousin Francisco, born 11 June 1908, was the sixth child of Manuel and Olimpia Marto. His sister, Jacinta, born in 1910, was a talkative, lively child who loved to dance; often wilful, she had begged her mother to allow her to tend sheep alongside her brother and adored cousin.

DAZZLING VISITATIONS

One day in April 1917 the children were playing near the grazing sheep when they saw a flash of lightning. The sight startled them, since the weather was calm and there was no sign of a storm. Suddenly a 'lady of dazzling light', smelling of roses, appeared before them. When Lúcia asked who she was, the Lady explained she was from Heaven and wanted them to come back to this spot at the same time on the 13th day of each month for the next six months. The Virgin Mary – for they were convinced it was her – requested that they repeat the rosary. They agreed, but after the apparition vanished Lúcia insisted to her cousins that they say nothing to anyone. Portugal had experienced a revolution in 1910, in which the monarch, King Manuel II,

Lúcia dos Santos with her cousins Francisco and Jacinta Marto, who saw the vision in 1917.

was replaced by a republic and the church separated from the state. The new government was strongly opposed to religion, even though most people's belief in Catholicism was undimmed. Portugal was also involved in the First World War, and the children, though very young, would no doubt have been aware of the instability all around them.

This was not the children's first spiritual experience. In the spring of 1916 an angel who was 'whiter than snow' had appeared to them while they played in an olive grove on Lúcia's parents' property. 'Do not be afraid,' he said, 'I am the angel of peace.' He asked them to join him in prayer for those who did not love God. He appeared again when they were playing by the well in Lúcia's garden, and on this occasion he chastised them for not praying frequently enough. He asked them to offer sacrifices to God for the redemption of sinners, telling them that Jesus and Mary had merciful plans for them. A few months later, as the children were on their knees praying while their flocks grazed, the angel appeared for a final time, holding a chalice and host that dripped with blood. He asked them again to pray for the redemption of sinners who had offended God. The host was given to Lúcia and the contents of the chalice to her cousins. Unbeknownst to them, the children had now been made ready to receive their vision of the Virgin Mary.

THE THREE SECRETS

Following the first apparition of the Virgin Mary, Jacinta was unable to keep the secret from her mother. Furious with her daughter for telling lies, Olimpia punished the girl – but at the same time she told her friends of Jacinta's claim. As a result, 60 villagers turned up for the second apparition, scheduled for May. The children began making voluntary sacrifices for redemption of sinners by giving up lunch, wearing knotted ropes around their waists, and not drinking water in the heat of the day. On 13 July, during the third vision, the Virgin Mary entrusted to the children three prophecies; these became known as the Three Secrets of Fátima. News of the apparition as well as the prophecies, which the children did not divulge, spread rapidly. The three children returned each month, as requested, on the 13th day – except in August, when they went on the 15th instead because they had been detained in prison. Arthur de Oliveira Santos, a Freemason and the mayor of Fátima, tried to frighten the children into revealing the secrets that the Lady had given them. He kidnapped them, threatened to boil them alive in burning oil, and jailed them when they refused to divulge the secrets.

The first two prophecies were revealed by Lúcia in 1941. The first was a vision of Hell, which frightened Jacinta especially, even though in the first apparition the children had been assured that they would all go to Heaven. The second secret described how to save souls from

‘ OUR LADY SHOWED US A GREAT SEA OF FIRE WHICH SEEMED TO BE UNDER THE EARTH. PLUNGED IN THIS FIRE WERE DEMONS AND SOULS IN HUMAN FORM, LIKE TRANSPARENT BURNING EMBERS, ALL BLACKENED OR BURNISHED BRONZE, FLOATING ABOUT IN THE CONFLAGRATION, NOW RAISED INTO THE AIR BY THE FLAMES THAT ISSUED FROM WITHIN THEMSELVES TOGETHER WITH GREAT CLOUDS OF SMOKE ... WHICH HORRIFIED US AND MADE US TREMBLE WITH FEAR. ’

Hell and reconvert the world to Roman Catholicism. The rise of communism in Russia was of particular concern to the Virgin Mary, who requested prayers be said for the reconsecration of Russia. If her requests were not met, then Russia's misdeeds would spread throughout the world, followed by war and famine. Furthermore, she proposed to the children that a strange light would illuminate the night sky during the pontificate of Pius XI (6 February 1922 – 10 February 1939), and that God would punish the world for its crimes. On 25 January 1938, there was indeed an unusual display of the aurora borealis that lit up the skies of Europe.

The third secret Lúcia believed too terrible to be revealed. After falling gravely ill in 1944 she was encouraged to write it down and send it in a sealed letter to the Vatican, with instructions that it should not be opened until after 1960, when it would be more fully understood. Pope John XXIII decided not to open it, and the letter was stored in the Vatican vaults. His successor, Pope Paul VI, opened it, without revealing its import, on 27 March 1965. However, rumours began circulating that the prophecy involved an impending apocalypse. In 1981 a 73-year-old former Trappist monk from Australia, Laurence James, even hijacked an Aer Lingus plane, threatening to blow it up if the secret was not revealed. French special forces stormed the plane at Le Touquet, in northern France, and James was jailed for five years.

Pope John Paul II finally divulged the third secret on 26 June 2000. It involved a 'bishop dressed in white' struggling towards a huge cross. He passed through a city in ruins, praying for the corpses felled by gunfire. At the foot of the cross he was killed by soldiers who then murdered the other men and women of the cloth. John Paul II interpreted the vision as a prophecy of his attempted assassination in 1981 by Mehmet Ali Agca. However, some people today still maintain that there is more to the prophecy than has thus far been revealed, and that it might be linked to Malachy's prediction of a last pope and the extinction of the papacy (see pages 56–59).

INSTRUCTIONS FROM THE VIRGIN

The Virgin Mary predicted that Francisco and Jacinta would die young, and they did indeed both die within a short time: as a result of complications from the pandemic of Spanish influenza, Francisco passed away in 1919 and Jacinta in 1920. Lúcia moved away from Fátima, becoming a nun and taking her final vows in 1928. She received two more visions of the Virgin Mary. In 1925 the Virgin told Lúcia, then in a convent in Spain, to reiterate her call for the faithful to attend Mass to offer prayers for Russia. In 1929 Lúcia was urged to tell the pope to pray with every Catholic bishop for the reconsecration of Russia and indeed the whole world.

FÁTIMA
PROPHECIES
Timeline

1917 (April) First appearance of the Virgin Mary to three young Portuguese children, including Lúcia dos Santos

1917 (July) During a gathering of the faithful at Cova da Iria, Our Lady of Fátima appears once more to the children, imparting three secrets to Lúcia

1928 Lúcia becomes a nun; work commences on construction of the Basilica of Our Lady of Fátima at the site of the vision

1941 Lúcia reveals two of the secrets imparted to her by the Virgin Mary

1944 Lúcia sends third secret to the Vatican

1953 The basilica at Fátima is consecrated

1981 Pope John Paul II survives an attempted assassination, believed to be the subject of Lúcia's third secret

2000 Francisco and Jacinta Marco, who experienced the vision with Lúcia are beatified by Pope John Paul II

2005 Lúcia dos Santos dies aged 97

2007 Church of the Holy Trinity opened next to the basilica

This event finally took place in 1984, during the papacy of Pope John Paul II. Many believers claim this act was responsible for the fall of the Iron Curtain in 1989.

The Virgin Mary also asked for a church to be built on the spot where she had appeared to the children on the Cova da Iria. Building commenced on the Basilica of Our Lady of Fátima in 1928, with consecration in 1953. Francisco and Jacinta were buried in the basilica in 1952, and on 13 May 2000 they were beatified by Pope John Paul II. Five years would have to elapse before Lúcia, who died aged 97 in February 2005, could also be beatified. She was then buried beside her cousins.

In October 2007 the Church of the Holy Trinity was opened near the Basilica of Our Lady. It cost £54 million ($108 million) to build and accommodates 9000 worshippers. Today five million people make pilgrimages to the site each year.

William Wadé Harris
1865–1929
The 'Black Elijah'

In 1914, a Ghanaian journalist witnessed a remarkable sight. Walking along the street ahead of him in the small town of Axim in the British Gold Coast was a barefoot Liberian man. Dressed in a white turban and robe with black bands across his chest, the man was carrying a tall cross made from cane. Awed passers-by were trembling and falling in convulsions while this charismatic evangelist baptized them with water from a bowl. The baptist in question was William Wadé Harris, a self-proclaimed prophet who claimed to receive 'messages from God' or 'telegrams from Heaven' as he gazed up at the sky.

Harris was born in 1865 at Half-Graway in Liberia. His parents, members of the Grebo tribe, belonged to the Kru coastal clan. The Kru had co-existed peacefully with the other indigenous peoples until 1821, when the American Colonization Society began sending freed African-American slaves to the Gold Coast. These new arrivals began acquiring land from the 16 tribes living in the area and in 1847 founded the independent nation of Liberia. It was not long before friction grew between the original inhabitants and the newcomers, with the Kru particularly hostile to their new rulers. To ease tensions, the African-Americans offered free education and other benefits in return for land. Yet discontent continued to simmer, and by 1875, relations had grown extremely strained between the settlers and the Grebo. The latter demanded the return of their land and accused the Americo-Liberians of breaking their promises. Fighting broke out, but with American aid the Grebos were suppressed.

Little is known of Harris's early life, but at the age of 12 he went to live with the Reverend Jesse Lowrie, a Grebo elder and Methodist Episcopal minister who had been heavily influenced both by white Christian missionaries and by the black American newcomers. Harris's Christian education set him apart from other Grebo, who adhered to a traditional animistic form of religion. This focused on a belief in the power of natural or ancestral spirits; anyone wishing to invoke these spiritual forces would obtain fetishes (amulets) from local shamans, who were able to activate them.

RELIGIOUS AND POLITICAL ENGAGEMENT

After leaving school, Harris went to work for a British shipping company, travelling twice on board ships to both Lagos and Gabon. In 1885 he married Rose Farr, daughter of a missionary schoolteacher, and they went on to produce six children. In 1886, he left the shipping industry and returned to Cape Palmas, where he worked as a bricklayer. That same year he became a lay member of the Methodist Episcopal Church, and in 1892 began teaching the catechism in an American Protestant Episcopal mission school in Half-Graway. Despite his increasingly outspoken opposition to the suppression of the Grebo, 11 years later Harris was appointed head teacher at the school. After just one year, however, he was dismissed from this post for alleged 'improper conduct' towards his supervisor.

By this time, the Americo-Liberian inhabitants of Liberia's capital, Monrovia, had become increasingly anti-British, as captains of British ships were refusing to pay berthing charges when they docked at Liberian ports. Predictably, the Kru sided with the British in this dispute, and by 1906 the settlers were finding it more and more difficult to quell Kru discontent. Even so, despite the political unrest, Harris was able to secure a post as head teacher in another school in Half-Graway and in addition to become a government interpreter. Yet once more his tenure of these posts was short-lived, as he was soon dismissed, probably for voicing his support for the Grebo. Furious at his sacking, Harris marched off to Monrovia to demand – unsuccessfully – an explanation from the president and secretary of the treasury.

Things came to a head in February 1909. When the Kru staged protests in Monrovia, Harris abandoned his mission work to join them. In anticipation of a successful coup d'état in Monrovia, Harris desecrated the Liberian flag and hoisted the Union Jack in its place in Cape Palmas. This act of treason earned him a prison sentence of more than a year as well as the nickname 'Old Union Jack'.

HARRIS'S EPIPHANY

It was while he was in prison that Harris had a dream in which the archangel Gabriel appeared to him, commanding him to discard his European clothes and to go forth and preach. He was told to warn Africans that Christ's return was imminent and that they must change their way of life and convert to Christianity in readiness. Harris immediately declared himself a prophet, and as soon as he was released from gaol followed the archangel's instructions, donning a tunic made from a white sheet and a turban fashioned from a pillowcase.

WILLIAM WADÉ HARRIS
A Life in Brief

1847 Foundation of the Republic of Liberia by emancipated American slaves

1865 William Wadé Harris born in Half-Graway, Liberia

1892–1903 Harris teaches at the American Protestant Episcopal mission in Half-Graway

1909 Harris imprisoned for political activism; he experiences a vision and becomes a self-styled prophet

1913–14 Harris preaches in the Ivory Coast, converting around 100,000 people to Christianity

1929 Death of Harris in Cape Palmas, Liberia

1998 Harrist Church joins the World Council of Churches (WCC)

Harris's prophetic career began inauspiciously in Liberia's Cape Palmas; many people simply considered him mad. It was even said that his wife, despairing of his actions, died of a broken heart shortly after his release from prison. Not until he moved to the neighbouring French Ivory Coast in 1913 did his star rise. According to Gordon Mackay Haliburton, author of *The Prophet Harris* (1971), his popularity there was due to the unsettling changes that Ivorians were experiencing under French colonial rule. Their gods and fetishes had failed to rid the country of its oppressors and as a result they were ripe for a new order to revitalize them. By contrast, the Grebo tribal leaders in Liberia had already united against their rulers and had no need of a prophet figure. Indeed, Harris's former brief stint as an interpreter raised suspicions among the Grebo that he might be a government collaborator.

EVANGELISTIC CRUSADE

Harris preached to the disparate tribes of the Ivory Coast, urging them to abandon their spirits, burn their fetishes and worship the one true God. He called on them to follow the Ten Commandments and observe the Sabbath; he also condemned extravagant tribal funerals and the tradition of excluding the newly widowed from society for eight days. He proscribed the custom of keeping menstruating women separate, prohibited people from having sex in public, and stopped the practice of allowing nubile young women to dress in nothing more than an apron in order to lure young men into paying a higher bridal price. He also recommended monogamy, although, to the distress of the missionaries, he stopped short of condemning polygamy. Harris may have had personal reasons for remaining silent on the subject. After his wife died, he travelled around the Ivory Coast with two women who dressed in white tunics and sang hymns; rumours circulated that they were actually his wives.

Harris did not form his own church, instead encouraging his followers to join any Christian church, an injunction that appealed to Catholic and Protestant missionaries alike. If there was no village church, one would be built by the locals to accommodate their new faith. A typical day for Harris would be to rise at 5 a.m. and approach a village, driving a flock of sheep before him and accompanied by his white-clad female choir. By 1914 he had converted thousands to Christianity. However, the French authorities became alarmed at the vast crowds he was attracting and expelled him from the country. After a brief sojourn in the Gold Coast, where his

The Indefatigable Preacher

In 1926, the French Methodist missionary Pierre Benoit gave the following account of Harris's power as a preacher:

He lives in a supernatural world in which the people, the ideas, the affirmations, the cosmogony and the eschatology of the Bible are more real than those which he sees and hears materially. He can adapt wonderfully some situation or some attitude of his adversary to a text and find an analogy in the scriptures ... He never doubts it {his mission}, above all he never derogates it. Neither money, nor threats, nor weariness deprive him of the pride he has in carrying through the world the message of the severe and just God, which he proclaims thus: 'Burn your fetishes and idols, or fire from Heaven will be upon you'.

message fell on deaf ears, he made his way back to the Ivory Coast, where his converts began calling him the 'Son of God'. This veneration made the French suspect he was a Protestant tool, and he was expelled for a second time. They then proceeded to burn down many of Harris's churches and to vilify him; during the First World War, rumours were put about that his disciples were German sympathizers and that Harris himself was a German agent.

Harris spent the next few years preaching in Liberia until, at the age of 60, he stopped travelling. In March 1929, realizing that he had not long to live, he appointed John (Jonas) Ahui, the 34-year-old son of a chief from the Ivory Coast, to carry on his work after his death. Harris died in October in the village of Spring Hill in Cape Palmas, aged 64.

Harris once said that he was 'a prophet like Elijah', as a result of which he became known as the 'Black Elijah'. He was reputed to have performed many miracles, including making a paralyzed woman walk again. Yet the most remarkable aspect of Harris's ministry was the sheer number of conversions to Christianity he made. In the early 20th century the Ivory Coast's population numbered 1,544,845. Harris converted over 100,000 people, equating to roughly a tenth of the population. Ahui continued to head Harris's ministry until his death in 1992. Today l'Église Harriste (the Harrist Church), which was founded by Ahui in 1931 and boasts 100,000 members and 1400 preachers, is found mainly in the Ivory Coast, with some congregations also in Ghana, Liberia and France. It joined the World Council of Churches in 1998.

wovoka
c.1854–1932
Prophet of the Ghost Dance

In 1891, James Mooney was sent to Nevada to investigate the events that had led to the massacre by the Seventh Cavalry of several hundred Lakota Sioux at Wounded Knee, South Dakota in 1890. There he received a transcription of words spoken some months earlier by a Paiute medicine man. Known as the 'Messiah Letter', it made dramatic claims: 'Jesus is now upon the Earth,' it declared. 'He appears like a cloud. The dead are still alive again. I do not know when they will be here; maybe this fall or in the spring. When the time comes there will be no more sickness and everyone will be young again.'

The Paiute shaman was Wovoka, a man responsible for a religious movement of hope and passive resistance that in less than two years had spread rapidly among the Native Indians of the American West. Born Quoitze Ow in Nevada in about 1854, he was the son of a Paiute medicine man named Tavibo. Nevada had begun changing dramatically in the years before Wovoka's birth and during his childhood. The United States acquired the Nevada territory from Mexico in 1848, and in 1864 it became the 36th state. During those 16 years it had witnessed

Wovoka, a Paiute shaman and prophet.

the arrival of the telegraph, the Pony Express, and the railroad. White settlements like Virginia City appeared almost overnight as thousands of people moved west to prospect for minerals, work in the gold and zinc mines or claim squatters' rights on the land. By the summer of 1860 battles had broken out between the white settlers and the Paiutes. In one battle, on 2 June 1860, 46 Paiute warriors were killed by a combined force of volunteers and US army regulars.

MAKING OF A PROPHET

Wovoka's father Tavibo, like many other Paiutes, had been deeply troubled by the arrival of the thousands of white settlers. Sometime after Wovoka's birth, he journeyed into the Sierra Nevada mountains to speak with the Great Spirits, returning with the revelation that the Earth would soon swallow the white settlers, and that the stolen lands would be returned to the Paiutes. When the Paiutes gave little credence to this prophecy, Tavibo twice more went into the mountains, both times returning with the same prophecy, which was received with the same gloomy scepticism.

Tavibo died in 1870, when his son was still an adolescent, and Wovoka went to work for a family named Wilson who ranched near the town of Yerington. He eventually befriended the son of the family, attended church with them, and became known as Jack Wilson, even remaining on the ranch after he married at the age of 20. He was interested in Christian teachings, but in about 1887, following a vision received while chopping wood (Wovoka, the

The Ghost Dance

In order to hasten the day when the Earth would be free of the scourge of the white man, Wovoka urged the Paiutes to perform the 'Ghost Dance', a ritual known to other Indians of the Great Basin and first introduced into Paiute culture - but seldom performed - around the time of Tavibo's death. It involved men and women coming together every six weeks to hold hands and dance in a circle for five straight days. 'I want you to dance every six weeks,' Wovoka told his followers. 'Make a feast at the dance and have food that everybody may eat. Then bathe in the water.'

The Ghost Dance found especially fervent adherents among the Sioux, who began wearing 'Ghost Shirts' - garments with a supposedly supernatural power to deflect the bullets fired by the whites - and boasting to the government agents on the reservation exactly what Wovoka had prophesied. Kicking Bear moreover declared that the Messiah forecast by Wovoka would appear in the spring of 1891.

name he assumed, means 'wood-chopper'), he returned to live among the Paiutes, becoming a shaman like his father. He soon developed a reputation for summoning rain – an invaluable talent in the arid lands of western Nevada.

Then, in the sudden darkness of a solar eclipse on New Year's Day in 1889, when he was in his mid-30s, he received a second vision. According to Mooney's report, the eclipse that fell over the valleys of western Nevada had made the Paiutes 'frantic with excitement', and they began firing their guns into the air to frighten the 'monster' that consumed their god. In the midst of these commotions, Wovoka, ill with scarlet fever, had a vision similar to the ones given to his father decades earlier. He was taken into the spirit world and told that Jesus had returned to Earth, and that the time would soon arrive when the white men would be wiped out in a great flood. Meanwhile all of the dead Paiute would return, resurrected along with the buffalo, to reclaim their land. Not only would these ancestors reappear, but the world they had inhabited – free from famine, disease and white settlers – would likewise return.

A decorated Ghost Shirt made of buckskin, which the wearers believed would deflect bullets fired at them.

‘ WHEN THE SUN DIED, I WENT UP TO HEAVEN AND
SAW GOD AND ALL THE PEOPLE WHO HAD DIED A
LONG TIME AGO. GOD TOLD ME TO COME BACK AND
TELL MY PEOPLE THEY MUST BE GOOD AND LOVE
ONE ANOTHER, AND NOT FIGHT, OR STEAL OR LIE. HE
GAVE ME THIS DANCE TO GIVE TO MY PEOPLE. ’

SPREADING THE WORD

While Tavibo's prophecies had fallen on deaf ears, those of Wovoka were eagerly received, and
not merely by the Paiutes. In 1889 the Ghost Dance ritual began spreading outwards from
western Nevada to the reservations of the Arapaho, Shoshone and Cheyenne. By the summer of
1890 it had found enthusiastic practitioners on the Great Plains among the Lakota Sioux. Two
members of the Lakota reservation at Pine Ridge in South Dakota, Short Bull and Kicking Bear,
travelled to Nevada to meet Wovoka, whom they claimed levitated in the air above them.
Wovoka's message had been a peaceful one, since he told his followers to 'be good and love one
another, and not fight, or steal or lie'. He also stressed that they were not to 'make any trouble'
with the whites. Yet despite the caution urged by Sitting Bull, the inspirational medicine man of
the Sioux and a veteran of dealing with the US army, the Ghost Dance was given a more
militant interpretation by the Lakota.

The Messiah Letter

The Messiah Letter was an address delivered by Wovoka to a Cheyenne-Arapaho delegation
that visited the prophet in Nevada in August 1891:

> When you get home you must make a dance to continue five days. Dance four successive
> nights, and the last night keep up the dance until the morning of the fifth day, when all must
> bathe in the river and then disperse to their homes. You must all do in the same way. I, Jack
> Wilson, love you all, and my heart is full of gladness for the gifts you have brought me ...
>
> You must not hurt anybody or do harm to anyone. You must not fight. Do right always. It
> will give you satisfaction in life ...
>
> Do not tell the white people about this. Jesus is now upon the Earth. He appears like a cloud.
> The dead are still alive again. I do not know when they will be here; maybe this fall or in the
> spring. When the time comes there will be no more sickness and everyone will be young
> again.
>
> Do not refuse to work for the whites and do not make any trouble with them until you leave
> them. When the earth shakes, do not be afraid. It will not hurt you.
>
> I want you to dance every six weeks. Make a feast at the dance and have food that everybody
> may eat. Then bathe in the water. That is all. You will receive good words again from me
> some time. Do not tell lies.

The Sioux nation had experienced terrible hardships as the buffalo disappeared from the plains, hunted to near-extinction by the settlers. In 1877 they lost their lands in the Black Hills and the Big Horn Mountain, and found themselves confined to reservations such as Pine Ridge. Little wonder, then, that the prophecy of the Ghost Dance found zealous adherents among them.

This spiritual revival among the Lakota alarmed both the government agents and the white settlers of South Dakota. The *Rapid City Journal* began publishing scare stories about a forthcoming Indian rebellion. One enterprising agent tried to distract the Lakota from their dancing by introducing them to the pastime of baseball – to no avail. Wovoka informed the American government that he would try to contain any violent uprising if Washington provided financial compensation as well as food. The offer was disregarded, and tribal police were dispatched to arrest Sitting Bull. On 15 December 1890, as several Lakota rallied to protect him, he and his son were shot dead. They would be only the first of many casualties. The Ghost Dance continued at the reservation, and two weeks later, in the dead of winter, the 7th Cavalry – the same regiment that General George Armstrong Custer had commanded at Little Big Horn in 1876 – ploughed through the snow to Pine Ridge. They had orders to disarm the Lakota and stop the Ghost Dance.

THE SLAUGHTER AT WOUNDED KNEE

At Little Big Horn, the Sioux and Cheyenne warriors led by Crazy Horse had wiped out the 7th Cavalry in under an hour. Fourteen years later, the regiment was taking no chances. In the bitter cold at Wounded Knee Creek, the heavily armed soldiers shot dead more than 150 Lakota, while many others died of hypothermia or simply went missing. These were not the valiant and ferocious legions of Crazy Horse: most were unarmed, and many women and children were among them. Short Bull and Kicking Bear survived, but among the dead was Big Foot, Sitting Bull's half-brother and leader of the Lakota Sioux.

The massacre at Wounded Knee brought the Ghost Dance movement to an abrupt and tragic end. Wovoka's prophecy had spectacularly failed to fulfill itself. Through no fault of his own, Wovoka's message of hope had brought about only misfortune and destruction – a sad end to a religious movement that, as James Mooney's report concluded, had been about peace, brotherhood and cultural revival among a desperate and discouraged people.

As for Wovoka, he quickly disappeared into obscurity, though in later years he could be found working as a sideshow exhibit at country fairs. He also had small roles in silent Western films. He eventually died in 1932, largely forgotten, and was buried in the Paiute cemetery in Schurz, Nevada, under the name Jack Wilson.

WOVOKA
A Life in Brief

c.1854 Birth of Wovoka in Nevada

1864 Nevada accedes to the Union as the 36th state

1869 Completion of the first trans-American railroad link

1876–7 The Great Sioux War brings the rout and massacre of General George Armstrong Custer and 200 US troopers at the Battle of Little Big Horn

1889 After experiencing a vision prophesying the demise of the white man, Wovoka institutes the Ghost Dance

1890 More than 150 Lakota Sioux slaughtered by the US 7th Cavalry at Wounded Knee Creek, South Dakota; the same year, the US government declares that the western frontier no longer exists

1932 Death of Wovoka in Nevada

nonteTha
nkwenkwe
1875-1935
Xhosa Prophetess

On 23 October 1998, several thousand people assembled at Khulile and sang hymns as the coffin of Nontetha Nkwenkwe was lowered gently into the ground. This village, near Debe Nek, in South Africa's Eastern Cape, was 600 miles (960 km) from the mental institution where Nontetha, a Xhosa healer and early black nationalist who died in 1935, had been buried in an unmarked grave. Over 60 years after her death, she had finally returned home.

had it not been for the persistence of Robert R. Edgar, an American professor at Howard University, Washington DC, Nontetha's burial place might never have been discovered. Once its whereabouts were confirmed, her followers finally understood the meaning of one of her many prophecies: 'Look to the Americans. They will help you one day.'

Nontetha was born in 1875 in Toyise, a Xhosa region of South Africa near King William's Town. Here Nontetha, whose name means 'She who speaks a lot', married a man named Bungu Nkwenkwe and produced ten children. However, like many African males, Bungu was forced to quit his village and earn his living as a migrant labourer, later dying at Saldanha Bay and leaving his wife to support her large family. Nontetha had received no formal education and spoke no English, which limited her employment prospects. However, she trained as a sangoma, a traditional healer who treated physical ailments and warded off evil spirits by means of herbal medicines. Though she never joined a Christian church, she had been exposed to Christianity through missionaries working in the area, and most of her children were baptized in the Wesleyan Methodist Church.

CHOSEN BY GOD

These Christian influences made themselves felt when Nontetha fell ill. In 1918 the worldwide influenza epidemic hit South Africa, killing a quarter of a million people. Nontetha caught the virus, and during her illness she experienced visions from God and Jesus. In one of them, she witnessed a rotten Bible wrapped in dirty cloth hanging from a tree. When she asked for a piece of it so she could testify on Earth, Jesus refused, saying that too many people had neglected the book. Further visions told her that witchcraft must be eradicated and that people were dying in the gold mines because they were failing to pray. In one vision, God commanded Nontetha to visit the African chiefs and instruct them to work together so that they could liberate themselves and rule their own country. He also told her that the Day of Judgement was imminent, and that the influenza epidemic was a foretaste of things to come.

Recovering from her influenza, Nontetha, then 43 years old, began sharing her visions with people around her – only to be mocked. She soon fell ill again, and further visions revealed that Jesus would appear in a cloud to judge the living and the dead on the Day of Judgement, and that ancestors who were asleep in their graves would be reunited with the living. She also dreamed of a bearded face that mutated into the mountain Ntaba Kandoda, a place where people would be freed of their sins. This vision was similar to that of a 19th-century Xhosa prophet named Ntsikana. Nontetha claimed that Ntsikana had also visited her in a dream, telling her she was the last angel sent from God, and that she was to preach all she had seen.

Nontetha pleaded with God, believing herself unequal to the task, to which God replied that in that case he would send her daughter to preach instead. Nontetha feared that prophesying among the Xhosa would create even more difficulties for her daughter, and so she agreed to submit to God's command. While she was still feverish, God came to her in yet more dreams, telling her that the only way she would recover was to bathe in the river. When she awoke, she instructed her daughter to wash her in river water, whereupon, as God had promised, she was healed. Nontetha then claimed to have been endowed with special powers from God, even believing she had died and been resurrected.

Although convinced that Judgement Day was approaching, Nontetha did not specify the date. She did, however, offer salvation for believers who agreed to change their ways. She preached against witchcraft, adultery, tobacco, alcohol, eating pork, traditional dancing and participation in circumcision ceremonies. She began her mission by approaching the traditional African authorities in the area, establishing her first ministry among the imiDushane and the Ndlambe people. Religious services regularly lasted between two and three hours. There was no dancing or beating of drums, though hymns were sung. During the services, Nontetha wore a white robe and headdress, with a white sash around her waist, and carried an umnqayi, the black stick taken by senior married women to important ceremonies. Since she was illiterate, she 'read' invisible phrases from the palm of her right hand, claiming that her pronouncements were the word of God.

A statue of the prophetess, Nontetha Nkwenkwe, by Lynnley Watson, outside the King William's Town magistrate's court, East Cape, South Africa. It was there that Nkwenkwe was first locked up for being 'troublesome'.

1875 Nontetha Nkwenkwe born in Toyise

1918 Nontetha receives visions from God and Jesus, commanding her to preach against witchcraft and other traditional practices and to encourage the black peoples of South Africa to unite

1921 Massacre by South African authorities of the Israelite sect at Bulhoek

1922 Fearing her preaching might foment uprising, the government incarcerates Nontetha in a mental hospital

1923 The Church of the Prophetesss Nontetha is founded by her followers

1926–7 Nontetha's followers organize 'Pilgrimages of Grace' to her hospital in Pretoria

1935 Death of Nontetha in custody and burial in an unmarked grave

1994 A black majority government comes to power in South Africa's first free elections

1998 Nontetha's remains are reinterred at Khulile in the Eastern Cape

FEAR OF SEDITION

By the summer of 1922, Nontetha had come to the attention of the white authorities. South Africa had been known as the Union of South Africa since 1910, when the British colony and former Boer Republics such as Transvaal came together as a self-governing dominion in the British empire. The country's official languages were English and Afrikaans, and only the white population had the right to vote. Nontetha's influence threatened to turn the black population against their white masters. She had been telling her followers that they must not only respect their own chiefs but also strive for solidarity between the tribes, so that one day Africans would be in a position to rule themselves. The opinion of the white authorities was divided: some regarded her new rules – her position against alcohol and witchcraft, for example – as a positive influence on the locals. Others believed her a threat to the stability of the whole region, especially as she was urging African independence.

Eighteen months after the massacre at nearby Bulhoek (see box feature), Nontetha was arrested and sent to Fort Beaufort Mental Hospital. Early in January 1923 she was released on probation, on condition that she refrain from preaching. When she refused, she was promptly returned to the mental hospital. Robert R. Edgar and Hilary Spire's biography of Nontetha, *African Apocalypse* (1999), points out that Africans were routinely incarcerated in mental institutions by colonial authorities fearing disruption to white rule. Prison conditions were appalling, with no medical treatment and no leisure facilities, and with inmates often sedated with a cocktail of drugs to keep them passive.

TRANSFERRED TO PRETORIA

Between 1923 and 1924, Nontetha received numerous visitors. She had prophesied that a plague of locusts would be sent from God as punishment for sins, decreeing that the insects should not be killed. When the locusts duly arrived in October 1923, the government, under the Agricultural Pest Act of 1911, ordered their destruction. Nontetha's followers refused, and over 100 of them were fined and imprisoned. To limit Nontetha's influence on her followers, the authorities decided to send her to Weskoppies Mental Hospital, over 600 miles (960 km) away in Pretoria. Once there, she was diagnosed by Dr Crosthwaite with dementia praecox (schizophrenia), since she remained adamant that God had entered her blood and placed writing in her head. Sometimes, the psychiatrist claimed, she preached over a fence to no one, was violent and hostile, attacked other inmates for no reason, and claimed that staff were trying to poison or burn her, and that they were hiding a letter addressed to her from the father of Queen Victoria. Nontetha later claimed that she was in regular communication with the deceased queen.

Nontetha's followers were persistently denied access to their prophetess. In 1926 and 1927, therefore, in order to highlight her incarceration, which they considered unjustified, they organized several Pilgrimages of Grace, travelling long distances *en masse* to Pretoria, praying and singing hymns as they went. On their arrival the authorities arrested many of them under the Urban Areas Act and, after they had served their sentences, shipped them back to their homes. Following the third Pilgrimage of Grace, Nontetha received few visitors.

On 20 May 1935, following years of ill health, Nontetha died of stomach and liver cancer at the age of 60. A telegram was sent to her family, requesting them to collect her body. However, it took weeks to arrive, and in the meantime, in accordance with government policy, Nontetha was buried two days after her death in an unmarked grave. On finally receiving the telegram, her son immediately travelled to Pretoria to request the release of his mother's remains, only to be turned away.

The Church of the Prophetess Nontetha was formed by her followers in 1923. Although it later split into two branches, it remains a small but thriving religion today, with over 1000 members.

The Bulhoek Massacre

In 1919, Enoch Mgijima, leader of a black South African millenarian sect known as the Israelites, warned his followers that the world would end in 1920 and urged them to gather in the villages of Bulhoek and Ntabelanga within the township of Kamastone in the Eastern Cape. The Israelites told local officials that they were assembling to observe the annual Passover festival. However, as the numbers of new arrivals continued to swell, the authorities grew concerned, and in December 1920 asked the squatters to leave. When they refused, and after three further unsuccessful attempts to evict them peacefully, on 24 May 1921 the authorities sent in 800 armed police to evict them by force. In the process, 183 Israelites were killed and a further 129 wounded. White church leaders in South Africa refused to condemn this atrocity, blaming the massacre on the supposedly 'threatening behaviour' of the Israelites.

‘ SHE (NONTETHA) STATED THAT SHE WAS INSPIRED DIRECTLY BY GOD, THAT SHE HAD TO OBEY HIM AND PREACH IF HE TOLD HER TO DO SO. GOD HAD PICKED HER TO PREACH TO THE NATIVES BECAUSE ALL THEIR SINS WOULD REST ON HER IF SHE DID NOT. ’

Guy Ballard
1878–1939

The 'I AM' Activity

In 1930 Guy Ballard, a 52-year-old American mining engineer, was prospecting for gold on Mount Shasta, in the Sierra Nevada in California. Yet he was also seeking treasures besides those in mineral form. Deeply interested in theosophy and the occult, Ballard had already undertaken many spiritual pilgrimages to this revered peak, eager to investigate rumours that the Brotherhood of Mount Shasta, a group of enlightened beings, lived there.

On this occasion, Ballard's devotion was rewarded with a miraculous encounter. Stopping to drink water from a stream, he suddenly felt an electrical current flowing from his head. When he raised his eyes, he saw a man with a dazzling countenance, a 'magnificent God-like figure in a white jewelled robe', who told him that he would fill his cup with a drink far more refreshing than water. The cup then filled with a creamy beverage that Ballard was informed came from a 'universal supply'. Asking the stranger's name, Ballard learned that he had just met the Comte de Saint Germain.

The Comte de Saint Germain (1710–84; not to be confused with King Louis XVI's military reformer of the same surname) was a real 18th-century alchemist and mystic who was a minor personage in the court of King Louis XV. However, he occupied a special place in early 20th-century theosophical and occult circles, having supposedly had several previous incarnations, including the prophet Samuel, Merlin, Roger Bacon, Christopher Columbus and Francis Bacon. He was even believed to have appeared to George Washington, inspiring him to draft the United States' Constitution. According to Ballard, Saint Germain was an Ascended Master – that is, a being who had completed all earthly cycles of reincarnation and karma and had become one of the Great White Brotherhood. This select band inhabited a higher plane of existence and was responsible for the destiny of the human race. To Saint Germain had been assigned the task of initiating the Seventh Golden Age, which would represent the permanent 'I AM Age' of perfection on Earth, and which was to begin, Ballard learned, in America. Saint Germain had spent centuries searching unsuccessfully for a messenger in human form to whom he could pass on the Great Law of Life. When Ballard accepted the drink from the source of 'Universal Life', he was introduced to the powers of the Ascended Masters and agreed to be their messenger.

MAN OF MANY PARTS

Guy Ballard was born in Newton, Kansas, in 1878. Little is known of his early life other than that he came from a large farming family. In 1916 he married Edna Anna Wheeler of Burlington, Iowa, and their son Donald was born two years later. He spent a short period in the army, took a business course, and went to work at his uncle's lead mine in Tucson, Arizona. When his uncle died, he moved with his family to Chicago.

These modest origins were at odds with Ballard's previous incarnations. In former lives, he claimed, he had been Aemilius, the Roman centurion present at Christ's crucifixion, King Richard the Lionheart (1157–99) and George Washington (1732–99). Over time, Saint

Mount Shasta in the Californian Sierra Nevada shown in this c.1870 wood engraving. It was here that Guy Ballard made many pilgrimages and first saw the Comte de Saint Germain.

Germain revealed to Ballard other of his previous lives, for example, in Ancient Egypt and among the Inca. On a touching domestic note, in these previous lives he had always been accompanied by both Edna and Donald. Their close union continued: while Ballard was in California he wrote frequently to Edna, keeping her informed of his experiences, and she and Donald also became Saint Germain's messengers.

'I [COMTE DE SAINT GERMAIN] HAVE COME TO TAKE YOU ON AN IMPORTANT JOURNEY. WE WILL BE GONE THIRTY-SIX HOURS. DRAW THE CURTAINS TO YOUR ROOM, LOCK THE DOORS, AND LEAVE YOUR BODY IN BED. IT WILL BE GUARDED UNTIL OUR RETURN. YOU HAVE MADE CERTAIN INNER ADVANCEMENT, AND A VERY INTERESTING, DELIGHTFUL EXPERIENCE AND JOURNEY LIE AHEAD OF YOU.'

GODFRÉ RAY KING *UNVEILED MYSTERIES* (1934)

The 'I AM' Presence

Scenes of the world's past and its future were disclosed by Saint Germain to Ballard, and eventually he was introduced to other Ascended Masters, including Jesus, all of whom worked in the invisible realms to help mankind. He was taught that God permeated all things, and that the 'I AM' presence of God inhabits all humans. 'I AM' was a reference to God's reply to Moses – 'I am who I am' – in Exodus 3:4. This 'I AM' presence was located, said Ballard, several feet above the head, and unlimited power could be drawn from it at any time. However, misuse of this divine spark had resulted in humanity's discord.

Ballard claimed to have travelled in 1931 to Europe, Egypt, Arabia and India. The following year he returned with his family to Chicago, where Saint Germain, via light and sound rays, imparted further spiritual messages, and where the Ballards began giving talks about the 'I AM' presence. In 1932 they founded the Saint Germain Press and the Saint Germain Foundation. The 'I AM' Religious Activity was also formed in that year with the purpose of teaching the wisdom of the Ascended Masters in order to bring perfection, illumination and freedom to mankind. These messages found a receptive audience. Thousands of people flocked to hear the Ballards speak or to attend their courses. Among their admirers was Saint Germain himself, who lavished praise on the Ballards via one of his discourses: 'They have proven their ability to stand in the Light, and with no personal desire, unselfishly to carry the pure unadulterated message of the Mighty "I AM" Presence.'

Seer or Charlatan?

Ballard's experiences on Mount Shasta were published in 1934 as *Unveiled Mysteries*, under the pseudonym Godfré Ray King. *The Magic Presence* was published the following year, detailing Ballard's travels in Europe, Egypt, Arabia and India. This latter work hinted at the existence of mineral wealth awaiting extraction and exploitation. Saint Germain had informed Ballard that there was gold to be found in Colorado, with one area containing 'over $20 million in gold, clear and above all generating expenses' – a statement inserted into *The Magic Presence* to attract potential investors. Yet it was claimed that material gain was not the principal reason for its extraction. According to Saint Germain, gold was vital because it 'purifies, vitalizes and balances the atomic structure of the world'.

Others imputed crasser motives to Ballard. According to a former follower of the 'I AM' Activity, Gerald B. Bryan, author of *Psychic Dictatorship in America* (1940), while Ballard was supposedly discoursing with Saint Germain and travelling the world in 1930 and 1931, he had in fact never left California and was, in between attending metaphysical lectures given by various teachers, prospecting for gold and touting for investors. Indeed, Ballard may have convinced Saint Germain of his ability to 'stand in the Light with no personal desire', but in 1929 he had been indicted by a Grand Jury in Chicago for 'obtaining money and goods by means of the confidence game'. Two women had fruitlessly invested thousands of dollars in the Gold Lake project in California, where Ballard was hoping to establish a mine. Ballard quickly departed for Los Angeles, where he assumed the name Dick Gilbert and embarked on his search for the Brotherhood of Mount Shasta. He did not stand trial, and the charges were dropped. He was summoned once again to a court in Chicago in 1938 after a 60-year-old woman sued him for $10,000. She had invested her life's savings in Ballard's Cottonwood Trust, founded to exploit a gold mining project in California. Although the press gleefully seized upon this latest impropriety, once again the charges failed to stick.

In response to criticism of the 'I AM' movement, the Ballards urged their followers to use their minds to conjure up blue lightning to zap their opponents. Decrees – mantras to effect this mind-zapping technique – were published in book form, covering a variety of situations, from dealing with mortal enemies to controlling the weather.

LEGAL WRANGLINGS

Despite stating that he had a body of 'immortal endurance', Ballard died at the age of 61 on 29 December 1939, bloated and in pain from liver and cardiac complications. Edna took over the leadership and, with Donald, weathered a mail fraud conviction in 1942. A score of prominent members of the 'I AM' Activity were charged with devising the 'I AM' religion knowing that it was a fabrication and a way of soliciting large sums of money through the mail. They were found guilty, but in 1944 the conviction was overturned by the US Supreme Court on the grounds that it was unacceptable under the Constitution to determine the truth or falsity of any religion – and that is what the jury would have had to have done to secure a conviction. The US postal service, however, denied them all use of the mail after the first conviction, a ban not revoked until 1954.

In the 1950s, Edna expanded the teachings, recording over 2000 dictations from the Ascended Masters, whom her husband had joined. In 1957 the 'I AM' Activity was given tax-exempt status. Donald eventually lost interest in the movement and opened an electrical shop in New Mexico. Edna died in 1971, at which point the governance of the religion passed to a five-member board, which in 1982 was expanded to 18. Today the headquarters of the organization are in Schaumburg, a suburb of Chicago, while more than 300 'I AM' centres have been established in over 25 countries.

'I CALL THE ANGELS OF BLUE LIGHTNING, THE LEGIONS OF LIGHT TO STAND GUARD OVER YOUR AMERICA; MY AMERICA; THAT EVERY PERSON WHO TRIES TO BRING DESTRUCTIVE CONDITIONS, QUALITIES OR ACTIVITIES INTO AMERICA, SHALL CEASE TO EXIST IN HIS HUMAN FORM.'

Wallace Fard muhammad
c.1891–?
The Nation of Islam

Wallace Fard Muhammad founded the Black Nationalist movement in the United States in 1933 to improve the economic, mental, social and spiritual condition of black people. Now known as the Nation of Islam, the movement is currently estimated to have more than 30,000 members. Fard Muhammad was, and still is, believed by some to be the Promised One – the Mahdi – who, according to Islamic prophecy, would restore a just Islamic society to the world.

There is, however, much confusion surrounding the identity of Fard Muhammad. The details of his early life, and his true identity, are still matters of debate, and according to the FBI the man who called himself Fard Muhammad had at least 28 aliases. He appears to

have been born in 1891, probably of mixed European and Polynesian parentage, either in New Zealand or Portland, Oregon. However, C. Eric Lincoln, author of *The Black Muslims in America* (1994), reports that Fard Muhammad was variously rumoured to be a black Jamaican with a Syrian mother, or a Palestinian. The FBI claimed that he was one and the same person as a man going by the name of Wallace Dodd Ford, who entered the United States in the early 1920s and was subsequently gaoled for drug offences between 1926 and 1929. The Nation of Islam (NOI), however, denies that Wallace Fard Muhammad and Wallace Dodd Ford are the same person, claiming that Fard Muhammad was born in Mecca in

Elijah Muhammad led the Nation of Islam from 1934, when he was put in charge by Fard Muhammad.

1877. Fard's successor in 1934, Elijah Muhammad (1897–1975), believed that Fard was actually the Allah incarnate but used the name Wallace Fard Muhammad on arrival in America from Mecca in 1930.

INTERNECINE FEUDING

According to one version of the Fard Muhammad story, on Dodd's release from prison he moved to Newark, New Jersey, where he joined the Moorish Science Temple of America (MST), founded in 1913, and adopted the name David Ford-el. The leader of the MST, Timothy Drew, known as Noble Drew Ali, was a former circus magician from North Carolina who travelled to Egypt and supposedly studied under a priestly member of a cult associated with the Pyramid of Cheops. Returning to America, he was told in a dream to found a new religion, which held that African-Americans were descended from Moabites or Moors and were therefore Islamic in origin. He preached that Christianity was for 'paleface' Europeans and 'Moslemism' for the dark-skinned 'Asiatics'. Only when each group had its own peculiar religion would there be peace on Earth. Drew Ali stressed loyalty to the United States, but at the same time he preached that black Americans were an oppressed race and that divine intervention would end white supremacy.

In June 1929, while Drew Ali was awaiting trial as an accessory to the murder of a rival, Dodd/Ford-el, who had become a charismatic preacher in the organization, was placed in charge of the MST, now based in Chicago. Drew Ali's controversial ideas had made him and his followers unwelcome in Newark and then Philadelphia and Detroit. A month later, Drew Ali was found dead in his house in suspicious circumstances: he was allegedly beaten by Chicago police and died shortly after his release from custody. His death caused friction within the 15,000-strong organization, particularly when Dodd/Ford-el claimed to be the reincarnation of Drew Ali and hence the rightful new leader. Two rival would-be leaders, who likewise claimed to be Drew Ali reincarnate, were Charles Kirkman Bey, an early convert, and Ira Johnson Bey. However, after a gun battle in one of the temples that left two policemen dead, Johnson Bey was imprisoned in a hospital for the criminally insane; he died in 1959. Eventually Charles took up the reins of the MST and Dodd/Ford-el left the organization, departing with loyal followers to Detroit, Michigan. Once again he changed his name, this time to Wallace Fard Muhammad, and renamed the fledgling sect he now controlled the Allah Temple of Islam (ATI).

SUCCOUR TO THE DOWNTRODDEN

Fard Muhammad's philosophy mixed traditional Islam with Theosophy (see pages 101–108). He preached that blacks in America had a duty to discover their true identities, which had been denied to them by the white slave owners. If Christianity was the religion of the whites, then

WALLACE FARD MUHAMMAD
A Life in Brief

c.1891 Possible date of birth of Wallace Fard Muhammad

1913 Noble Drew Ali founds the Moorish Science Temple of America in Newark, NJ

1929 Wallace Fard Muhammad joins the MST, but after losing a leadership struggle, founds the Allah Temple of Islam (later renamed the Nation of Islam)

1934 Disappearance of Wallace Fard Muhammad; Elijah Muhammad takes over leadership of the NOI

1965 Assassination by NOI members of the radical preacher Malcolm X

1975 Death of Elijah Muhammad

1977 Louis Farrakhan founds the new Nation of Islam

Islam was the original religion of the blacks. Black people, said Fard Muhammad, all belonged to the tribe Shabazz, which had originally come to Earth from another planet. They were by nature divine, having been created by Allah from the dark substance of space. White people, in contrast, were 'a race of white devils', created by an evil scientist named Yakub. Yakub had created the 'evil' white man in opposition to the 'good' black man, and the whiter the skin, the weaker, morally, a man was said to be. Armageddon, he stated, was imminent, and sometime in the near future a spaceship would appear to destroy all the 'blue-eyed devils'.

For many African-Americans, this legend provided an explanation of the desperate circumstances in which they found themselves. At the time there were 120,000 African-Americans living in Detroit, of whom 30,000 had been employed in the city's auto industries. With the onset of the Great Depression in 1929, many blacks lost their jobs to white workers, and Detroit's black population suffered severely, with 75 percent laid off. Fard Muhammad's message of hope spread among these disillusioned and impoverished African-Americans. He encouraged them to abandon their surnames, a lingering legacy of slavery, and adopt new Arabic ones.

In 1930, Fard Muhammad appointed one of his most devout followers, Elijah Poole, whom he renamed Elijah Muhammad, to establish a branch of the ATI in Chicago. Elijah began to preach that Fard Muhammad was the Mahdi, deifying his leader as the true and living God. However, by 1932 Fard Muhammad began experiencing difficulties in Detroit. In November of that year, an ATI member, Robert Harris (aka Elijah Karriem), sacrificially murdered another follower, James J. Smith, in what became known as the 'Voodoo Murder' (Smith had been stabbed to death on an altar). When captured, Karriem told police he killed Smith to bring himself closer to God. He quoted from Fard Muhammad's oral teaching *Secret Rituals of the Lost-Found Nation of Islam* a passage supposedly stating that 'the unbeliever must be stabbed through the heart', and he claimed that a free journey to Mecca was ensured for anyone who killed four whites.

MYSTERIOUS DISAPPEARANCE

Karriem was found insane during a trial in which he proclaimed himself 'King of Islam', but the police sought out Fard Muhammad who, when interviewed, told them he was 'the Supreme Ruler of the Universe'. Although not convicted of any crime, he was asked to leave Detroit. Before doing so, Fard Muhammad changed the name of the ATI to the Nation of Islam (NOI) in order to separate the organization from any links with ritual murder. He left Elijah Muhammad in charge until secretly returning to Detroit in 1934, whereupon he was re-arrested by the police and forced to leave for Chicago. He was never seen again.

The NOI after Fard

After Fard's disappearance, Elijah Muhammad assumed the leadership of the NOI. It expanded rapidly in the 1950s and 60s, especially under the dynamic young preacher Malcolm Little, better known as Malcolm X (who left the organization in 1964, after disagreements with Elijah Muhammad, and joined mainstream Islam). Following Malcolm X's assassination in 1965 and Elijah Muhammad's death in 1975, Elijah's son, Wallace D. Muhammad took over the NOI. He renamed the organization and distanced himself from Fard Muhammad's teachings. In 1977, Louis Farrakhan (b. 1933) and other members split away from Wallace's organization and founded their own group, once again calling it the Nation of Islam. Its membership represents only a small fraction of the total 2.5 million black Muslims in America.

The NOI claims that Fard Muhammad returned to Mecca. Others think he was murdered either by the police or by Elijah Muhammad, who wanted to take full control of the organization. Karl Evanzz, author of *The Messenger: The Rise and Fall of Elijah Muhammad* (1999), argues that Fard Muhammad was neither murdered nor did he return to Mecca, but took the alias of David Ford and eventually died in Chicago in 1971. Evanzz claims that Fard Muhammad was born Wali Dodd Fard in New Zealand in 1893, and emigrated to the United States in 1913, working as a restaurateur, gambler, bootlegger and travelling salesman before becoming involved with black nationalism.

Whatever his true identity and fate, within three years of founding the Allah Temple of Islam, Wallace Fard Muhammad had set up the University of Islam, elementary and secondary schools for Muslim children, and training courses for women and girls on being good Muslim wives and mothers. He also introduced the wearing of modest clothing and prohibited the eating of pork. Alongside his oral teaching, he also wrote *Teaching for the Lost-Found Nation of Islam in a Mathematical Way*.

❛ "FARD" IS A NAME MEANING AN INDEPENDENT ONE AND ONE WHO IS NOT ON THE LEVEL WITH THE AVERAGE GODS (ALLAHS). IT IS A NAME INDEPENDENT TO ITSELF WHICH ACTUALLY MEANS ONE WHOM WE MUST OBEY, OR ELSE HE DESTROYS US. THIS HONORABLE, MAJESTIC PERSON COMES IN THE LAST DAY. THE REASON WHY WE CALL HIM THE SUPREME BEING IS BECAUSE HE IS SUPREME OVER ALL BEINGS AND IS WISER THAN ALL. THE HOLY QUR'AN TEACHES: HE IS WISER THAN THEM, MEANING ALL THE GODS BEFORE AND ALL WHO ARE NOW PRESENT. ❜

ELIJAH MUHAMMAD *OUR SAVIOUR HAS ARRIVED* (1974)

edgar cayce
1877–1945

The Sleeping Prophet

At the age of 13, when his spelling lesson with his father was about to end, Edgar Cayce asked for a five-minute nap, insisting that if he slept with his head resting on the book he would learn the answers. On waking, the boy was indeed able to repeat its contents. As an adult, Cayce used these skills to 'channel' answers to questions on such diverse topics as health, astrology, reincarnation, Christ's work on Earth, the nature of the soul and the history of Atlantis.

One of five children, Edgar Cayce was born on 18 March 1877 in Beverly, Kentucky to Leslie ('Squire') Casey and his wife Carrie Elizabeth. The Cayces were farmers, with an extended family of aunts, uncles, grandparents and cousins living nearby, and likewise working the land. From the age of six, Cayce spoke of seeing visions and speaking to recently deceased relatives. Aged ten, he vowed to read the Bible from cover to cover once for every year of his life – which he did. At 15, Cayce was struck on the neck by a baseball. Recuperating in bed, he asked for a poultice of cornmeal, onions and herbs to be applied; by the following morning he had completely recovered, although he had no recollection of requesting the remedy. According to Thomas Sugrue's *There is a River: The Story of Edgar Cayce* (1945), this event provided the first proof of Cayce's clairvoyant diagnostic and prescriptive abilities.

' THUS AN UNSEEN FORCE, GRADUALLY GROWING, MUST RESULT IN AN ALMOST DIRECT OPPOSITION TO THE NAZI, OR ARYAN THEME. THIS WILL GRADUALLY PRODUCE A GROWTH OF ANIMOSITIES. AND UNLESS THERE IS INTERFERENCE BY WHAT MANY CALL SUPERNATURAL FORCES – WHICH ARE ACTIVE IN THE AFFAIRS OF NATIONS AND PEOPLE – THE WHOLE WORLD AS IT WERE ... WILL BE SET ON FIRE BY MILITARISTIC GROUPS AND PEOPLE WHO ARE FOR POWER EXPANSION. '

EDGAR CAYCE WARNS OF THE COMING WAR IN EUROPE (OCTOBER 1935)

HEALING THROUGH HYPNOTISM

In December 1893, the Cayce family moved to Hopkinsville, a few miles from Beverly. At 16, Cayce left school and worked first at Richard's Dry Goods Store and then in a bookshop where he came across occult books. By the turn of the century he had gone into business selling insurance with his father. However, his career as a travelling salesman was ended by a bout of laryngitis that silenced him for ten months, so he began an apprenticeship instead with a local photographer. His life changed its course in 1901 when a stage hypnotist, 'Hart the Laugh Man', arrived in Hopkinsville. Cayce, still unable to speak, agreed to be hypnotized on stage, and while under trance his voice returned. Unfortunately the restoration did not last, but a local hypnotist, Al Layne, continued treatment, during which an entranced Cayce instructed the hypnotist how to cure him.

Layne, who had himself been suffering from recurrent stomach problems, was so impressed that the following day he asked if he could hypnotize Cayce to discover a cure for his own ailments. Finding Cayce's advice helpful, he then suggested that Cayce offer his 'trance-healing' to the general public. As a member of the Protestant sect the Disciples of Christ, Cayce was worried that this might conflict with his Christian principles. However, he agreed to do so, provided the treatments were free. It is estimated that Cayce gave up to

EDGAR CAYCE
A Life in Brief

1877 Edgar Cayce born in Beverly, Kentucky

1892 Cayce gives first signs of his clairvoyance

1901 An encounter with a stage hypnotist convinces Cayce of his 'trance-reading' gift

1928 Opening of the Cayce Hospital for Research and Enlightenment in Virginia Beach

1932 Founding of the Association for Research and Enlightenment (ARE)

1943 Cayce comes to national attention through an article in the magazine *Coronet*

1945 Cayce dies aged 68 at Virginia Beach

Edgar Cayce and his wife, Gertrude, who conducted most of his readings.

30,000 'readings' during his 43 years as a psychic diagnostician. While in a trance, he would lie on his back with his hands crossed over his chest. These consultations appeared equally effective whether the patients were in the room with him or a long distance away. Once out of the trance, he would claim to recall nothing of what had taken place. It should be noted that for the first nine years of Cayce's consultations there was always someone in attendance who had knowledge of osteopathy, homeopathy or chiropractic treatments, which some say is reflected in his readings.

ANCIENT WISDOM FROM ATLANTIS

Cayce claimed that his trance-readings had an ancient pedigree. He revealed in one of his trances that he had once been known as Ra Ta, a healer from Atlantis – according to Cayce, a highly developed society that had destroyed itself in 10,000 BC. Cayce believed that his patients, too, had had previous incarnations. He therefore gave readings in which patients' present situations were analyzed and evaluated in terms of their past lives. Even so, he claimed it was not necessary to know all the details of their past, merely how past deeds affected the present life.

Cayce also gave more than 700 'business readings' pertaining to the stock market and business ventures, although many of these were unsuccessful. Indeed, Cayce himself, with his friend David Kahn, went to Texas to look for oil, only to return empty-handed. He also recorded 630 readings in which he interpreted patients' dreams. But he is perhaps best known for his prophecies. Cayce is said to have predicted the First and Second World Wars, and in 1939 foretold that two presidents would die in office. In 1935 he said that the Austrians, Germans and later the Japanese would form an alliance. He also foretold the discovery in 1958 of a 'death ray' from Atlantis, a prophecy perhaps fulfilled in 1960 when the first laser was demonstrated in California. He furthermore claimed that Atlantis would be found in 1968. In that year a causeway was discovered under the sea in the Bahamas, possibly indicating the site of Atlantis.

Some of Cayce's predictions have not come true, or at least have yet to fulfil themselves. He claimed in 1931 that the Depression would improve in the Spring of 1933, whereas economic historians agree that 1933 was one of the economy's most dire periods. China, he said, would become the 'cradle of Christianity' by 1968; and he claimed that in the year 2000 the Age of Aquarius, inaugurated by Jesus Christ, would commence. He also predicted that by the end of 2001 a huge chamber holding a magical library left by the Atlanteans would be found beneath the Sphinx in Egypt. More troublingly, he forecast that the Earth would shift on its axis, causing California, Japan and New York City to vanish into the sea.

Cayce on Health

Over 9000 of Cayce's recorded readings relate to health issues, for which he recommended poultices of castor oil, osteopathic adjustments, electrotherapy, colonic irrigation or massage. Other remedies included peach-tree poultices for convulsions, bedbug juice, heroin in liquid form, belladonna, and even turpentine and kerosene. He advised people to avoid red meat, white bread, fried foods and alcohol (except for red wine), and stated that a good diet should consist of 80 percent alkaline to 20 percent acidic foods. In some readings he recommended Jerusalem artichokes as a natural source of insulin. According to Jess Stearn, in *Edgar Cayce: The Sleeping Prophet* (1967), the blood and in some cases the raw side of the fur of a freshly skinned rabbit were prescribed for breast and thyroid cancers. Cayce is reputed to have cured his eight-year-old son Hugh Lynn of blindness and his wife, whom he married in 1903, of tuberculosis. Yet he was unable to save his other son Milton Porter, who died in infancy.

INSTITUTIONS AND FOUNDATIONS

In 1925, an 'inner voice' urged Cayce to move to Virginia Beach. Backed by a stockbroker named Morton Blumenthal, he founded the Association of National Investigators (ANI), which was devoted to his work. In 1928, the 60-bed Cayce Hospital for Research and Enlightenment opened its doors, followed two years later by the founding of the Atlantic University. Initially, Cayce's brother-in-law, a qualified medical doctor and osteopath, took charge of the hospital, but when he died in 1929, no doctor wished to be associated with Cayce's unique diagnostic methods. The hospital folded in 1931 after Blumenthal was ruined in the Wall Street crash of 1929, and the university closed soon after. In 1932, the now-defunct ANI was superseded by the Association for Research and Enlightenment (ARE) – which still exists today alongside the Edgar Cayce Foundation.

In the early 1940s, newspaper articles about Cayce and his healing methods helped boost his popularity. Requests for help arrived daily and, in an attempt to answer them all, he gave as many as eight readings a day. By now he was also charging a small fee, in order to support his family. However, Cayce was told under trance that he should reduce his readings to two a day or his health would suffer, leading to his death. In September 1944, when he finally stopped his readings, it was already too late: he suffered a stroke on 2 January 1945 and died the next day, aged 68.

Today, thousands of students study at Edgar Cayce Centres in 25 countries while there are members of his Association in a total of 60 countries. The Headquarters of the ARE are located in Cayce's former hospital in Virginia Beach. After his death, his son Hugh Lynn took over the leadership of the Association, a post he held until his retirement in 1976 when he was succeeded by Cayce's grandson, Charles Thomas Cayce.

‘THE LIFE OF A PERSON ENDOWED WITH SUCH POWERS IS NOT EASY. FOR MORE THAN FORTY YEARS NOW I HAVE BEEN GIVING READINGS TO THOSE WHO CAME SEEKING HELP. THIRTY-FIVE YEARS AGO THE JEERS, SCORN AND LAUGHTER WERE EVEN LOUDER THAN TODAY. I HAVE FACED THE LAUGHTER OF IGNORANT CROWDS, THE WITHERING SCORN OF TABLOID HEADLINES, AND THE COLD SMIRK OF SELF-SATISFIED INTELLECTUALS. BUT I HAVE ALSO KNOWN THE WORDLESS HAPPINESS OF LITTLE CHILDREN WHO HAVE BEEN HELPED, THE GRATITUDE OF FATHERS AND MOTHERS AND FRIENDS ... I BELIEVE THAT THE ATTITUDE OF THE SCIENTIFIC WORLD IS GRADUALLY CHANGING TOWARDS THESE SUBJECTS.’

EDGAR CAYCE ON SCEPTICS (1935)

L. RON HUBBARD
1911–86

Founder of Scientology

Late in the evening of 24 January 1986, a steady stream of cars could be seen coming and going from 'Whispering Winds', a luxurious 65-hectare (160-acre) property near Creston, California, 165 miles (264 km) north of Los Angeles. Until that night, the owners Lisa and Mike Mitchell, who lived there with their father Jack, had rarely received visitors. But now Jack Mitchell was dead. The funeral directors who were summoned to the house were instructed that Jack's religious views ruled out an autopsy and that cremation should take place as soon as possible.

however, when the owner of the funeral parlour in San Luis Obispo saw the overweight, white-haired, unkempt corpse, she immediately became suspicious and called the deputy coroner, Don Hines. Hines corroborated her opinion, and insisted that there could be no cremation until the body had been examined by an independent pathologist.

JACK MITCHELL, L. RON HUBBARD OR WALTER MITTY?

'Jack Mitchell', it soon transpired, was none other than L. Ron Hubbard, also known as the 'Source', who in 1952 had founded the Church of Scientology. The 'Mitchells' were in fact fellow-Scientologists Pat and Sue Broeker, who for the previous six years had helped to protect Hubbard from the IRS (Internal Revenue Service), the FBI and his own church.

Lafayette Ron Hubbard was born on 13 March 1911 in Tilden, Nebraska, to naval commander Harry Ross Hubbard and Ledora May, who soon afterwards moved with him to Montana and then Seattle. Hubbard's other biographical details vary, depending on the source. According to the Church of Scientology, he began reading and writing at a young age, rode horses at three, devoured Shakespeare and the classics, was befriended by Blackfoot Indians who made him a blood brother, and at the age of 13 became the youngest-ever Eagle Scout (a claim denied by the Boy Scouts of America). At 16, he began travelling, first with a companion and then alone, visiting China, Mongolia, Japan, Guam, the Philippines and certain Pacific islands, meeting gurus and other spiritual men. He returned to the United States in 1929 to attend high schools in Virginia and Washington DC.

According to Scientologists, Hubbard continued his stellar education by studying nuclear physics at George Washington University in 1930, pioneering experiments in this field. He was also alleged to be a Barnstormer stunt pilot and a decorated naval war hero, the recipient of a doctorate from the University of Sequoia, and an undercover agent for US Naval Intelligence, in which capacity he broke up a black magic ring connected to the British occultist Aleister Crowley.

Against these claims, however, Stewart Lamont, in his *Religion Inc: The Church of Scientology* (1986), argues that Hubbard's travelling adventures were a fabrication, that he failed his nuclear physics course (which was only one term), and that he was asked to leave his university after one year due to a lack of academic ability. Lamont further claims that Hubbard

L. Ron Hubbard, head of the Church of Scientology, in August 1973.

merely held a glider pilot's licence and was hardly a war hero. On the contrary, while commanding an escort vessel in 1943 Hubbard had ordered its guns to be fired for training purposes at an island belonging to neutral Mexico. For this act he was court-martialled and hospitalized on psychiatric grounds. Likewise, far from exposing Crowley's Satanic sex rituals, he was accused of participation in them. Finally, he was awarded a doctorate by Sequoia University – though this honour was acquired by mail order for $20.

SCI-FI AND DIANETICS

What is beyond dispute is that Hubbard enjoyed a very successful career as a science fiction writer. His first novel, *Buckskin Brigades*, published in 1937, was a fairly conventional western. Two years later he began establishing himself in the fantasy genre with *Slaves of Sleep*, a novel in which a man is cursed by a genie so that when he falls asleep he enters an alternative world in which he must battle against a genie who has enslaved the human race. Some six more fantasy novels followed over the next dozen years, as well as short stories such as '240,000 Miles Straight Up', published in 1948 in the pulp magazine *Thrilling Wonder Stories* and notable for coining the term 'moonbase'.

Hubbard was 39 when, in 1950, he published *Dianetics: The Modern Science of Mental Health* (*DMSMH*), which sold more than 100,000 copies in its first year and set him on a new

L. RON HUBBARD
A Life in Brief

1911 L. Ron Hubbard born in Tilden, Nebraska

1930 Hubbard enrols at the George Washington University, leaving without a degree after two semesters

1937 Hubbard publishes his first novel

1941 Hubbard enters service in the US navy, serving for nine years, during which time he is relieved of three commands

1950 Publication of *Dianetics: The Modern Science of Mental Health*, the key text of Scientology

1952 Hubbard founds the Church of Scientology

1959 Invention of the E-meter (later appropriated and repatented by Hubbard)

1966 Hubbard moves to Rhodesia (Zimbabwe) following Ian Smith's declaration of independence (UDI) and offers funding to the racist white minority government

1986 Death of Hubbard, under an asssumed name, in Creston, California

career path. Dianetics (a concept Hubbard originally introduced in the magazine *Astounding Science Fiction*) is the relationship between the mind, body and spirit. According to Hubbard, traumatic events called 'engrams' are stored in the mind, causing mental and psychosomatic problems. The goal of Dianetics is to remove these engrams and to help a person become an 'Operating Thetan VIII', that is, a person clear of any mental obstructions. Two years later, in 1952, Hubbard founded the first Church of Scientology in Camden, New Jersey. Dianetics was thereafter used to erase illness and unwanted bodily sensations, while Scientology was its religious application, designed to increase spiritual freedom, intelligence and ability – offering immortality into the bargain, as the Thetan never dies.

Hubbard's philosophy sees people as basically good, albeit polluted by painful experiences from past lives. The premise behind this theory reads like the plot of one of his sci-fi novels. Seventy-five million years ago, he claimed, there was a dictator named Xenu who ruled a galactic confederation of 76 planets. Due to overpopulation, Xenu, with the help of psychiatrists, enticed the entire population of these planets to Earth and vaporized their bodies with nuclear bombs placed in craters. Deprived of their bodies, the Thetans, or spirits, collected in billions of clusters that attached themselves like parasites to humans. The route to wellbeing, therefore, is for humans to rid themselves of these psychic limpets, a process that can only be achieved by 'auditing' a person back through his or her many lives, to the time when the Thetans first attached themselves. This is a very lengthy (and expensive) process, but it ultimately frees a person from ailments, makes him a balanced member of society, and even helps him to experience out-of-body experiences at will.

AUDITING, BULL-BAITING AND OTHER NEFARIOUS PRACTICES

Auditing is a one-way process designed to rehabilitate the human spirit under the guidance of a trained Scientology auditor. In 1959 the E-meter (now called the Hubbard Electrometer) was developed to assist in this process. Invented by a chiropractor named Volney G. Mathison, the device is still in use today, costing up to $4000 and working on similar lines to a lie detector, allegedly measuring thought processes. It helps to remove 'engrams', or past life incidents, in the Preclear (a person who hasn't reached the state of a Clear, i.e. someone free from engrams). In the United States, the Food and Drug Administration (FDA) became so concerned about the damaging effects of the E-meter that in 1963 agents raided the Church of Scientology in Washington DC. However, Scientology lawyers claimed that the meter was a religious artefact and, as such, protected by the First Amendment of the US Constitution.

'I HAVE LIVED NO CLOISTERED LIFE AND HOLD IN CONTEMPT THE WISE MAN WHO HAS NOT LIVED AND THE SCHOLAR WHO WILL NOT SHARE. THERE HAVE BEEN MANY WISER MEN THAN I, BUT FEW HAVE TRAVELLED AS MUCH ROAD. I HAVE SEEN LIFE FROM THE TOP DOWN AND THE BOTTOM UP. I KNOW HOW IT LOOKS BOTH WAYS. AND I KNOW THERE IS WISDOM AND THAT THERE IS HOPE.'

Many of Hubbard's other methods have also been criticized as extremely damaging. For instance, there is the 'bull-baiting' that takes place during the auditing process, when the coach is joined by others who tease, insult, shout and tickle the Preclear to get a reaction, while the use of robotic commands and punishments – which involve Preclears having to wear old clothes and being forbidden to bathe, shave, or cut hair, take any breaks or leave the premises – have been denounced as tantamount to brainwashing. Misdemeanours on board Hubbard's fleet of ships were punished by the perpetrator being thrown overboard, incarcerated below decks, or forced to climb to the crow's nest and remain there for hours on end.

By the end of the 1960s, Scientology was receiving widespread criticism. The church has been in conflict with governments and police forces throughout the world, notably in Germany, the United Kingdom and Australia, as well in the United States; and many countries do not deem Scientology a religion. The church has certainly not helped its image by harassing opponents and by launching 'Operation Snow White', in which Scientologists infiltrated the IRS and stole confidential documents – as a result of which 11 high-ranking Scientologists were gaoled.

SCIENTOLOGY AFTER HUBBARD

Hubbard's death in 1986 marked the end of neither Scientology as a movement nor the controversies that bedevilled it. Hubbard originally left his vast fortune to his family – he had seven children by three different women – and designated Pat Broeker as his executor and future leader. However, according to Russell Miller's *Bare-Faced Messiah* (1987), the day before he died Hubbard changed his will, leaving his entire fortune to the church. Norman Starkey was to become the new executor and David Miscavige the church's leader, replacing Broeker. Furthermore, observers were shocked to learn that laboratory tests revealed that Hubbard – a lifelong opponent of psychiatry and pharmaceuticals – had been taking Vistaril, a drug used to calm disturbed and hysterical patients. He also had needlemarks on his right buttock.

These controversies notwithstanding, the Church of Scientology continues to prosper more than 20 years after Hubbard's death. Hubbard may have suffered from paranoid schizophrenia – as once claimed by Dr E. Cunningham Crax, chairman of an Australian Mental Health Authority in the 1960s – but there is little doubt that he was a charismatic and talented man whose followers remain fiercely loyal and enthusiastic. His church boasts a membership of 10 million, though independent sources suggest a much lower figure. A prolific speaker, he left behind some 3000 lectures. In 2005 the *Guinness Book of World Records* claimed that his books (including his Scientology writings) had been translated into 65 languages – more than any other author.

David brandt berg

1919–94

The Children of God

David Brandt Berg – who latterly styled himself 'Moses David', 'Mo', 'Dad' or 'Grandpa' – was born on 18 February 1919 in Oakland, California, the youngest child of Hjalmer Berg, a preacher in a Protestant sect called the Disciples of Christ, and his wife Virginia Lee Brandt, also an ordained minister. Until his 50th year, Berg's life was an unremarkable continuation of his parents' evangelical mission. Thereafter, however, the cult he founded became increasingly embroiled in controversy over sexual licentiousness.

After graduating in 1935, Berg took a business administration course, later becoming his mother's chauffeur, secretary and singer when she went on the road to preach. In 1941 he was himself ordained a minister by the British-American Ministerial Federation. At the age of 25 he married Jane Miller (later to be known as Mother Eve), with whom he had four children. In 1948 he attended the Southern Bible College in Pasadena, the following year becoming a pastor in Valley Falls, Arizona, for the Christian and Missionary Alliance Church. He was dismissed from this post, officially on account of a difference of opinion, but according to his eldest daughter Linda in her damning book about her father, *The Children of God: The Inside Story* (1984), because of 'inappropriate behaviour'. His controversial career as a preacher and prophet was only just beginning.

ON THE ROAD

After leaving Arizona, Berg went on the road with his family as a travelling preacher, often sleeping rough. He formed his children into an evangelical singing group, 'Teens for Christ', who performed while he preached. In 1954, Berg met Fred Jordan, a TV minister who headed the Soul Clinic – a training school for missionaries – in Los Angeles. He persuaded Jordan to commission him to set up a Soul Clinic in Miami. However, Berg was twice thrown out of Florida on account of his aggressive evangelism and in due course he returned to work for a Soul Clinic Jordan had opened in Texas.

Berg's father, an authoritarian who had ruled his house with violence and beatings, died in 1964. The next year his widowed mother visited her son in an agitated state. She told Berg that she had received a vision of the Endtime and the coming of the Antichrist. 'Even now the skies are red, red with warning,' Virginia told her son, 'and black, black with clouds gathering for the great confusion which is almost upon you!' Berg immediately reread the Book of Revelation and became convinced that she was right, particularly as the United States, with the atom bomb, had acquired the means with which to destroy itself. Shortly after this, following a religious disagreement with Jordan, Berg and his family were asked to leave the Soul Clinic.

His mother suggested he join her at Huntingdon Beach, California, where she was preaching to hippies and drop-outs, and so the family moved on once more.

Berg had always been under the sway of his mother, although her influence was not always positive or benign. When she died in 1968, he violently repudiated her. Summoning his mother's friends, together with members of the press, to the Light House – the coffee shop where he preached – he damned everything she had stood for. 'After the death of my mother,' he stated, 'the Spirit of God rose up within me one night in public declaration of war on the religious system ...' Much to the horror of his mother's friends, he went on to say that he had now cast his lot in with outlaws, drug addicts, the younger generation, and 'maniacs'.

PLUNGING INTO THE PERMISSIVE SOCIETY

Up to this point, Berg had been a fairly straightforward Christian fundamentalist, accepting that the Bible was inspired by God and believing in the Virgin birth and salvation through faith in Christ. He also took literally the words of the Book of Revelation, believing that the Antichrist would soon appear. Contrary to traditional Christian belief, however, he now justified sex outside marriage as being God's expression of love – and this was to become the mainstay of his religion. According to Stephen A. Kent, author of *Lustful Prophet* (1994), Berg's unusual interpretation of Christianity derived from his negative sexual experiences as a child, which included being caught masturbating by his mother, who publicly humiliated him and threatened him with castration.

Shortly after his mother's death, Berg had a dream he was sure came directly from God. It involved naked hippies having sex in a basement while his mother condoned their behaviour, saying that this was a sign that they had been stripped of hypocrisy and 'all sham, cover-ups and fashions of the world'. This dream provided Berg with the justification to shed his own inhibitions and join in the sexual freedom of the Sixties. And so, in 1969, he founded the Children of God (COG) and left California, along with his family and a handful of followers, to preach his brand of 'liberal' Christianity. Berg's new beliefs also included a warning that people were living in the 'Last Days' – the time immediately preceding the return of the Antichrist and Jesus Christ.

He also received a revelation from God telling him that he was required to take a new wife to symbolize the establishment of the new church – and one of his followers, Karen Zerby, duly obliged. Berg's interest in sex soon became obsessive. He also took on yet another 'wife', a teenager named Rachel. Tales of wife-swapping and group sex soon abounded.

By 1970, the COG had over 200 members and the group began proselytizing in public. In Washington DC, members wore red sackcloth, carried Bibles and staffs and painted ash onto their foreheads. Around their necks they hung wooden yokes symbolizing the mourning of a

DAVID BERG
A Life in Brief

1919 David Berg born into a family of evangelical preachers in Oakland, California

1948 Berg becomes a pastor in Valley Falls, Arizona

1968 Berg publicly repudiates his domineering mother

1969 Children of God founded, a cult based on attaining divine grace through free love

1972 Berg proclaims himself God's prophet

1976 'Flirty Fishing' introduced: the winning of new converts to the COG by offering sexual favours

1987 Policy of 'Flirty Fishing' abandoned with the worldwide spread of HIV/AIDS

1994 Berg dies in Portugal; Karen Zerby, Berg's former partner, takes over leadership of the COG

2005 Suicide of Zerby's son Ricky Rodriguez

The cult's tour bus in London in 1972.

nation that had forsaken the Lord. The press called Berg the new Moses, a name (Mo for short) that he readily adopted. The COG soon began to experience public criticism in the United States, as a result of which members were encouraged to set up groups in other countries. Berg and Zerby moved to London. Once overseas, Berg communicated with COG leaders worldwide via letters that became known as the 'Mo Letters'. Today, over 3000 of these have been recorded. In 1972 Berg announced that his letters were the 'voice of God Himself' and that he, Berg, was His prophet.

PREACHING AND PROMISCUITY

COG members soon established communities in 40 countries and membership was fast approaching 2500. By 1974, members had begun calling themselves the Family of Love, and in 1976 they introduced the controversial practice of 'Flirty Fishing' (FFing), sanctioned by Berg as a legitimate way of proselytizing. This involved members picking up recruits in bars and discos – and often having sex with them. Children born as a result of FFing – by 1981 there were over 300 – were known as 'Jesus Babies'.

> ‘ THE DEVIL HATES SEX!
> BUT GOD LOVES IT! ’
>
> DAVID BERG, PUBLICATION DFO ['DISCIPLES
> AND FRIENDS ONLY'] 999, 20 MAY 1980

In 1978 Berg was forced to reorganize the COG due to financial mismanagement, abuse of position by senior members of the cult and opposition by some members to Flirty Fishing. Three hundred COG leaders were dismissed and the hierarchical chain of the organization was destroyed, Berg announcing that all members would now receive the Mo Letters. Fearing that the United States would be destroyed by nuclear war, he urged members to move to Latin America or Europe.

With sexual freedom at its peak in the early 1980s, Berg made the controversial announcement that God did not prohibit sex or incest with capable children. By 1988, after public outrage, he was forced to retract his words, stating that he forbade it. Despite allegations of child sexual abuse in many European and Latin American countries, as well as in Japan, Australia and the United States, no evidence has officially come to light.

A DYSFUNCTIONAL 'FAMILY'

The spread of HIV/AIDS in the 1980s put an end to Flirty Fishing. In 1987 Zerby replaced the activity with the FFing/DFing Revolution, i.e. flirting without sex. Members began returning to the United States and in 1992 the COG was renamed 'The Family'. Berg died in Portugal at the age of 75 in October 1994, whereupon Zerby took over the leadership. She then married her lover, Steven Douglas Kelly, also known as Peter Amsterdam or King Peter, who became her representative when she went into voluntary seclusion. In 1995 Karen Zerby introduced the Love Charter, defining the rules and regulations to which members of The Family were required to adhere.

Today Berg's church, having renamed itself once again, is known as 'The Family International'. It claims over 11,000 members in 100 countries. Controversy persists, however; as many as 31 former members have committed suicide, the most high-profile being 29-year-old Ricky Rodriguez. The son of Karen Zerby who was conceived during a Flirty Fishing episode in Spain, Rodriguez was raised in The Family as 'Davidito', a Messiah who would lead the attack against the Antichrist. But alleging sexual abuse throughout his childhood, he left The Family at the end of 2000. In January 2005, angry and disillusioned, he murdered his mother's longtime assistant, Angela Smith, then shot himself in the head. He left behind a videotape in which he denounced the 'sick fucking pervert' who had ruined his life.

Joseph Di mambro

1924–94
The Order of the Solar Temple

On 4 October 1994, firemen were shocked to discover five charred bodies in the burned-out shell of a house in Morin Heights, an exclusive ski resort 35 miles (56 km) north of Montreal. Among the dead was 3-month-old Christopher-Emmanuel Dutoit, whose heart had been pierced six times with a wooden stake before he was set alight. Later the same day, 21 corpses, some with bullets in their skulls and plastic bags over their heads, were found in a farmhouse destroyed by fire in Cheiry, Switzerland.

Eighteen of the bodies at Cheiry, wearing white, gold and black ceremonial costumes, lay in a radial pattern, like the spokes of a wheel. The room was decorated with shards of mirrors, red drapes and carpets; it also contained unexploded petrol bombs. The following day, 50 miles (80 km) south in the Swiss ski resort of Granges-sur-Salvan, three chalets were burned to the ground, killing the 25 occupants. A connection between the three tragedies was swiftly made: all five properties were owned by Joseph Di Mambro, co-founder in 1984 of the doomsday cult known as the Order of the Solar Temple.

FASCINATED BY THE TEMPLARS
Joseph Di Mambro was born on 19 August 1924, in Pont-Saint-Esprit, near Avignon in southern France. He apprenticed as a jeweller but from an early age showed an interest in the occult. In 1956 he joined an international spiritual group called the Ancient and Mystical

Order Rosae Crucis (AMORC), which was popular in France after the Second World War. He was accused of fraud in 1971, whereupon he moved to Annemasse, on the Swiss border. By 1973 he reappeared as president of a yoga and meditation school – the Centre for the Preparation of the New Age – whose members were expected to donate to him their worldly goods in exchange for spiritual and physical sustenance. Di Mambro told his followers that his previous incarnations included Osiris and Moses, which gave him the power to draw on centuries of metaphysical and mystical knowledge. In 1976 he bought a house near Geneva and founded an esoteric group that was later to become the Golden Way Foundation. He took complete control of the group, decreeing who should marry whom, and who should be allowed to have children.

Joseph di Mambro with his wife Jocelyne and their daughter Emmanuelle, whom he claimed was the Messiah.

Di Mambro's philosophy was heavily influenced by the beliefs of the Knights Templar, a sacred order formed in 1118 by nine knights from the First Crusade to protect pilgrims travelling to and from the Holy Land. The Knights Templar eventually developed into a secret organization whose members took monastic vows and for 200 years enjoyed the support of the European monarchies and the Holy See. In 1307, however, King Philip the Fair of France (r. 1285–1314), angered at their wealth and secrecy, began persecuting the Templars; 54 knights were tortured and burned at the stake in 1310, before Pope Clement V dissolved the order. In 1314 Jacques de Molay, the last of the Grand Masters, was put to death by fire.

Birth of the OTS

In 1980 Di Mambro met 33-year-old Luc Jouret, a charismatic Belgian who had been born in the Congo and trained as a medical doctor and homeopath. Jouret was also deeply interested in the resurgent Knights Templar movement, having joined a group called the Renewed Order of the Solar Temple. In 1982 he and his wife became the public face for Di Mambro's Golden Way Foundation. By 1983, Jouret was travelling throughout France, Switzerland and Canada, lecturing on homeopathy, New Age philosophies and impending environmental disaster. He declared himself to be a reincarnated Knight Templar – and the third incarnation of Jesus Christ. In Geneva in 1984, Di Mambro and Jouret founded what was to become the Ordre du Temple Solaire (OTS).

As Di Mambro and the Jourets lived a life of luxury on the money members had been ordered to hand over to the organization, their ideas became increasingly apocalyptic. Di Mambro, with his wife Jocelyne, set up a new headquarters in Quebec in 1984, where a Noah's Ark was to be built. He stated that he was working under the instructions of the Masters of Zurich – spiritual creatures that lived beneath the Swiss city. He also claimed that his daughter Emmanuelle, born in 1982, was the result of an immaculate conception, being one of nine 'cosmic' children who would escape the prophesied environmental doomsday by leading the chosen ones to a new life on a planet near the star Sirius. His son Elie, born in 1969, would also help shape the fate of the world. Membership had now reached over 400, and later that year the order published a detailed manual entitled *Survival Beyond the Year 2000*.

FAKERY AND FRAUD

Many events led to the cult's eventual demise. In the late 1980s, Elie Di Mambro discovered that his father's spiritual advisers, the Zurich Masters, did not exist: Di Mambro had been using cheap stage props and laser trickery to conjure them up at Solar Temple ceremonies, along with the Holy Grail and Excalibur. Tony Dutoit, a long-term member who had helped with the scam, also became disillusioned, and he and his wife Nicki resolved to leave the OTS. Dutoit and Elie informed other members of the deception, and several demanded their money back. Elie left the organization in 1990.

Matters came to a head in 1993, when both Di Mambro and Jouret found themselves under police surveillance. From Australia, which Di Mambro had visited several times, Canberra Interpol, suspecting him of money laundering, contacted the French authorities. Then the Canadian authorities refused to extend Di Mambro's wife's visa. Di Mambro claimed there was an international conspiracy against him and the OTS. Meanwhile, Jouret was linked by Quebec police to suspected political assassination conspiracies and arrested for purchasing illegal handguns and silencers. He was fined and sentenced to a year's probation, which effectively put an end to his lecturing career – and his credibility. The violent end to the 54-day siege in Waco, Texas, in 1993, in which 86 members of a cult called the Branch Davidians died, brought further defections from the OTS. It was also rumoured that Di Mambro was suffering from ill health, possibly cancer.

COUNTDOWN TO ARMAGEDDON

In November 1993, Nicki Dutoit defied the OTS and became pregnant. Di Mambro was outraged, claiming that her child was the Antichrist and a threat to his 11-year-old daughter, Messiah Emmanuelle, who was herself rebelling against being put on a pedestal and separated from the other children. According to Catherine Wessinger, author of *How the Millenium Comes Violently* (2000), in order to keep her purity 'intact' the girl was forced to wear a helmet and gloves and forbidden contact with anyone other than family.

During December 1993 and January 1994, Di Mambro allegedly received five messages from 'the Lady of Heaven' concerning the group's departure from Earth for their new home on Jupiter. Members were told to put their affairs in order. The couple stabbed to death at Morin Heights turned out to be none other than Tony and Nicki Dutoit, along with their baby son, the alleged Antichrist. Forensics revealed that Di Mambro, Jouret, Emmanuelle and Camille Pilet, a 68-year-old millionaire who had contributed vast sums of money to the cult, were among the dead in Granges-sur-Salvan; 24-year-old Elie Di Mambro also died at one of the chalets.

Texts and videotapes sent to the media by a surviving member, 26-year-old Patrick Vuarnet, son of a French ski champion, attempted to explain the deaths and the reason why some members had to be 'helped' (i.e. murdered) to make an exit. They explained that whenever

JOSEPH DI MAMBRO
A Life in Brief

1924 Di Mambro born in Pont-Saint-Esprit, near Avignon

1956 Di Mambro joins the Ancient and Mystical Order Rosae Crucis (AMORC)

1973 Presides over the Centre for the Preparation of the New Age

1978 Establishes the Golden Way Foundation

1980 First meeting between di Mambro and Luc Jouret, a self-styled Belgian mystic

1982 Birth of di Mambro's 'messianic' daughter Emmanuelle

1984 Di Mambro and Jouret found the Ordre du Temple Solaire (OTS); new HQ of the cult set up in Quebec

1994 First mass suicides/murders of OTS members

1995–8 Further mass killings of OTS members

Last Testament

The third video cassette left by the Order of the Solar Temple shows a doorway and inside people dressed in capuchin capes pulled around their faces. They are slowly walking, heads bowed holding candles as the narrator explains:

Brothers and sisters of the first and last hour ... Today ... as we are gathered here in this Holy Place ... the great Terrestrial cycle is closing in on itself. Alpha and Omega are fusing to initiate a new creation. The time of the Great Gathering is proclaiming the departure of the sons of Heaven. In the name of a Will above ... I am handing the seed of our Immortality and of our Transcendent nature to the Infinite Worlds ... and ascend toward its Point of Origin. Our Terrestrial Journey is coming to an end ... The work is being completed. Everyone must return to their position on the great celestial chessboard.

mankind needed to become more spiritual, the 'Blue Star' would appear. On its first appearance 26,000 years ago, it left on Earth beings known as the 'Sons of the One' (i.e. members of OTS), who would eventually return to their source. The Blue Star's departure in the 1990s was said to herald Armageddon, from which mankind would have no protection – hence the call to OTS members to leave the Earth. 'The idea of the passage from one world to another might worry some of you,' one document stated. However, members were assured 'that you are going towards a marvellous world which could not be, in any case, any worse than the one you are leaving', a place where 'your eternal body will be subject neither to ageing nor to pain or sickness'.

The deaths in October 1994 were not the end of the OTS. In December 1995 a further 16 burned bodies – 13 adults and 3 children – turned up in southeastern France. Most were wearing robes and were again positioned radially. Patrick Vuarnet and his mother were among the dead. Suicide notes suggested that more deaths might follow, so police monitored the remaining members of the OTS, particularly around the summer and winter solstices. In Quebec in 1997 a further five adults burnt themselves to death – though three teenagers who had begged to be spared were found drugged but safe next door. In 1998 Spanish police in the Canary Islands prevented a German psychologist from initiating another mass suicide attempt. Nothing has been heard of the OTS since.

'DO YOU UNDERSTAND WHAT WE REPRESENT? WE ARE THE PROMISE THAT THE ROSY CROSS MADE TO THE IMMUTABLE. WE ARE THE STAR SEEDS THAT GUARANTEE THE PERENNIAL EXISTENCE OF THE UNIVERSE. WE ARE THE HAND OF GOD THAT SHAPES CREATION ... WE HOLD THE KEY TO THE UNIVERSE AND MUST SECURE ITS ETERNITY.'

Jeane Dixon
1918–97
The Seeress of Washington

When she was eight years old, Jeane Pinckert had her hand read by a gypsy woman who announced to her mother that the markings on the child's palms indicated that she would become a great mystic. The gypsy then gave her a crystal ball, saying that it would do more good in her hands than it had in her own. Thus began the prophetical career of a latter-day Cassandra, many of whose remarkable predictions about tragic events were fulfilled.

The youngest of four children, Jeane Pinckert was born in Wisconsin but raised in California. She was very close to her mother; the family was well-to-do and the children enjoyed a comfortable upbringing. Her brother Erny remembers Jeane stopping her siblings from doing anything she thought was wrong: on one occasion she turned off Erny's alarm clock to prevent him from waking early to go squirrel hunting with his friends, as she had a bad feeling about the trip – which ended with one of the boys being shot in the foot. At an early age, Jeane was taught the art of astrology by a Jesuit priest.

SOCIETY STARGAZER

When Jeane married businessman James Dixon in 1939 she took on the role of Secretary-Treasurer of the James L. Dixon Real Estate Company in Washington DC. She soon began offering horoscope readings to servicemen during the Second World War. She also started writing a daily horoscope column that was eventually syndicated to 300 US newspapers.

Dixon and her husband lived in some style in Washington DC, where they mixed with the great and the good. Indeed many of Jeane's most notable predictions concerned well-known political figures, often foretelling death and disaster – though she was not above prophesying the winner of a horse race on occasion. She explained that her predictions came to her in different ways. Sometimes they arrived in the form of a revelation that would be preceded by three days of heightened awareness. These revelations were destiny, she believed, and could not be changed through foreknowledge. At other times she would see visions of what was to come, or experience thought transference or telepathy, and in such cases, disaster could be averted if the person involved acted on her warnings. She claimed to pick up people's thoughts, to the extent that she would sometimes 'take on another person's being'; she also received psychic information merely from touching someone's fingertips. Dixon claimed to have access to a sixth sense that she referred to as her 'gift of prophecy'.

PREDICTING POLITICAL ASSASSINATIONS

The prediction for which she became best known relates to the death of John F. Kennedy. In 1956 Dixon predicted in *Parade* magazine that the 1960 election would be won by a blue-eyed man with a full head of hair who would die violently while in office. Shortly before Kennedy's fateful visit to Dallas in November 1963, Dixon became very upset, saying that all she could see was a casket or shroud over the White House. Despite having received this information in

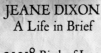

JEANE DIXON
A Life in Brief

c.1918 Birth of Jeane Pinckert in Wisconsin

1939 Jeane marries businessman James Dixon

1963 Assassination of John F. Kennedy, predicted by Dixon

1968 Dixon foresees the assassinations of both Robert Kennedy and Martin Luther King in this year

1972 President Richard M. Nixon takes office; he secretly consults Dixon as a soothsayer

1980 President Ronald Reagan's first term of office begins; Reagan and his wife Nancy both seek advice from Dixon

1988 Mathematician John Allen Paulos coins the term 'Jeane Dixon Effect' to describe manipulation of statistical probability

1997 Death of Jeane Dixon in Washington

the form of an irrevocable revelation, she nevertheless tried to get a message through to his family. Following the shooting, when she was told that the president had been wounded and was receiving a blood transfusion, she merely shook her head, saying: 'No, he's dead.' She was soon dubbed the 'Seeress of Washington', and her fame for having predicted Kennedy's assassination prompted a journalist, Ruth Montgomery, to write *The Gift of Prophecy: The Phenomenal Jeane Dixon* (1965).

When Robert Kennedy began campaigning for the Democrats in 1968, Dixon started to experience visions of another assassination. On this occasion she believed the victim could be saved, and again she tried, unsuccessfully, to pass warnings to him. In May 1968, Dixon was speaking in the Ambassador Hotel in Los Angeles; asked whether Robert Kennedy would become president, she responded that a tragedy 'right here in this hotel' would prevent him. A month later, Kennedy was shot dead in the kitchen of the Ambassador Hotel.

Jeane Dixon's prophecies were not confined to her own country. In 1944 she predicted that China would turn communist, becoming America's greatest concern. She continued for years to maintain that Russia had a grand plan to achieve world domination. In 1945 she prophesied the division of India, an event that took place two years later, and in 1947 she announced – correctly – that Mahatma Gandhi would be assassinated within six months. Predicting political assassinations seems to have been one of Dixon's specialities. She also predicted that Martin Luther King would be killed in 1968. She believed that he was using communists to help further his cause of equal rights for blacks, but that the communists would eliminate him when he no longer served their purpose. In April 1968, while she was lunching at a Washington hotel, a friend expressed concern over King's proposed march to Washington. Dixon told him that King would be shot dead before he could reach the capital. Dr King was killed by James Earl Ray a few days later – though not even the wildest conspiracy theorists suggest that Ray was acting on behalf of the shadowy communists envisaged by Dixon.

GAINING THE PRESIDENT'S EAR

There were more predictions concerning political figures in America. Early in her psychic career, Dixon claimed to have visited Franklin Roosevelt twice in the White House; a sick man, he apparently asked her how much time he had left to do his work. She replied 'very little' – and he died three months later. In 1949, she revealed to a friend that the young congressman Richard Nixon would one day become president of the United States; when he later achieved high office, he referred to her as his soothsayer, consulting her on several occasions, his secretary Rose Mary Woods acting as a go-between. She warned Nixon of the possibility of terrorist attacks or kidnappings, which caused him and his advisers to prepare for such possibilities. President Reagan and his wife

The psychic Jeane Dixon, soothsayer to two US presidents.

Nancy also consulted her during Reagan's presidency. Such consultations were conducted in secret as no president wanted to be seen as beholden to a soothsayer. However, Nancy Reagan apparently regarded Dixon as unreliable and so consulted the astrologer Joan Quigley instead.

A BYWORD FOR SKEWED STATISTICS

Not all Dixon's prophecies concerned well-known people and celebrities, and not all forecast tragedy, for she also appeared to have the gift of diagnosis and healing. Her prayers, and sometimes her touch, were said to be effective in curing illnesses. There were other times, though, when her predictions failed to come to pass, or were completely off-beam. She predicted, for example, that the Third World War would start in 1958, that a cure for cancer would be discovered in 1967, that the Soviet Union would be the first nation to put a man on the moon, and that George Bush Sr would beat Bill Clinton in the 1992 presidential election. She claimed that

Soothsayer of Woe

Jeane Dixon's renowned foretelling of the assassinations of prominent figures were characteristic of her repertoire. Many of her prophecies concerned disasters and fatalities. She apparently foresaw the death of both the actress Carole Lombard and the United Nations Secretary-General Dag Hammarskjöld in plane crashes (in 1942 and 1961 respectively) and the shooting that paralysed Governor George Wallace of Alabama in 1972. She predicted that three astronauts in the *Apollo* space programme would die, not in flight but on the ground: shortly afterwards, during a 'plugs-out' test in January 1967, astronauts Virgil ('Gus') Grissom, Ed White and Roger Chaffee were burned to death on the launchpad.

information picked up by telepathy could itself change if the person's own thoughts changed; she also explained her various failures by saying that she might sometimes incorrectly interpret the symbols that appeared in a psychic dream.

Sceptics say that many of Jeane Dixon's predictions were educated guesses resulting from her knowledge of the Washington political scene and information gained from her friends in high places. Her critics contend that, out of so many dozens of predictions, some were bound to come true, or alternatively that they were so vague they could be interpreted in many ways. The term 'Jeane Dixon Effect' was coined by Temple University mathematician John Allen Paulos in his 1988 book *Innumeracy: Mathematical Illiteracy and its Consequences*. In it he blames a misunderstanding or misuse of statistics for the fallacy by which a few correct predictions are loudly trumpeted and therefore offset the far more numerous incorrect ones.

Others believe every word she uttered came from the divine; certainly she herself felt that she had a channel to the Higher Power. Yet she always refused to put herself up for testing by parapsychologists, saying that her gift of prophecy came from God and she had no wish to act as a guinea pig for researchers. She was nevertheless persuaded to use her gift from God to author an astrology cookbook and a book of horoscopes for dogs.

Jeane Dixon died in Washington DC in January 1997. She always kept her private life secret, but her *New York Times* obituary gave her age as 79.

'I HAVE NO PACT WITH GOD THAT HE WILL SHOW ME EVERYTHING, BUT I AM ETERNALLY GRATEFUL FOR WHAT HE HAS ALLOWED ME TO SEE.'

marshall herff applewhite

1931–97

Heaven's Gate

In September 1975, 200 people gathered in Waldport, Oregon, to hear a lecture on UFOs by 'The Two', also known as 'Bo' and 'Peep'. Claiming to come from outer space, the pair revealed that the only way to attain eternal life on the 'Next Level' was to escape the Earth's spiritually toxic atmosphere by spaceship – one of which was ready and waiting in eastern Colorado. Humans could thus break the endless cycle of death and reincarnation and become androgynous beings in a state of perpetual growth.

More than 20 listeners joined the couple and were not seen again for the next two months, prompting a frenzy of stories in the American press about followers of a cult who had left families, friends and jobs for a life with aliens. But when the spaceship failed to materialize, many disillusioned followers returned to their former lives. Undaunted, Bo and Peep merely refrained from lecturing in public for a while.

Repressed Homosexual

Peep (a.k.a. Do and Pooh) was born Marshall Herff Applewhite, son of a Texan Presbyterian minister, on 17 May 1931. His childhood was spent moving around Texas where his father was founding new churches. Applewhite was a religious child and a talented singer who graduated with a degree in arts and music

Applewhite and Nettles ('Peep' and 'Bo') in 1974.

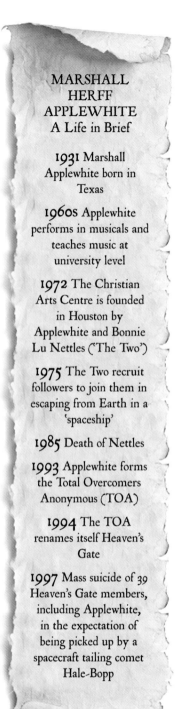

from Austin College. In 1954 he married Ann Pearce, with whom he had two children. By the 1960s he was teaching music at the University of St Thomas in Houston, directing the choir of the local Episcopal church, and singing in musicals such as *Oklahoma!* and *South Pacific*. Never comfortable in his marriage, he had several homosexual relationships, and in 1964 he left his young family. In 1970 he was dismissed from his university post after an affair with a student.

Following his dismissal, Applewhite became depressed and started hearing voices. In 1972 he met a 44-year-old nurse named Bonnie Lu Nettles. Some reports say that Applewhite met Nettles when he was suffering heart problems in hospital, during which time he experienced a near-death episode; others claim they met in a psychiatric hospital as he tried to come to terms with his homosexuality. Whatever the truth, Nettles convinced Applewhite that he should join her theosophical group that channelled messages from spiritual entities. Within a short while, the two of them had set up the Christian Arts Centre in Houston where Applewhite taught performing arts, and Nettles astrology and theosophy. Following the centre's closure a few months later, the couple began experiencing visions and other paranormal phenonena. During this time they were allegedly contacted by aliens.

AWAITING THE 'DEMONSTRATION'

Following a revelation, Applewhite became convinced that he and Nettles were the two witnesses mentioned in the Book of Revelation, and that they had been placed on Earth as prophets to save humanity. Eventually, he believed, they would be killed by their enemies but would be resurrected by God after three and a half days, at which point they would be taken on a spaceship to the Next Level – an event he called the Demonstration. In 1973, convinced of the importance of their mission, Nettles and Applewhite – now calling themselves Bo and Peep – set out for Oregon.

Applewhite and Nettles spent months in seclusion perfecting their mission, until in 1975 a New Age teacher, Clarence Klug, invited them to talk to his students in Los Angeles. Twenty-four students, along with Klug, decided to return with The Two to Oregon. Bo and Peep taught that those wishing to escape the endless cycle of death and reincarnation must first learn to abandon everything in their current lives. Spirits were believed to attach themselves to humans in the form of doubts, desires, old habits, and memories of friends and relatives, all of which needed to be eliminated before they could reach the next kingdom. Thus, members were to become isolated from their past lives; they were discouraged even from bonding with each other in case of contamination.

Followers split up and held talks in private homes and on university campuses. They had no income so were forced to beg for food and shelter. Applewhite and Nettles optimistically explained the universe would look after them and provide for their needs. However, after the spaceship failed to appear in 1975 and many disillusioned members left the cult, The Two disappeared for a while, abandoning their followers. According to Robert Balch, a sociology professor at the University of Montana who had infiltrated the cult, the former members were left wandering leaderless around the country. In 1976, however, The Two resurfaced, announcing that the doors to the Next Level had been closed and the Demonstration cancelled. All information from the Next Level would in future be channelled through them.

REGROUPING AND RECRUITING

In the late 1970s Applewhite and Nettles inherited money, which enabled them to rent properties instead of camping. Applewhite introduced a new set of rules: unisex uniforms were issued and celibacy enforced. Couples were separated and members given a 'partner' to watch out for 'misdemeanours'. Some members were encouraged to get jobs in order to support the group, and those who disagreed with these strictures were encouraged to leave.

In 1985 Nettles died of cancer, leaving Applewhite devastated – though he explained to his remaining followers that Nettles had deliberately gone ahead to the Next Level in order to help others make the journey. In 1993, he formed a new group – the Total Overcomers Anonymous (TOA). The group took out an advertisement in *USA Today* entitled '"UFO Cult" resurfaces with Final Offer', claiming that the Earth was about to be 'recycled' and 'spaded under. Its inhabitants are refusing to evolve. The weeds have taken over the garden and disturbed its usefulness beyond repair.' In 1994 Applewhite believed the lift-off was imminent. The group – at this stage only 24 strong, none of whom had seen their friends or families for years – gave up their conventional jobs and the communal houses in which they had been living, liquidated their assets and resumed public meetings. Their purpose this time was not so much to recruit new members as to locate past crew members who had come from the Next Level.

After nine months of searching for fellow crew members, the group moved with some new recruits to a rented mansion in Rancho Santa Fe, some 20 miles (32 km) north of San Diego, renaming themselves 'Heaven's Gate'. Isolating themselves from neighbours and the outside world, and only leaving the house at night, they told their landlord that they were a Christian sect. They supported themselves by setting up a web design company on the Internet, calling it Higher Source. They also created their own web page and in the autumn of 1995 posted several statements on their website. One was entitled 'Undercover "Jesus" Surfaces before Departure' (Applewhite was now claiming that he had been Jesus Christ in a previous incarnation). The other was a statement 'by an ET Presently Incarnate'. The ridicule and hostility with which the statements were received convinced Applewhite that the time was approaching to return 'home'.

TAILING THE COMET

The cue for action seems to have been the appearance in the sky of the comet Hale-Bopp. The comet came to hold great significance for Applewhite. From the Next Level he was apparently informed by Nettles that the spaceship that would collect the members of Heaven's Gate was tailing Hale-Bopp and would approach the Earth to pick up its passengers around the spring

Comet Hale-Bopp

Discovered in 1995, the comet became visible to the naked eye a year later, and remained so for a record 18 months. By early 1997 it was so bright that it became known as the 'Great Comet of 1997', with a NASA website tracking its progress recording 1.2 million hits on a single day in March 1997. Such enthusiasm had led to many stories - spread by the new medium of the Internet - that the appearance of the comet, coming so close to the end of the Second Millennium, portended great upheaval. A number of fundamentalist Christians contended that it was a sign of the 'end time', and that it could be identified with the 'death star' Wormwood described in the Book of Revelation (see pages 38-41).

equinox. Several days after the equinox, on 26 March 1997, 21 women and 18 men were found dead in the rented mansion at 18341 Colina Norte in Rancho Fe. All had committed suicide by drinking the sedative phenobarbital in apple sauce, washing the concoction down with vodka. When the bodies were first discovered, police assumed they were all male. All had short haircuts and were dressed in black sweat pants and shirts, wearing new black Nike footwear. Each body had been carefully laid out on a bed, and all but two were covered with a purple shroud. Next to each was a packed travelling bag; in the pocket of each was a $5 bill, and on their sleeves a badge reading 'Heaven's Gate Away Team'. Perhaps the most bizarre discovery was that six of the males, including Applewhite, had at some point undergone surgical castration. Over 100 videos were found on the premises, recording explanations of their actions by cult members, none of whom, it seemed, had been coerced into suicide.

Two months later, hoping to join Applewhite and his followers, two surviving members of Heaven's Gate – Charles Humphrey and Wayne Cooke – attempted suicide in a nearby Holiday Inn. Humphrey was unsuccessful but managed to kill himself in the Arizona desert a few months later. As recently as 2008, several remaining members were still maintaining the original Heaven's Gate website and distributing materials left behind by the group.

'IN THE EARLY 1970S, TWO INDIVIDUALS (MY TASK PARTNER AND MYSELF) FROM THE EVOLUTIONARY LEVEL ABOVE HUMAN (THE KINGDOM OF HEAVEN) INCARNATED INTO (MOVED INTO AND TOOK OVER) TWO HUMAN BODIES THAT WERE IN THEIR FORTIES. I MOVED INTO A MALE BODY, AND MY PARTNER, WHO IS AN OLDER MEMBER IN THE LEVEL ABOVE HUMAN, TOOK A FEMALE BODY ... WE BROUGHT TO EARTH WITH US A CREW OF STUDENTS WHOM WE HAD WORKED WITH (NURTURED) ON EARTH IN PREVIOUS MISSIONS. THEY WERE IN VARYING STAGES OF METAMORPHIC TRANSITION FROM MEMBERSHIP IN THE HUMAN KINGDOM TO MEMBERSHIP IN THE PHYSICAL EVOLUTIONARY LEVEL ABOVE HUMAN (WHAT YOUR HISTORY REFERS TO AS THE KINGDOM OF GOD OR KINGDOM OF HEAVEN).'

STATEMENT 'BY AN ET PRESENTLY INCARNATE' (1995)

Chief Dan evehema

c.1894–1999

The Hopi Prophecies

On 10 December 1992, Oren R. Lyons, Faithkeeper of the Six Nations of the Iroquois Confederacy, addressed the General Assembly of the United Nations in New York with three shouts. These cries were an announcement to the Great Spirit that the following speaker, an elder of the Wolf, Fox and Coyote clans, had a message of supreme importance to deliver. The elder, 82-year-old Thomas Banyacya, then stepped forward and sprinkled cornmeal around the podium.

anyacya and his companion that day, 98-year-old Chief Dan Evehema, were spiritual leaders of the Hopi Nation – a Native American people from the desert regions of the southwest. They had come to New York to warn world leaders of the Hopi Prophecies. 'Today, December 10, 1992,' Banyacya told his audience, 'you see increasing floods, more damaging hurricanes, hail storms, climate changes and earthquakes as our prophecies said would come.'

AN ANCIENT CULTURE UPROOTED

The Hopi migrated from Mexico into present-day Arizona around 500 BC, eventually settling around the 2500-metre (8000-ft) Black Mesa and growing corn. The arrival of the Spanish in 1540 severely disrupted the Hopi way of life. In 1824 their ancestral lands were ceded to Mexico by Spain, but in 1848 the United States laid claim to them, forcing the Hopi onto a reservation in 1882. Today the Hopi reservation is situated in northeastern Arizona, 100 miles (160 km) from the Grand Canyon. Covering 650,000 hectares (1.6 million acres), it is a mere

Paintings of kachina, *sacred ancestral spirits of the Hopi people.*

9 percent of their ancestral lands. The reservation of the 10,000-strong Hopi is now surrounded by that of the much larger Navajo Nation.

Chief Dan Evehema was born on the Hopi reservation in about 1894 and grew up in a village on the Black Mesa. His mother, Honvenka, and father, Kootsvayoema, produced a family of four boys and four girls. When the reservation was established in 1882, the Federal government attempted to eradicate Hopi culture by forcing children to attend English-language schools, often far from home, to have their hair cut, and to abandon the Hopi language and ceremonies. A rift developed within the Hopi community between assimilationists and traditionalists. Kootsvayoema, a traditionalist, was so appalled that he left Oraibi, his home village, and with other like-minded Hopi founded another village nearby, which they named Hotevilla. Kootsvayoema refused to let his children attend school and in 1907 was imprisoned along with other Hopi fathers. Evehema was sent to school for six years, three of them in a school 185 miles (296 km) away in Phoenix. Ultimately he returned to the reservation in 1913 to work on the land and marry. He would eventually become a spiritual leader, an elder of the Greasewood-Roadrunner clan, and a 'Snake Priest' who spent 16 days each year dancing with snakes and praying for rain.

KEEPERS OF THE LAND

The Hopi have a complex history that is intimately bound up with their stewardship of the land. Traditional beliefs hold that Hopiland is the microcosm of the planet and that a pact they made over 1000 years ago with Massau'u, the Great Spirit, makes them the keepers of the world's balance. Massau'u gave them instructions, inscribed on a set of sacred stone tablets, on how to live their lives; it included prophecies of what would happen if they failed to follow these instructions. These tablets allegedly still exist – one was given to the Fire clan and three to the Bear clan – but all remain hidden. Author Frank Waters, whose father was part Cheyenne, was shown one belonging to the Bear clan in 1960: it consisted of a small grey marble slab with hieroglyphic markings.

According to the Hopi, the human race has passed through three different worlds. At the end of each, Massau'u has punished humanity when they have turned away from his teachings, then purified them. The First World was destroyed by earthquakes, the Second World by the Great Freeze (the Ice Age), and the Third World by the Great Flood. Humanity now lives in the Fourth World.

The Hopi earned Massau'u's respect after the Great Flood that destroyed the Third World. With the help of Spider Woman, a female spirit, Massau'u had called together the leaders of the four surviving groups of people, placing corn of different colours and size in front of these leaders and telling them to choose what food they wanted in this world. The Hopi, who were the last to choose, picked the smallest, blue ear of corn. Massau'u then declared them the humblest and wisest of the peoples, naming them Hopi, which means 'people of peace'. He entrusted them to look after his land until he returned, keeping the world in balance through special prayers and rituals. Massau'u then gave the sacred stone tablets to Spider Woman's two grandsons and told the older brother to go to the rising sun in the east, remaining there until the younger brother's way of life was threatened. The Hopi are the descendants of the younger brother, who made the covenant with Massau'u and agreed to live according to his teachings. Massau'u instructed the Hopi to settle in Hopiland and mark the land with sacred footprints.

CHEATED AND DESPOILED

According to Dan Evehema, the ancient Hopi prophecy foretells that when the older brother returns to help the Hopi, he will place the stone tablet next to his brother's to show they are true brothers. He will wear a red cap and red cloak and, though belonging to no religion, will have many followers. Accompanying him will be two wise helpers: one will display the symbol of a swastika, which represents purity; the other will have a symbol of the sun. If these three fail in their mission to restore peace and brotherhood to Hopiland, then, according to the prophecies, merciless invaders from the west will come in large numbers. The Day of Purification will follow, and the Fifth World will commence. This prophecy has been interpreted by the Hopi as the start of a Third World War.

The Hopi Peace Prayer

This Hopi Prayer for Peace was read by Thomas Banyacya to the UN General Assembly and to the UN People's Assembly on 10 December 1992:

Great Spirit and all unseen, this day we pray and ask You for guidance, humbly we ask You to help us and fellow men to have recourse to peaceful ways of life, because of uncontrolled deceitfulness by humankind.

Help us all to love, not hate one another.

We ask you to be seen in an image of Love and Peace.

Let us be seen in beauty, the colours of the rainbow.

We respect our Mother, the plant, with our loving care, for from Her breast we receive our nourishment.

Let us not listen to the voice of the two-hearted, the destroyers of the mind, the haters and self-made leaders, whose lusts for power and wealth will lead us into confusion and darkness.

Seek visions always of world beauty, not violence nor battlefield.

It is our duty to pray always for harmony between man and Earth, so that the Earth will bloom once more.

Let us show our emblem of love and goodwill for all life and land.

Pray for the House of Glass (American Senate), for within it are minds clear and pure as ice and mountain streams.

Pray for the great leaders of nations in the House of Mica (UN) who in their own quiet ways help the Earth in balance.

We pray to the Great Spirit that one day our Mother Earth be purified into a healthy peaceful one.

Let us sing for strength of wisdom with all nations for the good of all people.

Our hope is not yet lost, purification must be to restore the health of our Mother Earth for lasting peace and happiness.

In 1944 strip mining for uranium for the Manhattan Project (the A-bomb programme) commenced in Hopiland, causing the traditionalists to fear the balance of the world was in jeopardy. Four years later, a young Hopi named Thomas Banyacya (1910–99) approached the UN with a warning of an apocalypse, claiming that material greed was distracting people from spiritual truths. He was refused an audience. By 1966, matters in Hopiland had worsened. The Hopi Council agreed to lease coalmining rights to the Peabody Energy Corporation, though most Hopi refused to acknowledge the council and abstained from voting. John Sterling Boydon, a Mormon attorney from Salt Lake City, was hired to represent the Hopi. After Boydon's death in 1980, he was found to have also been working for Peabody, a conflict of interest of which the Hopi were unaware. Traditionalists were dismayed as they witnessed the excavation of 12 million tons of coal annually from their land to fuel two huge power stations. The Black Mesa Mine on Hopiland also used 1.2 billion gallons of water a year from an ancient aquifer. The Hopi feared Massau'u's wrath for this despoliation of the land.

HARBINGERS OF DOOM

In their 1992 address to the UN, Evehema and Banyacya requested that it protect Hopiland because of its special role in balancing the world. The Hopi Prophecies warn that signs will appear when the Fourth World is about to end. Evehema, who co-authored *Hotevilla: Hopi Shrine of the Covenant* (1995) and *The Hopi Survival Kit* (1997), explained that many have already appeared. The first, he claimed, was when the 'Pahana' (white men) came to their land and tried to lead them astray. Other signs include the coming of wagons, strange beasts like buffalo with horns (longhorn cattle), snakes of iron (railroad tracks), giant spider webs (power and telephone lines), rivers of stone (asphalt roads), the sea turning black (oil spills) and youths with long hair (hippies). The final sign, yet to materialize, is a blue star, a 'dwelling-place in the heavens that will come crashing down'.

The two tribal elders, who died within days of each other in 1999, would have been delighted to witness the closure in 2005 of the Black Mesa Mine, after the Mohave Generating Station in Laughlin, Nevada, which it supplied with fuel, was condemned for harmful emissions and forced to cease operating. However, not all Hopi were pleased, since the mine was a major employer in an area scarce in jobs. The other mine, which is on Navajo land, remains open.

'WHEN THE END IS NEAR, WE WILL SEE A HALO OF MIST AROUND THE HEAVENLY BODIES. FOUR TIMES IT WILL APPEAR AROUND THE SUN AS A WARNING THAT WE MUST REFORM, TELLING US THAT PEOPLE OF ALL COLOUR MUST UNITE AND ARISE FOR SURVIVAL, AND THAT WE MUST UNCOVER THE CAUSES OF OUR DILEMMAS. UNLESS MAN-MADE WEAPONS ARE USED TO STRIKE FIRST, PEACE WILL THEN COME.'

DAN EVEHEMA, *HOTEVILLA: HOPI SHRINE OF THE COVENANT* (1995)

Sathya Sai baba

b.1926

India's God-Man

In March 1940, Sathyanarayana Raju, a 13-year-old boy from the remote southern Indian village of Puttaparthi, was stung by a large black scorpion. Unconscious for 24 hours, the boy awoke a different person, unwilling to eat, alternately weak and strong, laughing and weeping, talking of God and faraway places, and reciting long Sanskrit passages. Thinking him possessed by a demon, his parents summoned first an exorcist, then doctors and healers, all in vain. After almost three months of this strange behaviour, the boy announced he was a reincarnation of the wonder-worker Sai Baba of Shirdi (1835–1918).

Shirdi Sai Baba was said to have had supernatural powers, including the ability to turn water into oil for his lamps and to project himself through space. He had predicted before his death that he would reappear in the Madras area in eight years' time – and true to his word, Sathyanarayana was born on 23 November 1926, exactly eight years later. Sathya was a bright and charming child for whom his family had great hopes. Because of his hatred of cruelty to animals, he became a vegetarian when very young, while from the age of five he appeared to have an exceptional knowledge of God. He would sometimes produce sweets and pencils out of an apparently empty bag for his young school friends, telling them that he had an invisible helper.

FAMILY CONFLICT

At the age of ten, Sathya moved to the school where his elder brother Seshama Raju was a teacher. Here he excelled in music and dance, drama and poetry, while stories of his miraculous manifestations spread among students and teachers alike. When, following his startling announcement in 1940, Sathya started producing sweets for the villagers, his father, Pedda Venkama Raju, became furious and beat the boy, thinking him possessed by the spirit of a Muslim fakir – Baba being a Muslim name. A government officer from a nearby town who had known Shirdi Sai Baba came to see the family and at first refused to believe that the strange-looking boy was a reincarnation of his guru. Angrily, Sathya scattered ash that he had caused to appear from nowhere, then stormed out. Later, asked to prove that he really was Sai Baba, he requested some jasmine flowers; on receiving them he immediately threw them onto the floor – where they clearly formed the words Sai Baba. Throughout his life, whenever speaking of Shirdi Sai Baba, Sathya would refer to him as 'my previous body'.

Despite the fact that his younger brother had declared himself an avatar, or divine incarnation, Seshama Raju was unimpressed, insisting that the boy continue his education. By October of that year, however, Sathya finally threw away his books and announced that he was leaving school, saying that his devotees needed him and he had work to do. For three days he

1918 Death of the miracle worker Sai Baba of Shirdi; before dying, he predicts that he will be reincarnated near Madras (Chennai) within eight years

1926 Sathyanarayana Rahju born in Andhra Pradesh

1940 After being stung by a scorpion, Sathyanarayana has a mystical experience after which he proclaims himself the reincarnation of Shirdi Sai Baba

1950 The Prashanthi Nilayam ashram is built near Sathya Sai Baba's birthplace

1993 Disgruntled ex-students of Sai Baba attempt to assassinate the guru

2004 Controversy over the authenticity of Sai Baba is fuelled by a BBC documentary on alleged fraud and sexual abuse at the ashram

went to live at the house of a supportive excise inspector; it was only when his parents agreed not to interfere with what he regarded as his mission that he came home to Puttaparthi. Soon the 14-year-old gathered devotees around him, first in his father's home then in the larger house of a follower. Here, when people arrived, he insisted they be fed. If food ran short, Satya would pour the milk from two coconuts onto the remaining rice – and it would miraculously become sufficient to feed everyone. During this time he would sometimes be seen with a fiery wheel of light around his head or a blinding light coming from a third eye in the centre of his forehead.

In 1945 the growing number of visitors to Puttaparthi necessitated the building of a new four-roomed house. Five years later, a more spacious dwelling was constructed to the south of the village and given the name of Prashanthi Nilayam – the Abode of Supreme Peace. It is in this ashram that Sathya Sai Baba lives to this day, and it is here that he gives *darshan* – blessing by appearance – to his followers.

PARANORMAL ABILITIES?

During the first three decades of his life, Sathya Sai Baba spent much of his time in what have been called 'divine pranks' – the production of sacred ash known as *vibhuti*, sweets, jewels, rings and necklaces, coins, watches, pictures and photographs, which were given to followers, along with accounts of visions, healings and astral travel. Often in the afternoons, as the devotees gathered in the ashram, the short figure in an orange robe, his head crowned with a halo of frizzy black hair, would start playing with mounds of sand in any spot chosen by the crowd. From the sand he would then bring forth small statues of gods and goddesses – so hot they could hardly be handled. Or he might ask devotees what fruit they wanted, and pluck their choice from a nearby tamarind tree and give it to them. These seemingly miraculous happenings were perhaps designed to convince followers that he was a 'God-Man' – a divinity in human form. Later he was to spend more time in spiritual guidance and in teaching the right ways to live.

According to Sai Baba: 'miracles are the work of God coming through a purified person who incarnates.' Certainly there are thousands of first-hand accounts of Sai Baba's paranormal abilities, many recorded in the early days of his mission. A Madras businessman recalls empty dishes being magically refilled with hot food to feed the crowds: food for 1000 expanded to feed 10,000. Ash frequently formed on photographs; out-of-season fruits or, on one occasion, a large glass bowl of sweets materialized out of thin air. A diamond was produced from a flower bud. A tubercular woman, told her illness was incurable, was apparently healed with *vibhuti*, an ash whose healing powers have been acclaimed by many sufferers. Sometimes Sai Baba would take on the pain of his patients and become ill himself. Generally, however, his energy appeared to be inexhaustible as he gave talks to his followers at the ashram or travelled through villages to meet devotees.

The 'God-Man' Sai Baba passes among his devotees at the Puttaparthi ashram.

DEVOTEES AND DETRACTORS

Huge crowds of people from all over the world have visited Prashanthi Nilayam, overflowing the buildings and camping in the grounds in order to attend *darshan*. However, Sai Baba also has several detractors. He has said that he does not accept money from his followers, yet new devotees have been given details of a bank account to which donations can be sent. Sceptics look on him as a master of deception and refuse to believe in his miracles, saying that they could be reproduced by any conjurer. There is indeed evidence that he creates *vibhuti* by crushing tiny pills in his hand, and that much of the jewellery that he 'materializes' is actually purchased from a shop in Hyderabad. Disillusioned and often distraught students, scared to speak out while at the ashram, have contributed to *The Findings*, an investigation in 2000 by ex-devotees David and Faye Bailey. Their stories tell in detail of Sai Baba's alleged sexual abuse of young men and boys between the ages of 7 and 30. A 2004 BBC documentary, 'Secret Swami', recounted how he performed genital oilings on his alleged victims – a ritual otherwise

'I AM GOD. AND YOU TOO ARE GOD. THE ONLY DIFFERENCE BETWEEN YOU AND ME IS THAT WHILE I AM AWARE OF IT, YOU ARE COMPLETELY UNAWARE.'

unknown to Hinduism. He has also been involved in other controversies. In 1993 an attempt was made by a number of disgruntled ex-students to assassinate the guru: all four young men were killed by armed police after breaking into Sai Baba's bedroom and stabbing two of his aides.

Whatever the controversies, it would be difficult to argue with Sathya Sai Baba's message to the world: one of peace, right living, right feeling and right action. His self-imposed mission is to alleviate suffering and sorrow. He promotes the basic unity that exists between all religions, saying that 'the Lord can be addressed by any name that tastes sweet to your tongue', and that 'all religions lead man on the path to God'. There are over 1200 Sathya Sai Baba centres in 114 countries with an estimated 30 million devotees. To many he remains an avatar, a god in human form. As Michael Goldstein, international chairman of the Sathya Sai Organisation, told the BBC in 2004: 'We believe that Sathya Sai Baba is Jesus Christ. Sathya Sai Baba is Buddha. Sathya Sai Baba is the founder of all the world's religions. Sathya Sai Baba has always been God.'

hal lindsey
b.1929

'The Late, Great Planet Earth'

'This is a book about prophecy – Bible prophecy. If you have no interest in the future, this isn't for you.' So begins Hal Lindsey's *The Late, Great Planet Earth*, first printed in 1970 by Zondervan, a Michigan-based publisher of Bibles. Many people evidently did have an interest in the future as described by Lindsey, since the work became the best selling non-fiction book of the 1970s. It went through 40 printings and 4 million copies in its first four years, and to date it has sold 35 million copies and been translated into 54 languages.

For Lindsey, the Bible held the key to understanding contemporary political events, such as the Cold War and the Arab–Israeli conflict. It also offered a blueprint for future events, its ancient prophecies revealing when and how the rise of the Antichrist, Armageddon and the Second Coming of Christ would occur within the context of late 20th-century global politics. Writing during the height of the Cold War, when there was a threat of a nuclear holocaust and violent unrest in the Middle East, Lindsey believed these prophecies were on the brink of fulfilment. The last word of his book is the ancient Christian greeting 'marantha', which means 'the Lord is coming soon'.

Harold Lee Lindsey was born in Houston, Texas, in 1929. Very few details of his early life are available. However, on his website he states that he dropped out of the University of Houston in 1950 in order to serve as a tugboat captain in the Korean War. Having contemplated suicide after the breakdown of his first marriage, he was saved by reading the

New Testament. After remarrying, he graduated in 1958 with a degree from the Dallas Theological Seminary and, with his new wife, worked with Campus Crusade for Christ, an evangelical organization. In 1960, Lindsey established a Bible school in Los Angeles under the whimsical name of the 'JC Light and Power Company'.

CATALYST TO ARMAGEDDON

If the New Testament saved Lindsey's life, it was the Old Testament – and specifically its prophetic books – that gave him his vocation. In 1967 the Six-Day War was triggered by Egypt's expulsion of the UN peacekeeping force from the Sinai Peninsula, their massing of troops on Israel's border, and the closure of the Straits of Tiran to Israeli ships. Struck by the similarity of these political events to biblical prophecies, Lindsey became convinced that the Bible could be a reliable tool for predicting how war in the Middle East would lead to the Armageddon and the rise of the Antichrist. To outline his theory, he wrote (with the help of ghost writer Carole C. Carlson) *The Late, Great Planet Earth*. Giving a literal interpretation of biblical prophecies, he claimed that Armageddon would follow an invasion of Israeli territory and that the invading countries would be judged and destroyed. Ezekiel 38:15 had great significance for him: 'And thou shalt come out of thy place from the northern parts, thou and many people with thee, all of them riding upon horses, a great company and a mighty army.' This army, described in the Bible as coming from Magog, would be commanded by Gog, identified by Lindsey as the Soviet Union. According to his interpretation of Ezekiel 38:5, Gog's allies would be Iran, Ethiopia and Libya.

Hal Lindsey's prophecies of doom have fallen on receptive ears in the USA.

All geopolitical events could be seen, Lindsey believed, though the lens of biblical prophecy. He further claimed that Egypt, the Arab nations and the countries of Sub-Saharan Africa would form the alliance named in the Book of Revelation as the 'king of the South'; in time they would join with the Soviet Union to oppose Israel. The 'king of the East', also mentioned in the Book of Revelation, was identified by Lindsey as the Chinese. As described in the Book of Revelation (16:12), they would raise an army 200 million strong prior to Christ's return. This Asian horde would wipe out one-third of the Earth's population with fire, smoke and brimstone – or, as interpreted by Lindsey, by nuclear war.

IT AIN'T NECESSARILY SO...

The Book of Revelation describes torrents of fire and brimstone raining down on those from the north – the Russian alliance – and Israel. These torrents, in Lindsey's view, refer to nuclear weapons deployed by the EU. Lindsey claimed that the United States, which is not mentioned in the Bible, would not play a key role in these events. However, he forecast that the US would eventually join forces with the EU against the king of the East. Once Russia and the nations of the Middle East were annihilated, the EU would be faced with the king of the East who, needing to acquire resources, would renege on a peace agreement with Rome. China would move their 200 million troops towards Europe; the EU would then persuade the rest of the world to join them in their war against China, with nuclear weapons devastating the major cities of the world.

It is at this dire moment, just as mankind is about to destroy itself, that Christ will return. When his feet touch the earth on the Mount of Olives, from whence he departed to heaven, the mountain will split in half. Zachariah predicted that the Jews would run to this spot, knowing that God would protect them from the devastation to come. Lindsey claims there is a gigantic fault running east to west through the centre of the Mount of Olives, further proof, in his view, that the Bible is genuinely prophetic. When all has been destroyed, as predicted in the Bible, Christ will rule for 1000 years. At the end of this time, those who rebel will be judged; and finally, a new Earth, where there is no war or famine, will be created for true believers in Christ.

Lindsey was careful not to commit to specific dates on which these biblical prophecies would fulfil themselves. 'I have never taken to the hills with my possessions and loved ones to await Doomsday,' he wrote. However, his literal interpretation of certain passages has involved him in mathematical calculations with highly specific conclusions. He predicted that Armageddon would take place within a generation of the creation in 1948 of the state of Israel, that is, 20 to 40 years from that date. Thus the nuclear devastation was projected to occur by 1988 at the latest. By the 1980s Lindsey therefore appeared to believe that Armageddon was imminent. In his 1983 book *The 1980s: Countdown to Armageddon*, he claimed that the 1980s might be 'the last decade of history as we know it'. Other publications by him include *Satan is Alive and Well on Planet Earth* (1972) and *There's a New World Coming* (1973).

TAILORING THE MESSAGE
Since the fall of the Berlin Wall and the collapse of the Soviet Union removed the Russians from their prophetic role, Lindsey has recently turned his attention to the Islamic world,

*'*TO THE SCEPTIC WHO SAYS THAT CHRIST IS NOT COMING SOON, I WOULD ASK HIM TO PUT THE BOOK OF REVELATION IN ONE HAND, AND THE DAILY NEWSPAPER IN THE OTHER, AND THEN SINCERELY ASK GOD TO SHOW HIM WHERE WE ARE ON HIS PROPHETIC TIME-CLOCK.*'*

The EU Enters the Fray

Lindsey did not take his inspiration from the Book of Revelation alone. The Book of Daniel prophesied that three kingdoms would rise to power from the ruins of Babylon. According to Lindsey, the second of these kingdoms - the Medean-Persian empire - had been conquered by Alexander the Great, leader of the third kingdom. The fourth kingdom, destined to be 'strong as iron', would be a revived Rome. This kingdom would consist of a ten-nation confederacy understood by Lindsey to be the European Union. (In 1970, when Lindsey's book appeared, the EEC had six members, expanding to nine in 1973; it has never consisted of ten members.) The leader of the EU, a charismatic dictator, would be the Antichrist described in the Book of Revelation. Revelation 13:3 forecast that this leader would recover from a seemingly fatal head wound, after which men would worship him. So powerful would he become that he would establish himself in the Temple of God (Thessalonians 2:4), eventually proclaiming himself God incarnate and ruling for 43 months, during which time he would control the world's economies. Believers in Christ who attempted to oppose him would be declared traitors and barred from buying, selling or holding down a job. Many would be executed.

In Lindsey's reading, the EU leader would make a pact with Israel in order to protect her, whereupon the Israelis will rebuild the Temple of Jerusalem. However, this pact, according to the Book of Isaiah, was destined to trigger a seven-year Tribulation. The king of the South - the Egypt/Arab/African confederacy - would then attack Israel, unleashing the Armageddon. The king of the North - the Soviet Union and her allies - would also attack Israel which, according to Lindsey, the EU would protect on account of its need for access to mineral resources under the Dead Sea.

publishing *The Everlasting Hatred: the Roots of Jihad* (2002). Lindsey's beliefs about Islam have plunged him into controversy. For 12 years until 2006 he hosted the International Intelligence Briefing on the Trinity Broadcasting Network (TBN), a Christian television network. However, he resigned early in 2006, complaining that his broadcast had been pulled from the schedule because of his pro-Israel, anti-Muslim stance, although TBN claimed the change was due to seasonal Christmas programming. Yet TBN spokesman John Casoria did later admit that the network was concerned about how Lindsey's prophecies 'placed Arabs in a negative light'. An unrepentant Lindsey responded with an interview on the Fox Network in which he called Islam a violent religion. Since February 2006, he has broadcast 'The Hal Lindsey Report' on the Sky Angel Nationwide, another Christian TV network. The programme focuses on links between biblical prophecies and current events.

Lindsey still prophesies the end times, Armageddon, and the Second Coming of Christ. Although he gives no precise dates, he continues to maintain that an army from far to the north of Israel will trigger an invasion by a confederacy of nations. Now, however, 'all the nations of this confederacy are Muslim', and he sees the Muslim leader as an Iranian. As ever, his interpretation fits nicely with contemporary anxieties over current events.

billy meıer

b.1937

The Henoch Prophecies

On a cold afternoon in January 1975, a one-armed man named Eduard Meier was seen by curious neighbours in Hinwil, 30 miles (48 km) southeast of Zurich, seated on his moped and towing a tiny wagon towards the dense forest outside the village. Soon after, he returned, but was later spotted making further furtive excursions into the woods at all hours of the day and night. After a while the inquisitive villagers asked his wife what her husband was up to, but Kalliope Meier, nicknamed Popi, had no idea. Only after several months did Meier show her photographs of 'spaceships' in order to explain his actions.

The tattooed, grey-bearded Eduard Albert Meier has led a colourful life. Known in later life as Billy, he was born on 3 February 1937 to a farming family in Bülach, Switzerland. Aged only five, he witnessed his first UFO sightings while with his father. In 1944, he claimed to have made contact with an elderly male named Sfath, an extraterrestrial from the planet Erra, in a star system beyond the Pleiades. That summer, Sfath took Meier on a four-hour ride in his spacecraft high above the Earth's orbit and revealed his destiny to him. Soon after his return to Earth, Meier began hearing Sfath's voice in his head.

AN ERRANT EXISTENCE

As he grew up, Meier showed little enthusiasm for education or a career. In 1949 he spent eight months in a tuberculosis sanatorium; at 14 was sent to a boys' home for truants in Alibisbrunn, from which he absconded three times. He was eventually returned to his parents' farm but left school before completing the sixth grade. Later, after having been caught stealing, he was sent to a detention centre in Aarburg; he escaped from this institution to join the French Foreign Legion, only to go AWOL after his initial training. He then headed back to the Swiss detention centre to finish his sentence.

Meanwhile Meier's extraterrestrial experiences were continuing. In 1953, according to Meier, Sfath left the planet and was replaced by a female named Asket from the DAL, a parallel universe to Earth. In 1958, having been advised by Asket to broaden his horizons by travelling to countries in which, according to Asket, he had experienced past lives, Meier set off for Israel, Jordan, Pakistan, India and the Himalayas. During this period, he learned from Asket that he had once been a 'Plejaran' – someone from Sfath's star system – who had travelled on an expedition to Earth. Once there, Meier had deviously exploited humans, as a result of which he was reincarnated as a 'terrestrial primitive' in order to experience exploitation at first hand. In this incarnation, he had inspired a rebellion against his oppressors and organized a movement designed to recognize the 'Creation' – the source of everything. Since then, he had reincarnated many times. He furthermore claimed to have operated as 'The Phantom', a secret agent who apprehended serial killers in the Middle East, and who had been in contact with world leaders such as Mahatma Gandhi.

Hotline to extraterrestrials? Meier at home (with a portrait of his alien contact Semjase).

In 1964 Meier arrived in India, where he lived for five months in a cave near Mehrauli. He told an Indian reporter that he had visited many planets, showing photographs of spaceships as evidence. Before leaving India with his pet monkey, Meier informed the journalist that he had to complete a mysterious mission, details of which he would disclose within a year. However, in 1965, before he could share his mission with earthlings, Meier's left arm was severed in a bus accident while he was travelling near the coastal city of Iskenderun, Turkey.

Meier recuperated in hospital but then continued his wanderings. In Thessaloniki, Greece, he met his future wife, 17-year-old Kalliope. Her parents disapproved of the one-armed Swiss drifter, and so the couple were forced to elope. Over the next four years they travelled widely and had three children. In 1971 they returned to Hinwil and two years later moved into a council farmhouse in the village. Meier received a disability pension, but the family were far from well off.

THE LONG-LIVED PLEJARANS

Also in 1975, Meier made contact with a female extraterrestrial named Semjase, who replaced Asket. The arrival of this attractive alien caused friction in the Meier marriage. Popi had not been convinced by her husband's photographs of the 'beamships' when he first produced them, although her doubts did not deter Meier. He showed them to a friend named Jakobus Bertschinger, who was so impressed by them, and by Meier's description of Semjase, that he agreed to pay for an advertisement in a German magazine; interested people were invited to come and discuss UFOs with Meier. Meier then founded the Free Community of Interests for the Fringe and Spiritual Sciences and UFOlogical Studies (FIGU). Hinwil soon found itself overrun by visitors coming to Meier's farmhouse to participate in the discussions. The shy Popi, unable to cope with Meier's newfound fame, attempted suicide the following year. The couple eventually divorced in 1995.

The Talmud Jmmanuel

In 1975, Meier published in Germany translations of ancient Aramaic scrolls supposedly written by Jmmanuel, previously known (erroneously) as Jesus Christ. Meier claimed that he, along with a mysterious Greek friend named Isa Rashid, a Roman Catholic priest, had discovered them in Jerusalem in 1963. These 'original teachings', which threatened to overturn all major religions, suggested an extraterrestrial origin to the New Testament. Rashid allegedly translated 36 chapters from Aramaic into German and sent them to Meier – before being assassinated, apparently by Jewish and Christian leaders. However, critics argue that since the original scrolls have been destroyed and there are no photocopies, since no location details of the cave in which they were discovered have been made public, and since no records whatsoever exist of Rashid's life, the Jmmanuel scrolls (or Talmud Jmmanuel) must be a hoax perpetrated by Meier.

According to Meier, Semjase was Sfath's granddaughter. He was able to produce a photograph that showed her to be extremely pretty, with sparkling eyes, fair skin and human features. Like Sfath, she came from the planet Erra and was highly developed spiritually. She returned to her own planet in 1977, later returning to Earth where she remained until 1984, making contact with Meier on numerous occasions. Semjase revealed to Meier that Erra had a population of 500 million, with robots and androids to do the work. There was no government as the spiritual leaders simply made suggestions to the populace rather than ruling. Plejarans were essentially human, having the same ancestors as earthlings, though they had developed in a different way. Plejarans could live for up to 1000 years; aged 350, Semjase herself was relatively youthful. They did not show themselves to most earthlings, Semjase explained, because they feared humans would either become hysterical or revere them as gods. The Plejarans were aware of the aggressive nature of Earth humans and their unachievable need to control the universe.

Part of Meier's mission was to publish these conversations with Semjase and the other Plejarans, which he continues to do under the titles *Contact Notes* and *Contact Reports*. He claims he has also been instructed to raise human consciousness. The Plejarans allowed him to take pictures of their beamships to convince earthlings of their existence. They also gave him multi-tone sound recordings, metal alloy samples from one of their ships, and temporary use of a laser gun.

THE DARK PROPHECIES OF HENOCH

During his 215th contact with extraterrestrials, on 28 February 1987, Meier was told by the Plejaran commander Quetzal of the Henoch Prophecies. Henoch, whose name recalls the Hebrew prophet Enoch, predicted dire future events that would occur if humans did not learn to live peacefully together. This face-to-face meeting apparently furnished Meier with a prophecy about the terrorist attack on the World Trade Center in New York. Further contacts with extraterrestrials in the ensuing years told of imminent earthquakes in California, landslides in Brazil and volcanic eruptions in Alaska and Sicily. Contact with aliens in 1994 informed Meier that meat infected with Bovine Spongiform Encephalopathy (BSE) pathogens should be cooked at temperatures as high as 1000°C (1832°F). In the following year, Meier learned that 'hybrid warriors' would be created by mixing human DNA with that of pigs, and that people would soon have biochips attached to their nerve endings.

The most unsettling of the Henoch Prophecies have to do with a Third World War. According to Meier, the war was to begin sometime between 2006 and 2011, during the month of November. It would occur if Israel and the United States did not refrain from interfering in Middle Eastern affairs. He also denounces Muslim terrorists who could trigger war. A sign that his prophecies will begin fulfilling themselves will be when a pope no longer resides in Rome, causing the Christian religion and its churches to collapse. Then, for 888 days, millions of people throughout the world will be killed by weapons deployed by both governments and terrorists. Cloned humans devoid of compassion will be created for use as killer machines. The United States will be destroyed and Britain conquered and 'thrown down to the lowest level of misery'.

EVIDENCE OF FRAUD

Meier's claims have met with much scepticism. Critics such as Robert Shaeffer, author of *UFO Sightings: The Evidence* (1988), and Kal K. Korff, in *Spaceships of the Pleiades* (1995), claim that Meier's photographs are faked and that many have simply been taken from science fiction books, paintings and television programmes. The picture of Semjase, they argue, came from a Sears catalogue, while the picture of another supposed Plejaran was an actress who had appeared on Dean Martin's television show. Meier, however, says that the intelligence agencies altered many of his photographs and slipped them into his collection in an attempt to discredit him. Popi, Meier's ex-wife, claims that she saw models of spaceships in her husband's possession and passed photographs of them to a reporter. Meier does not dispute her claim, stating that he built the models to explain how the beamships worked. Marcel Vogel, the scientist who tested the sample that allegedly came from the beamships, found an unusual metal mixed in with other more common ones; after testing, however, the sample mysteriously disappeared and so could not be examined further.

Despite a reported 21 attempts on his life and the failure of his marriage, Meier has not done badly from his claims of extraterrestrial prophecy. He has published numerous books and articles, and founded in Switzerland the Semjase Silver Star Centre, headquarters of the FIGU, offering spiritual teachings and research facilities. There are FIGU organizations in Japan, Canada, the United States, Germany and Italy. He maintains that he still keeps in contact with extraterrestrials.

‘ BEFORE I GIVE YOU A CLEAR ACCOUNT OF THE PROPHECIES OF HENOCH, I WOULD LIKE TO POINT OUT THAT PROPHECIES ARE ALWAYS CHANGEABLE AND CAN BE CHANGED FOR THE BETTER IF MAN MAKES POSITIVE CHANGES IN HIS THOUGHTS, FEELINGS AND ACTIONS, LEADING TO THAT WHICH IS BETTER AND POSITIVELY PROGRESSIVE. ’

215TH CONTACT, 28 FEBRUARY 1987

elizabeth clare PROPHET

b.1939

The Summit Lighthouse Prophecies

Elizabeth Clare Wulf was born in 1939 in Red Bank, New Jersey, to former First World War German U-boat commander Hans Wulf and his Swiss wife Frida. Her father ran a construction company, while her mother raised Elizabeth as a Christian Scientist. The girl received a good education, completing her French studies in Switzerland, attending Antioch College in Ohio, and later transferring to Boston University. After gaining a degree in political science, she completed an internship at the United Nations.

Despite her upbringing as a Christian Scientist, as a young woman Elizabeth explored various different religions, claiming that as a child Jesus had spoken to her of the inadequacy of the Judaeo-Christian faiths. At the age of 18 she saw a picture of the Comte de Saint Germain – an 18th-century French mystic (see pages 124–127) – and immediately recognized him as her oldest friend. In that instant she realized that she must undertake a mission for him. First of all, though, she needed to discover just what her mission was.

INFATUATED WITH A MYSTIC

In 1960, Elizabeth married Dag Ytreberg, a Norwegian law student. However, the following year she met Mark Prophet at a meeting of the Summit Lighthouse, a church in Boston. Prophet, who had founded the Summit Lighthouse three years previously, made a profound impression on the young woman. He claimed to be a messenger for the Ascended Masters who belonged to the Great White Brotherhood – an organization with which both Madame Blavatsky (see pages 101–104) and Guy Ballard had allegedly been in contact. According to Prophet, Saint Germain, Jesus Christ, Gautama Buddha and some of the Hindu gods were also members of the Brotherhood. Prophet himself claimed to have been communicating since the age of 17 with another Ascended Master, El Morya, the reincarnation of King Arthur and Sir Thomas More. Prophet had also founded the Keepers of the Flame, a fraternity for élite members of the Summit Lighthouse who received advanced teachings from the Ascended Masters. These students were said to be descended from cosmic beings once led by Master Sanat Kumara from the planet Venus. Their mission was to save the soul of humanity from self-destruction.

Elizabeth not only became a member of the Summit Lighthouse, she also fell in love with Prophet, 21 years her senior. In 1963, they divorced their respective spouses and married each other. At first Elizabeth played a secondary role to Prophet, training to become a messenger of the Ascended Masters while her new husband organized the Summit Lighthouse's move to Fairfax, Virginia. He also published *The Soulless Ones* (1965), which described how ancient astronauts had come to Earth to conduct genetic experiments on humans, with the aim of creating a race of soulless automatons to control the remaining humans; these mutants, Prophet said, were now in 'high places', controlling the world.

THE LIGHTHOUSE AT COLORADO SPRINGS

Between 1966 and 1972, the Summit Lighthouse again moved its headquarters, this time to Colorado Springs. The Summit Press, for publishing their ideas, and the Summit University, for those who wished to study mystical religions and to gain knowledge of the Ascended Masters, were founded during this time. The Prophets themselves travelled to India, Ghana and the Middle East and in 1972 published *Climb the Highest Mountain*, which contained the tenets of their beliefs.

In addition to Mark Prophet's five children from his first marriage, the Prophets had four of their own. In February 1973, Mark Prophet died of a stroke at the age of 56. Elizabeth, only 33 years old, was devastated. However, she took over the leadership of the organizations, purchasing a 10-hectare (24-acre) property outside Colorado Springs. Shortly after her husband's death, she claimed to have been contacted telepathically by aliens in spacecraft with sinister intent. At a crossroads between good and evil, she chose good and the Ascended Masters. Indeed, Elizabeth's ministry was to focus on the battle against the

A young Elizabeth Clare Wulf, before her marriage to Mark Prophet.

forces of evil, which included UFOs and extraterrestrials; these, according to Elizabeth, were instruments of 'dark forces' attempting to lead humanity away from God.

Within a year of Prophet's death, Elizabeth married Randall King, a member of the board of the Summit Lighthouse. In 1973, however, King used church funds to speculate on the silver futures market, losing $697,000. Clayton Commodities Brokerage filed a lawsuit against the church, which resulted in an IRS investigation of the Summit Lighthouse's tax-free status and in King's removal from the board.

THE CHURCH UNIVERSAL AND TRIUMPHANT

Another move soon followed. In 1974 Elizabeth became concerned about the Summit Lighthouse's proximity to the North American Aerospace Defence Command (NORAD) in Colorado Springs. Nuclear weapons were sited outside Denver, and Elizabeth feared that Colorado would be targeted in the event of war. She therefore moved the Summit Lighthouse to Santa Barbara, California, and soon afterwards restructured the organization. She founded the Church Universal and Triumphant (CUT), introducing religious and ceremonial practices. Pork, processed foods, tobacco, recreational drugs, alcohol and rock music were banned. Tight clothing as well as the colours red, chartreuse and fuchsia were also proscribed. Celibacy was mandatory for single members, while sex was permitted only twice a week for married couples. Members were expected to tithe 10 percent of their income to CUT.

Elizabeth claimed that Mark Prophet had become an Ascended Master called Lanello, guiding members of CUT wherever he could. She maintained his original ideas but made CUT uniquely her own. Like her late husband, she combined various of the world's religions. She was particularly influenced by both theosophy and Guy Ballard's 'I AM' movement. CUT's main theme was 'the Ascension' – the moment when the soul finally reunites with God. It also encompassed reincarnation, the balancing of karma and the evolution of souls. She taught that human negativity could be destroyed by visualizing the 'violet flame' – a ray of cosmic light – while chanting prayers and mantras that she called 'decrees'. These were to be used for spiritual assistance in dealing with political, environmental and social problems.

In 1978, Elizabeth again moved the church's headquarters, this time to a 88-hectare (218-acre) property in Calabasas, California, 25 miles (40 km) northwest of Los Angeles. She also visited Africa, where she had a small following. After only a few years of marriage, she and King divorced in 1980. Before marrying her fourth husband, Edward Francis, in 1981, she received a 'dictation' from the Ascended Masters informing her that although she had balanced her karma, she must remain on Earth to help others. With Francis at her side, Elizabeth moved CUT yet again, this time to a 50-square kilometre (12,000-acre) property outside Yellowstone National Park, near Gardiner, Montana, renaming it Royal Teton.

WAITING FOR THE END OF THE WORLD

The 1980s proved to be a disturbing time for Elizabeth Prophet, for she was convinced that nuclear war was imminent. In 1979, when the Soviet Union invaded Afghanistan, she feared that the superpower would next mount an attack on the United States. Persuading her followers that it was the duty of CUT members to survive and recolonize the world in the aftermath of a nuclear war, she urged them to start building shelters. At Royal Teton, followers spent up to 16 hours a day building a huge bomb shelter, named Mol Herron, designed to accommodate 756 people, with enough food to last for seven years. Forty-five smaller shelters were also built nearby. The cost of this massive building project was estimated at $20 million.

In 1989, Francis was imprisoned for a month for buying $100,000-worth of semi-automatic weapons under a false name, to protect survivors of the expected holocaust. The IRS decided to investigate alleged unpaid taxes, and to make matters worse, the church's 20,000-gallon fuel tanks, buried

'I AM A MESSENGER, SPEAKING ON BEHALF OF GOD. I PRAY REGULARLY THAT THIS PROPHECY (NUCLEAR WAR) WILL FAIL, I WOULD BE HAPPY TO BE A FOOL FOR CHRIST.'

for use after the war, began to leak, requiring an expensive clean-up. Meanwhile, Elizabeth prophesied that nuclear war would commence on 2 October 1989; when the holocaust failed to occur, she revised the date to 15 March 1990. Media crews turned up in the spring of 1990 to witness members of CUT huddled in their shelters and praying for the world to end, believing they would survive and, from the ashes, create a new, God-fearing society. Instead of the Russians launching the first strike, as Elizabeth was convinced they would, the world witnessed the collapse of the Soviet empire. One-third of CUT members left at this point, while Elizabeth announced that their prayers had in fact saved the world from nuclear disaster.

The 1990s were not kind to Elizabeth. Despite the birth of her fifth child when she was 52, her marriage to Francis ended in 1998. By 1999, with her health failing, she was diagnosed with Alzheimer's disease. Forced to withdraw from the church, she was admitted to a nursing home in Bozeman, Montana.

At its peak in the 1980s, CUT had a staff of 750 and a membership of 10,000. However, by 2005, staffing was reduced to 75 and it is not known how many members remain. Since Elizabeth's departure, CUT is run by a two-person presidency, a board of directors and a council of leaders. The Summit Lighthouse, the Summit University, the Summit Press and the Keepers of the Flame fraternity still operate. Mark and Elizabeth Prophet have left a legacy of over 75 published works, including over 3000 dictations from the Masters, entitled *Pearls of Wisdom*.

ÒΑVΊΌ ΙCKE

b.1952

Extraterrestrial Lizards

David Icke, ex-footballer, ex-journalist, ex-TV sports presenter, ex-Green Party spokesman, has made his mark as a controversial proponent of New Age philosophies. Born in 1952, Icke (pronounced 'Ike') was brought up on an English council housing estate. From this unremarkable beginning, he claims to have been guided over the years by mediums, voices and powerful spiritual energies, compelled by them to denounce totalitarian conspiracies and to reveal the truth behind suppressed spiritual knowledge. Ridiculed by many, he nevertheless continues to reach ever-growing audiences.

Icke's first ambition was to be a professional soccer player. After leaving school, he realized his dream by keeping goal for Coventry City and Hereford United football clubs. However, after five years of growing pain in his joints, rheumatoid arthritis forced him to retire from sport. Undaunted, at the age of 21 he got a job as a reporter on a local newspaper, rising through local journalism, radio and television to become a national sports presenter and anchor man.

Icke's Peruvian Awakening

In 1991 an intuitive urge impelled Icke to visit Peru. While staying in Puno, near Lake Titicaca, he visited an ancient Inca burial site called Sillustani. Approaching a mound topped with ruins, he heard a voice in his head calling 'come to me, come to me ...' and he knew he must go to the mound. Once there, he again felt himself anchored to the ground by a magnetic force, and as the sun beat down, his arms shot up above his head, where they remained unmoving for over an hour. Powerful energy flowed in through the top of his head and he heard another voice say clearly: 'It will be over when you feel the rain.' Eventually the sky darkened, a storm materialized, rain fell – and the power surge ceased instantly, although energy still poured from his hands, and his feet burned and vibrated for 24 hours.

Moving to the rural Isle of Wight, off the south coast of England, Icke then became interested in environmental issues and was soon acting as national spokesman for the Green Party. It was in 1989, while writing a book on the Green's agenda entitled *It Doesn't Have To Be Like This*, that he first began to feel a presence around him – a presence so strong that he begged it to reveal itself. And it was not long before it did just that.

THE CHOSEN ONE

Standing in a newsagent's doorway, his feet seemingly stuck to the ground as if attached by magnets, he was aware of a voice telling him to go and look at the books at the far side of the shop. Following this instruction, he picked out a book by a psychic and healer and decided to visit her, hoping that his arthritis might be healed. On his third visit, as he lay on the couch, he felt a spider's web touch his face – a well-attested sensation of spiritual contact. Sure enough, the psychic told him that a figure wanted to pass messages on to him. The same happened on his fourth and final visit. From these contacts in March 1990, Icke learned that his mission was to heal the Earth. Despite meeting opposition, he was told he would be protected by the spirits and would become world-famous, his courage and discipline having been tested through his involvement in sport. He learnt that knowledge would come to him when the time was right, that he would leave politics in order to communicate messages that would change the world, and that he would write five books within three years.

Other facts revealed to Icke were that there would be great earthquakes and the sea would reclaim the land, following the destabilizing of the inner Earth by mankind's removal of oil from the seabed; and that within 20 years people would be transported in time-defying flying machines. The reaction of those to whom Icke spoke of these matters was one of disbelief and he began to be regarded as crazy.

Icke went on television in 1991 to promote his latest book, *Truth Vibrations*; the result was widespread ridicule throughout Britain. As if to add fuel to the fire, at the same time he began to wear turquoise clothes as part of his spiritual beliefs, and announced that he was 'a channel for the Christ spirit'. However, it

Seer in a shellsuit: Icke strikes a pious attitude at a news conference in 1991.

was the statement that David Icke regarded himself as 'the son of God' that caused the most derision (and his expulsion from the Green Party) – although he insists that he was misinterpreted by a sensation-seeking press and that he had used the phrase only in the sense that all people are 'like droplets of water in an ocean of infinite consciousness'.

Icke states that everything forecast by the psychic has come to pass and that by acquiring the courage to disregard conventional beliefs, he no longer fears what people may think of him; he has thus been able to communicate the extraordinary knowledge that is continually given to him and which he pours into his books and reveals at his lectures.

A WELTER OF CONSPIRACY THEORIES

For there was much more to come. In his numerous publications, he has set out his views on conspiracy theories, New Age philosophies, the suppression of spiritual knowledge, the control of the world by a global élite, his belief in shape-shifting reptilian humanoids, and the Great Awakening and Transformation that is to come. He has also produced books and videos on subjects such as alien invasions, the faked moon landings and the effects of shamans interacting with the Earth's energy fields. As can be imagined, the confrontational nature of his revelations has not made for an easy life.

In his books, David Icke introduces the notion of the Brotherhood, a network of secret societies headed by the Global Élite, alternatively known as the Illuminati, that commands world economies using mind-control techniques. Almost every aspect of western society is said to be involved – religion, big business, banking, education, intelligence agencies, organized crime, pharmaceutical companies and the media. Icke states that the Global Élite controls the world through a 'pyramid of manipulation', at the top of which are the 'prison warders', a non-human race under their master, the Luciferic Consciousness. He states that major catastrophes such as the Holocaust, the 9/11 attacks and many others were organized by the Global Élite in order to dupe the masses into willingly handing over power to those in charge so that they could bring in a New World Order with a single world government.

Icke has been accused of anti-Semitism on account of his statement that the Global Élite includes prominent Jewish bankers – although he denies this charge. Nevertheless, he is on record as stating that he believes in the truth of *The Protocols of the Elders of Zion* – a notorious early 20th-century tract, supposedly written by Jewish leaders and 'revealing' a plot for world domination, which was proved to have been fabricated by Russian anti-Semites. He also has links with far-right organizations in Canada and the USA, in particular neo-Nazis and the armed militia movement.

He is further thought to support conspiracy theories that regard much of the Bible to be false. Certainly he claims that most organized religions have been created in order to divide the

DAVID ICKE
A Life in Brief

1952 Icke born in Leicester, England

1973 Forced by arthritis to retire from his career as a professional footballer

1983-5 Icke presents the sports news on BBC's national TV show Breakfast Time

1989 Publication of Icke's first book (on environmental issues) *It Doesn't Have to Be Like This*

1990 Icke experiences his first spirit visions

1991 On a trip to Peru, Icke has a revelation that he has been chosen to heal the Earth

1994 Icke publishes *The Robots' Rebellion*, the first book to expound his theory of the 'Global Elite'

1999 Theory of reptilian humanoids elaborated in Icke's *The Biggest Secret*

human race through continual conflict, and he maintains that racism adds fuel to the fire of the Illuminati/Global Élite agenda. He also speaks of the suppression of spiritual knowledge that prevents us from understanding our purpose and indeed the nature of life itself.

RULED BY REPTILES

Icke's most controversial theory is expounded in his 1999 book *The Biggest Secret*, in which he portrays the Illuminati as a race of reptilian humanoids known as the Babylonian Brotherhood. This belief in reptoids or lizard men occurs in many ancient cultures throughout the world and is not exclusive to Icke. Snake-like creatures were said to live underground or beneath the sea and Native Americans refer to the 'snake brothers'. In China it is believed that emperors were descended from dragon kings; serpent men were mentioned in the Middle East, while in Africa a reptilian race was thought to have controlled the Earth. Icke states that reptilian humanoids are the force behind the worldwide conspiracy mentioned above and that they promote racial and ethnic division in order to increase conflict worldwide. He further states that most of the world's leaders (and, bizarrely, some entertainers) – including members of the British royal family, George W. Bush, Hillary Clinton, Kris Kristofferson and Bob Hope –

> ' I BELIEVE THAT PEOPLE HAVE A RIGHT TO BELIEVE, TO READ, AND HAVE ACCESS TO ALL INFORMATION, SO THAT THEY CAN THEN MAKE UP THEIR OWN MINDS. '

are related to reptilians originally from the star system Alpha Draconis. The 'prison warders' working for the Global Élite are reptilian; what is more, cross-breeding with humans has altered their genetic structure, allowing them to change from reptile to human form at will, after drinking human blood.

This reads like a particularly outlandish piece of science fiction. The theories David Icke expounds are certainly controversial: his books were removed from bookshops after protests by the Canadian Jewish Congress in Ontario and several speeches were cancelled. They also have lucrative box-office appeal to those inclined to heed them: supporters gave him a standing ovation following a four-hour speech he delivered in Toronto. Some might ask why an ostensibly intelligent man, a fluent speaker with a promising career, should voluntarily put himself in the firing line of ridicule without good reason. Critics suggest that absence of reason is precisely the problem, and that Icke is in the grip of a mental illness that manifests itself in an intricately crafted, endlessly self-justifying messianic complex. Icke's response to this is that he is merely a conduit for the knowledge that comes to him and that it is up to individuals to form their own opinions as to its validity.

mother meera
b.1960
Union of All Faiths

In a large house in the German village of Balduinstein, a group of people silently await the arrival of the Divine Mother and the ritual of *darshan* – a wordless offering of love and light. A slight figure in a richly coloured sari enters and sits in an armchair facing her devotees. As they kneel, one by one, before her, Mother Meera takes each person's head in her hands. She looks deep into their eyes to discover where they need healing; she then unties knots in their subtle body and permeates them with the divine Light. When she has finished, she looks down at the ground, indicating that the *darshan* has ended.

Mother Meera and the Divine Mother are believed to be part of the same consciousness, for Mother Meera is perceived as an avatar – a god in human form – and is worshipped in India as an incarnation of the Divine Mother. Since the beginning of time, the Divine Mother has been worshipped under many different names; Mother Meera is just one of her incarnations, called to Earth at a time when 'there is a need to uplift and protect humanity'.

DESTINED FOR DIVINITY

Mother Meera – birth name Kamala Reddy – was born on 26 December 1960 in the small town of Chandepalle, in Andhra Pradesh, southern India. Her parents soon realized that there was something unusual about their daughter, for from the age of three she spoke of 'going to various lights', while at six she experienced her first Samadhi – a state of spiritual absorption – that lasted for a whole day. She spent much time on her own as a young child and it was through the guides that she encountered whilst in an exalted state that she received spiritual help and love. Her family were poor members of the Reddy clan, however, and Kamala was sent at the age of eight to work as a servant in the house of rich Reddy neighbours. It was here that she later met Venkat Reddy, son-in-law and heir to the estate, who would become her mentor.

Venkat Reddy had spent 42 years of his life moving from ashram to ashram in search of the Divine Mother. Leaving his young wife and baby daughter in Pondicherry at the Sri Aurobindo ashram, which, following the death of the founder, was in the care of the elderly Sweet Mother, Venkat returned to Chandepalle on the death of his father-in-

During darshan, *devotees of Mother Meera claim she has manifested herself as various Hindu goddesses such as Parvati (seen here).*

> '**I HAVE MY OWN WAY OF TRAVELLING TO OTHER PLACES. I KNOW PAST, PRESENT AND FUTURE SIMULTANEOUSLY, SO THERE IS NO DUALITY.**'

law. It was here that he first set eyes on the young servant girl, the 12-year-old Kamala, whom he instantly recognized as the divine one, the object of his lifelong search. Venkat, sometimes known by the courtesy title of 'uncle', spent the next two years helping the girl to develop her visionary and spiritual powers.

Meanwhile, the Aurobindo ashram was going through hard times following the death of Sweet Mother. In 1974 Venkat returned to Pondicherry with Kamala, declaring that Sweet Mother's divine powers had entered into the girl. The trio was completed by Adilakshmi, a woman some 17 years older than Kamala, who had come to Pondicherry ten years earlier in search of the Sweet Mother and who had remained there as a teacher. Now that Sweet Mother had died, Kamala became the focus of the lives of both Venkat and Adilakshmi – although it should be said that Venkat's wife and daughter were less than happy with this turn of events. Although fully aware since birth of her divine status, Kamala continued her education, both under the instruction of Venkat and also at a girls' hostel. Eventually she was accepted as successor to Sweet Mother and given the name Mother Meera. Initially her presence at the ashram attracted much attention; she met many Westerners seeking enlightenment and it was there that she gave her first *darshan*.

BRINGING LIGHT TO GERMANY

Before leaving the ashram, Mother Meera visited devotees in Canada. Then, in 1981, she moved to West Germany, saying that, following two world wars, the country was in need of healing. She stayed there with Venkat Reddy and Adilakshmi; later both women married German devotees, ensuring their right to stay in the country. Now living with her husband in Germany, she regularly receives thousands of visitors for *darshan*. Mother Meera is not involved in any specific religion, dogma or belief system, nor does she follow any particular tradition other than a devotion to God. 'My work is not for one country or one race or one people only; it is for the world,' she has stated. She offers *darshan* to all those who seek it, regardless of their faith, or indeed lack of faith. She makes no charges and gives no lectures, saying that 'the power of the Divine works in the silence'. The aim of her work is to purify the consciousness of the Earth and to transform humanity into God. In collaboration with saints and other divine beings, she claims to call to Earth a divine Light from the Supreme Self – the

Invoking the Divine Light-Force

Mother Meera claims that there are two fine white lines starting at a person's toes and joining together at the base of the spine to form a single line that then rises to the top of the head. As she holds the head of the devotee, she is able to unravel the knots that have formed in the lines and to study the stage of development of the person's *sadhana* - that is, the degree of their self-discipline and spiritual practice. If the person is developing spiritually, the Light moves up the white line; where there has been deterioration, the Light moves downwards; it is part of Mother Meera's task to stop this deterioration. When the white line flows uninterruptedly from the toes to the top of the head, the person may experience visions, such is the intense state of their spirituality. At the front of the body, two red lines also grow from the toes to unite at the base of the spine. If and when the red lines meet the white lines at this spot - and this is rare - the person can achieve a state of complete detachment, or maybe enlightenment.

Paramatman – and she uses this Light to aid the spiritual progress of mankind. She has said that the divine Light is everywhere and that her mission is to activate it.

Mother Meera has explained that as she gives *darshan*, she sees into every corner of the person's being, at the same time spreading Light throughout their body and opening them to the Light. Her task is to open all people who come to her to the power of the Light, thus preparing for the transformation of humanity into God. 'Enjoy the Light' she says, 'It is here; let it change you. The transformation will come in its own time.'

DEVOTEES AND CRITICS

In 1985 Venkat Reddy died, following years of failing health. The following year, in order to cope with an ever-increasing number of visitors, Mother Meera bought a second house in Germany, which she and the devotees renovated themselves. In 1988 she bought a further property, including farmland, in Madanapalle – Adlilakshmi's home town – near Bangalore in India, which she visits from time to time and where members of her extended family are now able to live.

Unaffected by people's opinions of her, Mother Meera quietly continues her mission of bringing down the divine Light. Some visitors remain permanent devotees whilst others feel the need to break away from her influence. As she herself has warned: 'The visions that come from the Divine change you.' Some Westerners in particular find that the sudden surge of power they receive from her during *darshan* changes their lives too forcefully for comfort, while others decide to follow a different spiritual path. She has had her detractors too: unsurprisingly, Venkat Reddy's abandoned wife, who is said to have simply announced: 'I do not believe.' There has also been criticism from the writer Andrew Harvey. A one-time devoted follower who claimed to have become enlightened through his connection with Mother Meera, he later accused her of homophobia, saying that she had disapproved of his marriage to another man. Although one of his former lovers contested this accusation, she does appear to have made further homophobic statements that have caused distress.

So what is it about this woman who has no wish to found a religion yet who attracts thousands of devotees? This woman who claims to pass on the divine Light in silence, saying only that 'I do not speak but my force changes people'. Perhaps it is her statement that: 'The Divine is the sea. All religions are rivers leading to the sea; some rivers wind a great deal. Why not go to the sea directly?' that strikes a chord in today's chaotic world. Certainly there seem to be many people who are prepared to subscribe to Mother Meera's way.

MOTHER MEERA
A Life in Brief

1960 Mother Meera born Kamala Reddy in Andhra Pradesh state, India

1966 Kamal experiences her first Samadhi

1974 Kamala's relative 'Uncle' Venkat Reddy takes her to the Sri Aurobindo ashram in Pondicherry, proclaiming her a divine being; Kamala takes the name Mother Meera

1981 Mother Meera moves to Germany to bring the country healing

1985 Mother Meera's long-time mentor Venkat Reddy dies

2002 Former devotee Andrew Harvey accuses Mother Meera of homophobia in his book *The Sun at Midnight*

The Medjugorje
Sightings
1981–

Seers of the Virgin Mary

On 24 June 1981, 15-year-old Ivanka Ivankovic, an ethnic Croat from the village of Medjugorje in Yugoslavia (now in Bosnia-Herzegovina), was walking with her friend Mirjana Dragicevic, 16, when she noticed a bright light on the hill behind her village. The girls were on a rocky slope, covered in thorn bushes, that overlooked the village of Bijakovic in one direction and, in the other, the 518-metre (1700-ft) high Mount Kirzevac, on top of which stood a 8.5-metre (28-ft) high white cross erected in 1934.

Looking more closely, Ivanka was able to make out the figure of a woman on a hovering cloud, with a child in her arms. Ivanka joked to Mirjana that it was the Gospa – the Croatian name for Our Lady. Her friend, frightened, refused at first to look, but when they were joined by two other young girls, Milka Pavlovic and Vicka Ivankovic, all four witnessed the apparition. Vicka fled, terrified. Halfway down the hillside, she met two local boys, Ivan Dragicevic and Ivan Ivankovic, both of whom hurried to the top where they, too, saw the vision.

Virgin of the Balkans

Medjugorje, meaning 'rugged place between the hills', lies 20 miles (32 km) southwest of Mostar. In 1981 it had a population of some 4000 people, predominantly Croats who grew grapes and tobacco, and who worshipped in the Roman Catholic church of St James, begun in 1940 and still unfinished four decades later. There were more than 7 million Roman Catholics, mostly ethnic Croats and Slovenes, in the Socialist Federal Republic of Yugoslavia, which had been ruled for 35 years by the dictator Tito (Josip Broz). While the official policy of communist governments in Eastern Europe was to suppress and restrict religious practices, in 1966 Tito had signed a protocol with the Vatican promising to recognize freedom of conscience in return for a ban on priests involving themselves in politics. His death in May 1980, a little more than a year before the apparition on the hillside, meant Yugoslavia would begin its slow and ultimately violent disintegration along religious and ethnic lines.

The six young people who witnessed the vision on the hillside were curious as to what they had seen. On the following day, 25 June, four of them – Ivanka, Mirjana, Vicka and Ivan Dragicevic – returned with two other children, Marija Pavlovic and Jakov Colo, who, at 12, was the youngest. Ivan Ivankovic and Milka Pavlovic did not accompany the others on this occasion. Once again the figure appeared on the hillside, though this time she was without the child. She was later described by the children in precise detail: of slim build, 1.6 metres (5ft 5ins) tall, weighing 60 kilograms (132 lbs), with blue eyes, black hair, a blue-grey dress, manicured fingernails and a crown of gold stars. Her head was covered by a veil and she stood on a white cloud, looking serene and beautiful.

*In 2004, on the anniversary of the vision, pilgrims climb
Apparition Hill in Medjugorje.*

The six young people believed the woman to be the Virgin Mary. They returned each day
to the site for further visions. Ivan Ivankovic and Milka Pavlovic, who missed the apparition on
the second day, also returned, though, unlike the others, they never again received a vision.

INSTRUCTIONS AND PROPHECIES

News of the apparition spread quickly, and by the fifth day more than 15,000 people had
gathered to witness the event, but no one other than the children saw the Gospa. Concerned
by the number of visitors descending on their hamlet, the authorities closed the site to the
public and turned sightseers away. Sealing off Apparition Hill, as it had become known,
temporarily halted the influx of visitors but could not prevent the apparitions from appearing
to the youngsters. In fact, they now began witnessing the visions in the surrounding fields, in
St James's Church in Medjugorje, and even their own homes. The parish priest, Father Jozo
Zovko, was at first sceptical of the children's visions, questioning them thoroughly and
checking the stories against each other. On the sixth day of the Virgin's appearance, the
children were all taken to Mostar for medical examinations. All, however, were declared
healthy and of sound mind. Father Zovko soon changed his mind about the visions, having
received a message from God, while praying, that he should protect the children. The children

'DEAR CHILDREN, THIS IS THE REASON FOR MY PRESENCE AMONG YOU FOR SUCH A LONG TIME: TO LEAD YOU ON THE PATH OF JESUS. I WANT TO SAVE YOU AND, THROUGH YOU, TO SAVE THE WHOLE WORLD. MANY PEOPLE NOW LIVE WITHOUT FAITH; SOME DON'T EVEN WANT TO HEAR ABOUT JESUS, BUT THEY STILL WANT PEACE AND SATISFACTION! CHILDREN, HERE IS THE REASON WHY I NEED YOUR PRAYER: PRAYER IS THE ONLY WAY TO SAVE THE HUMAN RACE.'

THE VIRGIN MARY, 30 JULY 1987

also received support from Bishop Pavao Zanic, of the local diocese, who supported their claims, telling a Croatian newspaper that the children had not been influenced by the Church or by anyone else.

The Virgin soon began passing messages of peace and love to the children, in order to help them guide people to a closer relationship with God. She told the youngsters to encourage everyone to read the Bible each day, to pray daily with the rosary, to fast on Wednesdays and Fridays, to attend monthly confession and to take Holy Communion. Each child was instructed to pray for particular things: Vicka and Jakov were to pray especially for the sick, Mirjana for unbelievers, Ivanka for families, Ivan for priests and the youth of the world, and Marija for the souls in purgatory and for religious nuns. Ivanka claimed that on five occasions God had allowed her to see and speak to her mother, who had died earlier in 1981.

The Virgin Mary also promised to confide ten prophetic secrets to each of the youngsters. She eventually revealed nine to Ivan, Marija and Vicka, and ten to the other three. So far, the visionaries have revealed only the first of these prophecies: the Virgin's promise to leave a

Studied by Scholars

Several scientific studies have been conducted on the six Croatian visionaries, quite apart from the enquiries by the Catholic Church. In 1986, a French-Italian scientific theological commission examined the apparitions and announced that - unlike the bishops five years later - they recognized a 'supernatural origin' to the events at Medjugorje. Later that year in Paris, a French team headed by Henri Joyeux used EEG and EKG machines to examine the visionaries. Their conclusion, published in *Études Medicales et Scientifiques sur les Apparitions de Medjugorje* (1986), was that the visionaries were seeing something external and that there was no visible evidence of external stimulation. This finding was confirmed by several other institutes, including the Innsbruck Centre for Study and Research on Psychophsysiology of States of Consciousness, while the Parapsychology Centre of Bologna stated that the visionaries showed no signs of pathological symptoms and were not under a state of hypnosis.

supernatural, indestructible and visible sign on Apparition Hill as a sign for atheists. The faithful were told not to wait for this sign, however, but to embrace God's love long before it appeared. When all the ten secrets have been revealed, the Virgin Mary will cease to appear.

OFFICIAL SCEPTICISM, POPULAR ACCLAIM

The Yugoslav authorities soon became anxious to discredit the visions. The secret police, the sinister UDBA, ordered both Father Zovko and Bishop Zanic to stop supporting the children's claims. The former refused and was imprisoned for 18 months, but Bishop Zanic complied, becoming an ardent opponent of the validity of the visions. In 1984 he established a commission of 14 people to investigate the sightings. He made it clear that he was sceptical, forbidding priests from organizing any further pilgrimages to Medjugorje until the investigations were completed. In April 1985, in a memorandum from the Vatican State Secretariat's Office, Cardinal Franjo Kuharic was ordered to convey to Zanic that he should: 'suspend the airing of his own personal statements and renounce making judgements until such time as all elements could be conclusively gathered together and the happenings could be clarified.' In 1987, the investigation was handed over to the Yugoslav Bishops' Conference. In 1991 the commission reported that it could not confirm the 'supernatural character' of the sightings. Plans for a second study were interrupted by the bloody civil war.

Since 1981, more than 20 million pilgrims have travelled to Apparition Hill in Medjugorje to pray to the Virgin Mary, to attend one of the services at St James's Church in the town in the company of one of the six visionaries, or to climb to the cross at the top of Mount Kvizevac; 1.6 million pilgrims came in the year 2007 alone. According to Father Ljudevic Rupcic, author of *The Truth of Medjugorje* (1990), there were 56 healings in the early days of the sightings. The village now has a visitor centre, a souvenir shop and an outdoor altar with seating for 5000. A wooden cross has been erected on the site of the first apparition.

By 2008, all of the visionaries were married; most had children of their own. Several still have daily apparitions, while Jakov Colo receives a vision once a year, at Christmas, and Ivanka Ivankovic-Elez, the first to see the Virgin, does so on each anniversary of the apparition. Investigations by the Catholic Church continue, but private pilgrimages to the site are condoned.

THE MEDJUGORJE SIGHTINGS Timeline

1981 The Virgin Mary (Gospa) appears to six Croat children at Medjugorje in Bosnia-Herzegovina

1984 Encouraged by the Yugoslav authorities, Bishop Pavao Zanic establishes an investigative committee with the aim of discrediting the sightings

1986 An independent French-Italian theological commission finds evidence of supernatural activity in the Medjugorje sightings

1987 The Vatican orders the investigation to be transferred to the Yugoslav Bishops' Conference

1991 Interim report of the commission concludes that there is no evidence the sightings were supernatural; outbreak of civil war in Yugoslavia

2007 As the fame of Medjugorje spreads, 1.6 million pilgrims arrive there in this year alone

JOHN TITOR
b.1998?

Time Traveller from 2036

If at some stage in the future, time travel becomes a reality, why then, asks the eminent British physicist Stephen Hawking, has no one ever returned to show us how it is done? Why are we not overrun with what he calls 'tourists from the future'? And yet, in the year 2000 an alleged time traveller did appear. Less a tourist than a man with a mission, he was the bearer of depressing news.

Time Travel_0, or John Titor, as he later became known, made his first appearance in November 2000 on the Internet's Time Travel Institute Forum, an entirely fictional organization dedicated to the research and explanation of time travel. In a story recalling the *Back to the Future* and *Terminator* film franchises, Titor claimed to be 38 years old and to have travelled back in time from the year 2036. He was supposedly a soldier who had returned to the year 1975 to retrieve the 5100 IBM computer system; in addition to APL and Basic, this system was able to read older computer languages and would be capable of debugging a problem with the UNIX system that would occur in 2038. Titor was chosen for the mission as his paternal grandfather had worked on the 5100 system. After completing this mission, Titor decided to stop over in 1998 to pick up family photographs from his infancy, remaining a time traveller in the years of his early childhood, 1998–2001.

PILOT OF THE TIME MACHINE

Titor claimed to have been born in 1998 in Florida, and on his return in time he went back to his parents' house, introducing himself as their son from the future. Mr and Mrs Titor apparently accepted the stranger's story and invited him to stay. His baby self, who had been asleep in the house when he arrived, took to calling him 'uncle'. There is apparently no record of Titor's activities from the time of his 1998 arrival on Earth until his first Internet posting in November 2000.

Tips from the Future

Before he 'departed', John Titor dispensed some final pieces of advice on how people could improve their chances of survival:
- Do not eat or use animal products where the animal had eaten parts of other animals
- Avoid intimate relations with strangers
- Learn how to purify water and to shoot, and get a first-aid kit
- Identify five people within 100 miles (160 km) you can trust with your life
- Read the US Constitution
- Eat less, buy a bicycle and ride it regularly

*John Titor's military insignia.
The Latin motto means* Time,
the Devourer of all Things.

JOHN TITOR
Timeline

1998 Claimed birth
date of John Titor

2000 (November) John
Titor begins posting on
the Internet, claiming to
be a returned US soldier
from the year 2036

2001 (March) Titor's
Internet postings cease

2003 The John Titor
Foundation publishes
*John Titor: A Time
Traveller's Tale*

2004 A rock opera,
*Time Traveller Zero
Zero*, is staged, based on
Titor's predictions

2005 The documentary
'Obsessed & Scientific'
investigates time travel
and Titor's 'life'

2008 An Italian
television documentary
on the Titor
phenomenon fails to
unearth any evidence of
the existence of a Titor
family in the United
States

For four months between November 2000 and March 2001 Titor held discussions on Internet forums with anyone who expressed an interest in time travel. He posted pictures of his time-travelling vehicle, the 'C204 time distortion gravity displacement machine'. He also included extracts from the machine's manual that detailed its workings. The C204 had, he claimed, been made by General Electrics in 2034; it contained two magnetic housing units for the dual micro singularities, three main computer units, four caesium clocks, gravity sensors, a cooling and X-ray venting system, and an electron injection manifold to alter mass and gravity micro singularities. It was allegedly capable of manipulating a miniature black hole that would enable time travel. Titor explained that it takes one hour to cover every ten years of time travel, and that the C204 is accurate for up to 60 years. Titor said that, at the start of his journey, he felt a gravitational pull of up to 2G as light bent around the machine. For the trip back to 1975, the device was installed – like the DeLorean car used in the 1985 movie *Back to the Future* – in a 1967 Chevrolet Corvette convertible. On his 1998 arrival, in order to avoid any unnecessary attention, it was relocated to a 1987 four-wheel drive truck.

A GLOOMY PROGNOSIS

Over the same four months (November 2000–March 2001), Titor made many predictions about the future. He prophesied that in 2004 the United States would suffer a civil war, caused by increasingly intrusive police-state tactics and culminating in pitched battles between urban areas, which sympathized with such methods, and the rural regions, which did not. By 2008 this civil war would have engulfed the entire nation, ceasing only in 2015, at the start of the Third World War, when Russia would attack most American cities with nuclear warheads. Most major nations of the world would be dragged into the war, with Europe, Africa and Australia badly affected and three billion people dead. As the West grew increasingly unstable, China would annex Japan, Taiwan and Korea. Washington DC would be destroyed and the American capital moved to Omaha, Nebraska. The United States would separate into five states, each with its own president who would be voted in and out in staggered elections. The five vice presidents, elected separately, would preside over the Senate. In Titor's account, there would be more than ten political parties in the United States after the Third World War.

Titor made numerous further predictions. He implied that in early 2001 America would wage war on Iraq, claiming that Iraq harboured nuclear weapons, although these, he predicted, would not be found: 'Are you really surprised that Iraq has nukes now, or is that just BS [bullshit] to whip everyone up into accepting the next war?' He forecast that weapons of mass destruction would be used against Israel by her neighbours, that Bovine Spongiform Encephalopathy (BSE), or mad cow disease, would become a problem in the United States, that genetically modified foods would cause health problems, and that the European Organisation for Nuclear Research (CERN) would announce in 2001 that it had discovered the foundations for time travel. Titor also stated that the 2004 summer Olympics would be the last to be held.

Many of Titor's predictions, notably those of civil war in America and the discovery of the foundations of time travel, did not come true. CERN has not to date created mini black holes to make time travel possible, as Titor predicted (though the first beam from the Large Hadron Collider, CERN's particle accelerator, was activated on 10 September 2008). Moreover, the photograph he posted on the Internet to show how a laser beam is bent by gravity looks more like an optical fibre beam, as neither the objects around the beam nor the window frame in the background is distorted. One serious omission from Titor's prophecies would appear to have been the terrorist attacks on the United States on 11 September 2001 or the world financial crisis that began in 2008.

A SIMPLER, SLOWER FUTURE

Besides his prophecies, Titor gave a description of his life in the future. The Third World War brought a drastic change to American society. He grew up with his parents in a community of tree houses by a large river. The family business was picking, sorting and shipping oranges by sailboat up and down the Florida coast, in return for which his parents were given electricity, heat, water and food from their community. Food and livestock were grown and sold locally, and people tended to live in small communities of between 1000 and 4000 people. These communities were usually based near universities, where books and knowledge were stored. In order to move to another community, the applicant had to be interviewed and evaluated as to what he or she could contribute to the community.

In this society, everyone did farm work as well as military and community service. Life was much more rural, although technology was used for communication and travel. There was no health care, with the average life expectancy just 60 years. Due to environmental damage caused by the nuclear conflagration, women found it difficult to conceive (as in Margaret Atwood's 1986 novel *The Handmaid's Tale*). Much communal effort therefore went into repairing the damage caused to the environment, such as cleaning the water supplies and soil where vegetables were grown.

THE MESSENGER DEPARTS

John Titor sent his final Internet post on 24 March 2001. He explained that the window for his return to 2036 was approaching and that only a handful of people knew when and where it

> '**IMAGINE YOU ARE JEWISH AND YOU ARE ABLE TO TRAVEL BACK IN TIME TO GERMANY IN 1935. ALL AROUND YOU ARE THE PATTERNS OF THINKING AND ACTION THAT WILL LEAD TO A GREAT DEAL OF HARM, DEATH AND DESTRUCTION IN JUST A FEW YEARS. YOU HAVE THE ADVANTAGE OF KNOWING WHAT WILL COME BUT NO ONE WILL LISTEN TO YOU. IN FACT, THEY THINK YOU'RE INSANE AND THE SITUATIONS YOU DESCRIBE COULD NEVER HAPPEN.**'
>
> JOHN TITOR, 29 JANUARY 2001

would be. His 'father' agreed to videotape his departure and to make this available on the Internet to the public. Since that last posting, nothing further has been heard from Titor, the promised videotape of his departure has not surfaced, and his 'parents' have disappeared.

Even if John Titor was merely an elaborate (and not entirely original) Internet hoax, the Titor postings attracted the interest of thousands of people, including many believers in time travel. A book, *John Titor: A Time Traveller's Tale*, was published in 2003, and in 2004 Cyburbia Productions presented a rock opera, *Time Traveller Zero Zero*, at George Mason University in Fairfax, Virginia. A short documentary, 'Obsessed & Scientific', about time travel and Titor's life, was aired in 2005.

Titor's record of prophesying future events is, at best, hit and miss. However, he claimed that a 2 percent discrepancy between two timelines exists, and so it is logical to presume that some of his predictions will not come true. Using this logic, it is also impossible to prove categorically that he does or did not exist, or that some of his prophecies will not be realized in the future. Yet the point of his prophecies may well have been – like those of so many other prophets of doom – not to foretell the future so much as to make people in the present change their ways of living.

index

Page numbers in **bold** type indicate main references to the various topics; those in *italic* refer to illustrations

Picture credits

Author's Acknowledgements

For my sister Destine.

I would like to thank my dear friend Sue Adams for her brilliant input and my husband, Ross King, for his continuous love and support. Thank you also to Heather Holden-Brown and James Pryor from hhb agency ltd; Len Kehoe, my computer whiz; and Richard Milbank from Quercus Books for his enthusiastic support.

Quercus Publishing Plc
21 Bloomsbury Square
London
WC1A 2NS

First published in 2009

A CIP catalogue record for this book is available from the British Library

Printed case edition: ISBN–978 1 84724 192 4

Printed and bound in China

1 3 5 7 9 10 8 6 4 2

Designed and edited by BCS Publishing Limited, Oxford.